Free and Easy Website Design for Museums and Historic Sites

About the Series

The American Association for State and Local History Book Series addresses issues critical to the field of state and local history through interpretive, intellectual, scholarly, and educational texts. To submit a proposal or manuscript to the series, please request proposal guidelines from AASLH headquarters: AASLH Editorial Board, 1717 Church St., Nashville, Tennessee 37203. Telephone: (615) 320-3203. Website: www.aaslh.org.

About the Organization

The American Association for State and Local History (AASLH) is a national history membership association headquartered in Nashville, Tennessee. AASLH provides leadership and support for its members who preserve and interpret state and local history in order to make the past more meaningful to all Americans. AASLH members are leaders in preserving, researching, and interpreting traces of the American past to connect the people, thoughts, and events of yesterday with the creative memories and abiding concerns of people, communities, and our nation today. In addition to sponsorship of this book series, AASLH publishes *History News* magazine, a newsletter, technical leaflets and reports, and other materials; confers prizes and awards in recognition of outstanding achievement in the field; supports a broad education program and other activities designed to help members work more effectively; and advocates on behalf of the discipline of history. To join AASLH, go to www.aaslh.org or contact Membership Services, AASLH, 1717 Church St., Nashville, TN 37203.

Free and Easy Website Design for Museums and Historic Sites

Kelsey J. S. Ransick

ROWMAN & LITTLEFIELD
Lanham • Boulder • New York • London

Published by Rowman & Littlefield
A wholly owned subsidary of The Rowman & Littlefield Publishing Group, Inc.
4501 Forbes Boulevard, Suite 200, Lanham, Maryland 20706
www.rowman.com

Unit A, Whitacre Mews, 26-34 Stannary Street, London SE11 4AB

British Library Cataloguing in Publication Information Available

Library of Congress Cataloging-in-Publication Data

Ransick, Kelsey J. S., author.
Free and easy website design for museums and historic sites / Kelsey J. S. Ransick.
   pages cm. — (American Association for State and Local History book series)
Includes bibliographical references and index.
ISBN 978-1-4422-5579-1 (cloth : alk. paper) — ISBN 978-1-4422-5580-7
(pbk. : alk. paper) — ISBN 978-1-4422-5581-4 (electronic)
1. Web sites—Design. 2. Web site development. 3. Museum information networks—
United States. 4. Historic sites—United States—Information services. 5. Museum
visitors—Education. I. American Association for State and Local History. II. Title.
TK5105.888.R364 2015
006.7—dc23   2015030313

Printed in the United States of America

For my grandmothers, Jean and Judy

Contents

Do not miss the free website extras that come with this book! These include additional design tips and tools, an HTML tester, and updated WYSIWYG editor guides. Find them all at freethemuseum.net using your special access code: 239clwaej34lsg.

Foreword

Kelsey Ransick is a young museum professional with a mission. She wants every museum and historic site, no matter how small, to be able to present its unique story and attract visitors through a good-looking, information-packed website. And in this easy-to-follow book, Kelsey offers clear instructions on how your organization can prepare for, build, and maintain an appealing website.

Kelsey Ransick is just the person to make the case for small-museum websites. As one of the graduate assistants attached to "Sustaining Places," a three-year project developed by the University of Delaware Museum Studies Program and funded by the Institute for Museum and Library Services, Kelsey created the first iteration of our "online encyclopedia" of resources for small historical organizations, www.sustainingplaces.com. Adapting a WordPress template to our needs, Kelsey built a site notable for both its clarity and utility and trained other graduate students to take over the project when she graduated.

From the Museum Studies Program's collaborations with small museums through Sustaining Places and course-based projects, I have learned that the "digital divide" between small community-based museums and larger organizations is still growing—and that's not a good thing. While small organizations like yours may never be in the business of building "apps" or creating complex digital projects, they need to be present online. Your appealing stories, remarkable collections, and enjoyable public programs deserve the exposure that an attractive and informative website, findable through standard search engines and updated regularly, can bring.

Let Kelsey Ransick be your guide to the increasingly accessible world of website construction. With some planning and commitment, you'll find that building a website can even be fun. Good luck!

Katherine C. Grier
Director, Museum Studies Program
University of Delaware

Preface

In the twenty-five years or so since the World Wide Web became worldwide, a lot has changed. Programmers and engineers continue to develop software and write code, but some now have careers focused wholly on mobile app development. Whole new theories and schools of study have sprung up around Internet usage.[1] Social media for museums and cultural institutions now includes Twitter, Facebook, Pinterest, LinkedIn, and scores more sites that were certainly not part of the Web's original infrastructure. The explosion of Web-based phone technologies, such as Skype and Talkatone, is proof enough that the way we interact with the Web changes quickly and constantly. The words "Internet" and "Web site" have become so ingrained in our daily vocabulary that they have undergone the ultimate acknowledgment of acceptance in the English language—they have been modified by everyday speech, and now neither requires capitalization! Though this may seem trivial, what it ultimately shows is that the internet of the twenty-first century is, in many ways, a new beast, and we must reevaluate a number of the conventional rules regarding its use. *Free and Easy Website Design for Museums and Historic Sites* is here to help.

WHY BOTHER?

Convention holds that small and local businesses, including museums and other nonprofits, are notoriously slow at adopting new technology. Unfortunately, this all-too-often proves true. A 2013 survey by website host Weebly noted that over 55 percent of businesses and almost 40 percent of nonprofits do not have a website.[2] While perhaps not an issue fifteen years ago in a world of phonebooks and directory assistance, this is increasingly detrimental to such institutions—the same survey found that 56 percent of consumers do not trust businesses that do not have a website.³ Without a website, a business often seems inaccessible and unreliable, and consumers are increasingly liable to seek out another organization whose information is easier to access.

Researchers have long noted a few trends in page visitation habits on museum websites. Even in 2007, a paper presented by Judy Haynes and Dan Zambonini at the International Conference for Culture and Heritage On-Line reported⁴ that the top-viewed pages on a museum website are generally those that list the open hours, directions, event calendar, and other visitor information.⁵ Easy access to your hours, address, email, and mission is often a deciding factor in whether or not a visitor will come to your physical site over another, and this is especially so in the case of smartphone-wielding generations, who are used to having this information quite literally at their fingertips. To their thinking, if it can be digitized and accessed on a smartphone, why would it *not* be.

Those sites that have taken the leap and launched an online presence have noticed an increase in museum visits of almost 75 percent.⁶ Instead of detracting from on-site visitors, having a web presence entices visitors, urging them to seek out more information and deeper connections—in the museum itself. Zambonini, who works for British software development consultant agency Box UK, which serves numerous museums and non-profits, writes:

> Traditional retailers can offer their retail services online. Content providers can offer their content services online. . . . Museums and galleries, however, have always had the monopoly on the experiences that they offer. *That's* why you make the effort to visit the building: because you can't see this stuff—this real, physical, *unique* stuff—anywhere else. . . . The website you make, however, in no way *replaces* such experiences except for those who cannot physically make it to the museum because of where they live. Your website will supplement your physical site. It will direct people to your site and your collections.⁷

At a conference about the intersection of museums and technology, Australian museum blogger Jen Griffiths made a similarly poignant point when asked the importance of "all this . . . online stuff":

> If museums' point of difference is objects . . . how important is [it?] . . . Then I remembered the other part about museums that dovetails so neatly into technology/internet [is] that they were made for each other. The conversations. These conversations, traditionally held while standing in the museum, can be banal, fascinating, surprising, and everything in between, but they are the way we make sense of our world and the way we connect to people around us. . . . Museums are the custodians of the objects that make these connections possible. And if you could make these conversations easier to have, if you could expand the

people able to have the conversations, if you could include yourself [or institution] in the conversations, wouldn't you want to?[8]

Zambonini and Griffiths's words bespeak another major benefit of establishing an online presence: a growing audience. Without the merit of being the major art museum of a metropolitan area, many small museums and historic sites are restricted to audiences that they can personally reach out to. Having a blog or website widens the potential demographics of audience members and increases their number.

Other benefits of being online include a "near-zero variable cost for storage and distribution"[9] of data in the form of membership management and digital collections that are accessible online. In fact, as historic sites have created more videos highlighting their collections and organized donor and membership information online, repositories like Google and YouTube have become prime caches for museums' digital assets.[10] Digital curation has been on the rise, and its interactivity encourages responses, personal narratives, feedback, and more.[11]

The bottom line is: your website is there when you are not. It always picks up the phone. The doorbell is always answered. Thanks to in-browser translators, it knows multiple languages. Having a website expands your audience and boosts access to your collections. It lends credence to your site's expertise, building an active, reliable reputation for your site. A website is built-in media exposure online—where lifestyle journalists across the country hunt for interesting local activities to fill their spreads. A website is a vital part of any business—be it Starbucks or your museum.

HOW TO BOTHER

However valuable a website may be, many museums faced with small budgets and staff find it intimidating to redesign a current website or create a new one from scratch. Concerns over resources make coding and designing (or hiring someone to do so) daunting and expensive. Fortunately, it does not have to be so, and it is never too late to start making a viable online presence for your historic site. Gone are the days of relying on a web designer who lives halfway across the country and has never been to your site. By far, the easiest and cheapest way to build and maintain a website is by using an online WYSIWYG[12] (What You See Is What You Get) editor. Dreamweaver has a WYSIWYG component, so anyone familiar with that software will understand the virtues of being able to see your content as you build it.

Newer WYSIWYG platforms are often free, in-browser editors, meaning that you immediately save a few hundred dollars on software. Moreover, you do not have to have specialized training in creating code or learning how to use complicated software. These programs provide website hosting, domains, and drag-and-drop design platforms and templates, eliminating the need to know HTML coding. They also simplify the design process, requiring much less time to become familiar with the editor's features. These editors are more abundant and easier to use than ever before, and they are the ideal tool for small- and medium-sized museums and historic sites that cannot afford the time or the cost of maintaining a coded website through an outside webmaster. Websites and blogs created on WYSIWYG editors[13] can be beautiful, professional, and as simple or complex as needed. They are, with a bit of practice, easy to create and maintain. They are flexible. And most importantly, they generally carry no more cost than that of just hosting the website's data.

HOW TO USE *FREE AND EASY WEBSITE DESIGN FOR MUSEUMS AND HISTORIC SITES*

This book seeks to guide you through the process of writing, designing, compiling, and maintaining a website that is professional, accessible, and relevant. All of the tools discussed in the book are free at the base level, and some offer upgrade packages with even more features. The advice and techniques are all created with an eye to making websites work for smaller institutions with limited budgets and timeframes. Chapter 1 will help you plan your website, from site goals and content to design and usability testing. Once you have mapped out and developed your site, Chapter 2 will help you lay out the actual web pages. You will find theories and techniques of basic web design, including a discussion of colors, graphics, layouts, and multimedia usage. Next, Chapters 3–6 provide guidance for selecting the best WYSIWYG editor for your needs and step-by-step instructions for getting your content online. Chapter 7 is an optional section that helps you make your site uniquely yours by tweaking basic HTML. In Chapter 8, you will explore ways to showcase your collection using blogs, online photo-sharing platforms, and Omeka—a collections-hosting platform designed specifically for museums, libraries, and archives. At the end, you will find a fully equipped glossary and a list of additional resources of interest. Throughout the book, there are tips geared uniquely toward museums and historic sites, as well as pointers on how to make your website accessible to all your visitors, including those using web readers for the visually impaired.

Lastly, the purchase of *Free and Easy Website Design for Museums and Historic Sites* gives you access to routinely updated online resources that pair with the material found here. The how-to guides for each WYSIWYG editor are routinely revised, and you have access to an interactive community forum for questions that arise during your planning and design process. Visit www. freethemuseum.net to get started. You will need to request access to the site using passcode: 239clwaej34lsg.

NOTES

1. For instance, web science, which studies the relationship between people and technology like the World Wide Web, is now a common degree in universities and colleges across the world. It draws from diverse fields, such as computer science, psychology, sociology, and mathematics. As an example, look to Fitt's Law—the idea that both the distance and size of, for example, a button, affect the rapidity with which a user can click on it. Fitt's Law has significantly influenced web design techniques and even print design. Additionally, homophily, or "love of the same" is a long-studied tendency of human interaction. Psychologists have found new ways to explore how "birds of a feather flock together" by tracing online interaction and browsing habits. Clearly, widespread usage of the Internet has prompted the flourishing of studies of humans' interaction with and through the web.

2. Weebly, "The Power of Sites in 2013," accessed October 20, 2014, http://www.weebly.com/power-of-sites.

3. Ibid.

4. Based on their review of the websites of the Imperial War Museum, the San Francisco Museum of Modern Art, the Powerhouse Museum, and various others.

5. Judy Haynes and Dan Zambonini, "Why Are They Doing That!? How Users Interact With Museum Web Sites," in J. Trant and D. Bearman, eds., *Museums and the Web 2007: Proceedings, Toronto: Archives & Museum Informatics*, March 1, 2007, accessed October 20, 2014, http://www.archimuse.com/mw2007/papers/haynes/haynes.html.

6. Kronkosky Charitable Foundation, *Museums Research Brief*, December 2013, accessed September 6, 2014, http://kronkosky.org/research/Research_Briefs/Museums%20%20December%202013.pdf. Having an online presence means having an active blog, website, artifact database, Facebook page, or some combination thereof. Moreover, it should be updated at least monthly to keep visitors engaged.

7. Dan Zambonini, "The Museum and Gallery Website: A Thing of the Past?" *Box UK Blog*, March 18, 2009, accessed September 6, 2014, www.boxuk.com/blog/museum-gallery-websites.

8. Jen Griffiths, "Why I Think Small Museums Should Have a Web Presence," *Historian @ Work*, November 3, 2010, accessed September 6, 2014, http://historianatwork.wordpress.com/2010/11/03/why-i-think-small-museums-should-have-a-web-presence.

9. American Association of Museums—Center for the Future of Museums, *Museums & Society 2034: Trends and Potential Futures*, December 2008, accessed September 6, 2014, www.aam-us.org/docs/center-for-the-future-of-museums/museumssociety2034.pdf.

10. Ibid.

11. Betty Farrell and Maria Medvedeva, *Demographic Transformation and the Future of Museums*, American Association of Museums—Center for the Future of Museums, 2010, accessed September 6, 2014, www.aam-us.org/docs/center-for-the-future-of-museums/demotransaam2010.pdf.

12. Pronounced "wissy-wig" in the web design world.

13. For the purposes of this book, the terms "WYSIWYG editor" or "WYSIWYG platform" refers specifically to those that are hosted online, including Weebly, Wix, WordPress, and Google Sites. These terms do not refer to WYSIWYG software programs available for purchase that must be installed on your computer.

Acknowledgments

So much energy and tech-savviness went into this book, not all of it mine, that I have a fair number of acknowledgments to make. A huge debt of gratitude goes to Dr. Kasey Grier and Tracy Jentzsch at the University of Delaware for giving me the opportunity to stretch my "web-design wings" as the webmaster for the Sustaining Places grant. Another goes to Lenore Bailey, Della Hall, and Ashley Hlebinsky for being sounding boards for my ideas and plans over the years.

I am indebted to the folks at the Arden Craft Shop Museum and Newlin Grist Mill for giving me the opportunity to experiment with their websites, which allowed me to learn how to use each of these platforms. Robin Valencia MacDonald and Barbara Macklem have been especially helpful in supporting me in my work in Arden while also trying to write a book. Test groups that gave me exceedingly valuable feedback on the material include KB Inglee, Sheila Jones, Jen Matthews, and Robin Valencia MacDonald. Your comments shaped this book in many ways, giving it usefulness that it would not have had otherwise. Many thanks go to my testers and readers for assistance with technical accuracy. Your help was vital in balancing the fine line between "giving sufficiently comprehensive details" and "avoiding information overload." Thank you to AASLH and Rowman & Littlefield for giving me a platform to spread the knowledge of website development that I have gained by working with such amazing and passionate groups of people as are found in the museum field.

Finally, thank you to my family: To Allan, without whom this book would not have been written (almost literally, as I wrote it on a new computer courtesy of the gentleman, who could not put up with my complaints of my "dinosaur laptop" anymore). To my father, Chris, whose writing models the style, humor, and clarity I hope to achieve in my own writing. You have read every draft I ever asked you to, and you truly are every daughter-writer's dream. To my mother, Shannon, who has always supported me in my goals and helped me think about them in a realistic way. You answer the phone every time, are ready to comfort and advise, and that is invaluable to me. To my brother, Sean, who always knew his sister needed to be simultaneously kept in line and encouraged. *Muchas gracias, mi hermano.*

Introduction

Mythbusting

Many smaller institutions find the prospect of creating a website intimidating or time consuming. While a quality website will certainly take time to build, there are a lot of common misconceptions about website design and development that can hinder the process unnecessarily. These misconceptions should not be a barrier to creating what is one of the best marketing and community-building tools available to museums and historic sites. Below, you will find a discussion of some of these common myths, some of which address the concerns of those who doubt a website is worth the trouble, and some of which concern changes to the web design field that have opened up flexible new possibilities.

Myth #1: Websites are not really worth it, plus we do not have the time or money to maintain a website.

Websites no longer cost hundreds of dollars to establish and maintain, and website creation and maintenance can now be done—and done quite easily—on-site. All you need is creative energy and an updated computer browser. Your website offers up your hours, address, mission, and other vital information to every potential visitor, including those that you cannot possibly reach with your physical site. In fact, the availability of this information online can be a deciding factor in whether a potential visitor comes to your museum. This is especially true for smartphone-wielding visitors, whose often on-the-go lifestyle comes with the expectation that that information will be easily accessible via the internet. Your online presence extends your potential reach, and is available to your audience even when you are not. A well-developed website boosts your visibility, offering a sense of professionalism and expertise. In the twenty-first century, having a website is, simply, a great idea.

Myth #2: Someone on staff has to know HTML or CSS to make a website, or we will have to pay someone who does know.

Not at all! Though an understanding of HTML, XML, and CSS can be helpful in tweaking your final product on a WYSIWYG platform, most of these platforms require *absolutely no programming knowledge.*

Myth #3: We have to have a specific computer to make a website and Macs/PCs are better.

First and foremost, this is one of the greatest marketing gimmicks of all time. PC merely means a "personal computer." The marketing team at Apple has enforced the idea that the term "Mac" is fundamentally opposed to the term "PC," when in fact, a Macintosh is just another competitor in the PC business (just like when the cleaning commercials compare their product to the "leading dishwashing brand"). This is not to say that Mac is not at a distinct advantage when it comes to accessibility, intuitiveness, and design quality, but do not let Mac's flashy advertising distract you from what really matters when it comes to outfitting your institution with technology. Below is some information for your consideration.

The advantages of a Wintel (or Windows-Intel-based) PC lie mostly in the price. Mac can easily run two or three times the price of a technically comparable Wintel computer. Wintels are often easier to link into existing computer networks because most institutions already have Wintel systems. They can be cheaper to repair because parts are sold by a greater number of retailers. This, however, points to one of the problems with Wintel computers: breakdowns and viruses. Computer hackers, spammers, etc. often target non-Mac systems because a greater portion of the population uses them so there is potential for a larger impact. Macs often have more built-in spyware and virus protection, though most Wintel computers come with free or cheap spyware already installed.

Macs are generally acknowledged to have a more aesthetically pleasing and intuitive interface, though a lot of this depends on the user's familiarity with each system. Though a large generalization, it is often alleged that Macs are for designers and other people with artistic endeavors and Wintels are for gamers, computer builders, and business people (who do a lot of networking and work in Excel).

What matters more than any specific computer brand is the web browser you use and how up-to-date your version is. Before you ever begin exploring WYSIWYG editors, download the most recent version of your chosen web browser; keep it updated throughout the process. See chapter 2 for more information about using web browsers.

Myth #4: Sans-serif fonts look better online, so all of our text has to be Arial or Helvetica.

Designers and psychologists alike have used up a lot of ink debating whether serif fonts "push" the eye across the page better than sans-serif fonts and whether computers have high enough resolutions to handle serif fonts. The conclusion seems to be that while serif fonts can lessen eye fatigue in traditional print, this does not necessarily mean much to websites.[1] Visitors do not read a website the way they read a book. Their eyes jump from the header to the page title and around succeeding paragraphs to find the information they seek, so there is no need to push their eye forward along the lines as book typefaces do. Sans-serif fonts make for great body text and easy navigation of menus, and serif fonts are easy enough to skim when looking for important information. More important is the *number* of fonts you use on a given page.

Myth #5: We can only use web-safe colors on our website.

Web-safe colors are an increasingly unimportant consideration in web design. When the internet first appeared, most computers could only display 256 colors, and for various browser-computer compatibility reasons, only 216 of these were considered "web-safe" colors. These colors were developed so that, in theory, any computer would display these exactly the same way that the designer intended them to be displayed. Though never completely universally standardized, web-safe colors were most important when the majority of users had devices with 8-bit displays.

At this point in time, however, most PCs have at least a 24-bit display and most mobile devices have at least a 12-bit display. As such, pretty much any color you pick will be displayed correctly on most devices. If you are using Wix, Weebly, or another WYSIWYG editor, however, you probably will not even have to worry about editing colors. There will be preset colors you can choose from, so you can just click on the one that you like the most and the code for that color will be automatically updated. Some of these platforms do offer the ability to define specific colors using RGB and hexadecimal codes, and those are addressed in the individual subsections in Part II. Check out some of the quick tools to convert colors from one color system discussed in Chapter 2 and listed in Appendix A.

Myth #6: I need to use two spaces after periods.

The internet is plagued with dozens of arguments back and forth about using two versus one space, and both sides have valid reasons for their assertions. The most commonly named reason for the debate is that word processing on typewriters before modern computers came around merited two spaces due to the use of monospaced type. Each letter of a monospaced font, such as Courier, takes up the same width on the page. Two spaces after the period in monospaced documents helped the eye quickly find the period, and therefore the end of the sentence. Modern word processors, however, often automatically adjust their kerning (i.e., they automatically make the space after a period ever-so-slightly larger than that between words). Most typographers and graphic designers agree that one space is the best rule to follow because the eye can still quickly find those pesky periods and you save space in the long run. More on the history of monospaced versus proportional typesets can be found at theworldsgreatestbook.com/how-many-spaces-after-a-period.

Vitriolic accounts of the history of monospaced fonts aside, at the end of the day, consistency is what matters. Habit, more than aesthetics, determines the number of spaces each person types, so check each page carefully for consistency in these spaces before finalizing your text. A quick way to find and change all spaces in a document at once is to click Command+F (on a Mac), Control+F (on Windows) or navigate to Find and Replace. In the Find field, type ". " to find one space at the end of a sentence or ". " to find two spaces at the end of a sentence. In the Replace field, type ". " to insert the second space at the end of every sentence or ". " to eliminate the second space, depending on which style you decide on.

☙

After reading the preface and dispelling these common myths, you should feel confident that creating your website is both feasible and well worth the effort. If any of the discussions above delved into unfamiliar territory, never fear. Working through Chapters 1 and 2 before moving on to building your website will give you a gradual introduction to some of the more challenging aspects of website development and design.

NOTE

1. Look to webdesignerdepot.com/2013/03/serif-vs-sans-the-final-battle for an excellent summary of the debate.

Part I

PREPARE YOUR WEBSITE

CAB

The first part of this book will help you plan your website. The first chapter guides you through the seven steps of developing a website—from writing your website text to creating an update schedule for the final product. Read through these two chapters in order first, before moving on to Parts II and III. This will help you avoid jumping ahead in the process and having to come back later and redo foundational parts of your website.

...SEO settings if you know this category or [...] on page of your website. For instance, you may want to sell educations [...] on your Education page and memberships for golf tournaments [...]

Under the Orders menu, you can see a list of past orders [...] with their [...] and other details. After you have your first order, you'll begin managing your orders here by marking them as shipped, [...] customers about order details or missing information, and exporting your emails to a spreadsheet program like Excel.

Adjust Online Store Settings

As with the general site settings mentioned earlier, the online store settings are not all included in the free package, so they will not all be addressed. For example, settings for shipping and taxes are only available with an upgrade to the Business Package or higher. You can also just figure these costs into your product listing. Settings you should be aware of include:

- Store → General
  - Currency and Weight Unit are determined by your location.
  - Store Mode indicates whether visitors buy items all at once (Add to Cart) or one-by-one (Buy Now).
  - *Make sure you fill out your store information so that confirmations and receipts can be sent to your customers.*
  - Your shipping and return policies provide important information to your customers about the turnaround time for their orders, their options for returning unwanted merchandise, and any extra charges of shipping [...] will have on their order. Any details customers need will be given to your customer at checkout, on their receipt, or both.
  - If you want your customer to have the option of including a message with special requests or other details, slide the Note to Seller switch to on.
- Store → Checkout: This is where you will select which payment processor you will use. You can choose between Weebly (via Stripe), Square, Authorize.net, and PayPal. As Weebly's preferred integration, Stripe is available with the free Weebly package. The nice part about this option is only the designers have made the Stripe checkout integrate seamlessly with your store. Visitors will never have to leave your site or create another account to check out. You pay for this integration—literally—with a 3 percent merchant fee to Weebly in *addition* to the Stripe fee of 2.9 percent + $0.30 per transaction. You may want to take these costs into consideration when choosing/setting the type and price of items for sale on your site. For anyone intent on using PayPal to collect donations, and not sell items, the free option in this section [...]

Chapter 1

Planning Your Website

The bulk of the work that goes into developing a site actually happens before you ever set mouse to monitor. Picking colors and fonts must wait until you have what your visitors actually come for—the content. Taking the time to plan your goals, map out your site, evaluate your audience, and develop the prose that will represent your institution to the public is crucial to making a successful website. The best first step you can take is to gather together the leaders of your institution and every person who will be contributing to your website and brainstorm the details reviewed below. The planning committee does not need to meet for every stage, but you should have an initial meeting to brainstorm and assign tasks.

STEP 1A: STREAMLINE EMAIL ACCOUNT

Before you sign up for any WYSIWYG (What You See Is What You Get) editors or other accounts, create an email address to which *all your website information* will be connected. It behooves your organization to have a single receptacle for all website-related information and accounts because:

- Using a personal account can make things difficult if the owner of that account leaves the organization or someone else needs to access the content.
- Using multiple accounts makes it harder to track down information on the website or website accounts.
- Having a single, professional email account for your organization makes it easy for visitors to remember and looks cleaner on promotional materials, letterhead, and the like.

Google and Yahoo, among many others, offer free email services, so try signing up for one with a name like yourmuseum@gmail.com.[1] Chances are, you can snag a unique email (no more kr5482@hotmail.com). This will boost your recognizability among your visitors and make it easy for staff and volunteers to remember.

STEP 1B: IDENTIFY AUDIENCE

Contrary to what you might think, the audience for your website may not be the same as the audience for your physical site. There will likely be overlap, especially for those visitors who come to your website for your contact information, address, and directions. However, the difference lies not only in *what* visitors look for on your site or what they intend to do with the information they find, but also in *how* they will access the site and what their expectations for that access are. Therefore, the first task is to consider who your audience is—or if you have more than one.

For instance, you might have a great relationship with a local school that brings all its sixth graders to your museum for a presentation on civil rights during the month of November. With this relationship in mind, you know that parents might look at your site to see what the presentation curriculum is. Chaperones for the field trip will want to know about parking. Teachers from neighboring schools want to know who they can contact to set up their own field trips like this. On the other hand, you might be situated near a retirement community with an active ceramics group. They often look for places to exhibit, and your institution has a small rotating gallery space that you look to switch out once or twice per year. Your new website is the perfect place to include information on rental space, an "artist of the month" submission form, or details on the latest round of pottery displays from the Woodland Senior Center.

As you may have surmised, the new website is your chance not only to identify your current audience(s) but also to think about what audiences you want to reach that you might not currently be reaching. Once identified, you can incorporate strategies for reaching these audiences into your site plan. Cast a wide net, thinking of all your current audiences and potential audiences, then narrow it down to focus on the most important or realistically reachable ones. Consider how these different audiences will use your site. The teachers, for example, will likely be accessing your site through a web browser on their work computer. Parents might be on the go and using their smartphones. The ceramics group leader might do either of the above—do not assume that only teenagers use their phones and every senior center uses a dial-up modem.

Once you have a list of your audience members, write a corresponding list of how users might choose to access your site. Think about both access route and access device: on an iPhone, through a Google search, using Internet Explorer, navigating directly to your URL, at home, through a link on a local historical coalition, etc. Though you cannot anticipate all scenarios, having a general idea of your audience will help you anticipate their needs during their online visit. In turn, this will help you in planning and testing your website. Many website developers find it helpful to paint a picture of their "ideal visitor,"[2] meaning one of the people they consider most likely to visit their website. Is your ideal visitor male? Is your ideal visitor young? Is your ideal visitor a parent? Does your ideal visitor work in the humanities? Develop three to four profiles for ideal visitors, and use these to help guide your design and development. For each major stage, ask yourself or your team how Ideal Visitor 1 would respond to the layout. Posit how Ideal Visitor 2 would navigate to your Calendar of Events. Discuss what ways Ideal Visitor 3 might contact you through the website.

STEP 2: ESTABLISH SITE GOALS

Keeping your audience in mind, the planning committee should next establish what the goals for the site are. This means determining what basic functions the site should fulfill (e.g., providing contact information and location details) as well as what new or unique services your site can provide (e.g., hosting a permanent online exhibit about local history that teachers in the area can use in their curriculum—which boosts your audience count, expands your reach into classrooms, and piques the interest of young minds that might convince their families to come visit your physical site). To begin, ask your team the following questions:

1. Whom do we want to reach with our site? *Remember that "everyone" or the similarly vague "a diverse group" will not help us develop specific, measurable goals for our site.*
2. What are our expectations for the site?
3. What will our audience(s) expect from the site?
4. How will people access our site?
5. How much time can we commit to our site each month (or, how often do we want to update the site or post to the blog)?
6. What are the limitations of our online presence (or, what does our physical site offer that our website cannot—and vice versa)?
7. What can our site offer visitors who cannot come to our physical location?
8. How can the website engage with or supplement in-person visits?

9. How can we engage new visitors? Maintain current visitors?
10. How will we measure the effectiveness of our site?

Another way to direct thinking about your website is by describing what you want it to portray using single adjectives, almost like you are describing the personality of a person. Do you want it to be professional? Casual? Friendly? Cultured? Savvy? Technological? Contemporary? Identifying a group of these words will help you direct both the content and the design of your site later on.

Throughout, be specific with numbers and timelines (e.g., "In the next year, we want to reach five new classrooms through our online exhibit and we will measure that by emailing newsletters and surveys to local teachers."). Create achievable goals—you will probably not be able to garner 500,000 new visitors to your physical site in the first month after launching your website, but you might be able to entice twenty families to the yearly "Family Night at the Museum" that you announce on the front page of your website. Make sure you include both short- and long-term goals, as this will help you see the impact your site has and adjust your aims and plans accordingly. There is no "right" number of goals; perhaps you only have one. The important part is asking your team these kinds of questions and thinking of your website as more than just a page on the internet where visitors can see your open hours (though this, too, is of supreme import).

STEP 3: CREATE SITEMAP

After you know where your site is headed conceptually, you need to figure out where your site is headed in a more literal sense: you need to create a sitemap. A sitemap shows all the connections between pages, almost like a family tree. It traces all possible routes of navigation between pages. A well-done sitemap, developed before site construction ever begins, will make your website easier to navigate, both for your visitors and for search engines—meaning that those who do not already know where or what your museum is can find it more easily through a Google or Yahoo search.[3] Simple sitemaps will show a home page, contact page, and a few other content pages. More complex sitemaps will show all links on a site. Starting with a simple sitemap and building out from there is best for determining the basic structure of your site.

On a large piece of paper, write down all the pages you will need. Include any of the following that are appropriate:

- About Us
- Blog

- Calendar of Events
- Collections
- Donate
- Education/Field Trips
- Employment/Opportunities
- Exhibitions
- FAQs
- Get Involved/Volunteer
- Gift Shop
- Home
- Interns
- Location & Directions
- Membership
- News
- Newsletter
- Programs
- Rentals
- Research
- Special Events
- Staff List/Contact
- Visit Us

Using your site goals as a guide, include in the master list any other pages you will need, keeping in mind that some pages can be combined (e.g., Contact Us and Staff List often include the same information, so why design two pages when you can do one coherent one?).

Decide what your top menu items will be. The big ticket items are Home, Visit Us, Get Involved, Events & Programs, Blog, etc. Then, underneath the appropriate top-level pages, list your second-level pages: Location & Directions (under Visit Us), Volunteer (under Get Involved), Calendar of Events (under Events & Programs), etc. If you have third-level pages, list those as well. If you know that you will want to link *between* pages, include this in your sitemap. For example, you may want to link to your Calendar of Events page from both your Programs page and your Special Events page. In that case, you will include the link on both pages in addition to putting the calendar as a menu or submenu item, and representing this on the sitemap is a reminder to review the relationship between all your pages.

As you decide these relationships, keep in mind that visitors want to be able to navigate quickly and without a lot of guesswork. Avoid over-layering your site. You do not want to hide your Location & Directions page three pages down in the menu. With the exception of collections database items, if something cannot be accessed from within four or five clicks of the home page, it is probably buried too deeply. Consider what pages should have links in the header and footer of your site and therefore show up on every single page. These pages are often pages like Contact Us, Employment, and Location & Directions. These are the pages that most visitors will want to look at or that otherwise contain the most sought-after information. Moreover, do not structure your site so that every page is linked to every other page, except through menu items. The menu is a valuable tool for organizing your website, so take advantage of its built-in organization but do not overburden it with too many items or submenus. Once you feel comfortable with your sitemap, move on to listing the elements you will need on each page.

STEP 4: LIST ELEMENTS

Before delving too deep into creating written content for your site, take the time to list the nontext elements you will need to create. This includes your institution's logo, a summary of photos for each page, YouTube videos, audio files, PDFs, and other multimedia components. If you do not have an institutional logo, seriously consider developing one. It can be as simple as your museum name in a fancy font or as complex as one you hire a professional graphic designer to create.[4] If you decide to create a logo yourself, look in the Additional Resources section at the back of the book for free or generic software you can use to lay out and design your logo. No matter what logo route you decide on, having a single logo for your website and official documents is vital for presenting a unified, professional image of your institution. Logos help you create brand recognition, just like the "Nike swoosh" or the "best part of waking up" Folgers jingle. Do not underestimate how much a logo can do for your organization.

When choosing images for your website, keep both copyright and quality in mind. One of the great things about running a museum or historic site is that you generally own the right to reproduce your collection, so you have built-in subject matter—all you have to do is produce a high-quality photograph or scan.[5] For information on generating your own images by photographing or scanning, look to Chapter 2 on basic web design. Use stock photos with reservation; people visit your website to learn about *you* and *your institution*, so showing them photos of your events or your volunteers will draw them in more readily than an unimaginative, generic photo. If you do not have such photos readily on hand, now is the time to start taking them! Bring a camera along to all your functions, be they board meetings, public lectures, or work nights.

If you plan to have downloadable documents, such as volunteer interest forms or research requests, prepare these by turning them into PDFs. Turning documents into PDFs ensures that they are consistently readable by all your viewers; to wit, you do not have to worry whether your visitors have the same fonts or computer programs as you because the PDF displays the content of the document almost like an image and nothing becomes distorted or out of alignment due to a change in machinery. Again, look to Chapter 2 for specifics on preparing your images, documents, and other media for use on your website.

STEP 5: GENERATE CONTENT

You will be creating your site's text content in Word, Pages, or another word processing program, so once you feel comfortable with your sitemap and element list, create a Word document for *each* page, no matter how little content will actually be on the page. Writing your text content in a Word document makes it easier to focus on the content itself rather than the form or layout. Make a single folder titled [Your Website] and a single document for each page with the page as the document title.[6] This aids in the sharing of documents for review and editing as well, and it will be especially helpful if you are working with a group to complete the website.

If you are working with a group, think about how to structure the responsibility for the website. Ideally, you will have one webmaster, the person to whom all content is submitted for "publication." This person then reviews it for consistency, designs the layout of the page, and puts the content up online. If you have a large website, give the content responsibility for sections or individual pages to those most involved in the events or areas it describes. For example, if you have a volunteer coordinator, he will have the best grip on what information needs to be conveyed about joining the museum as a volunteer. Your curator, however, will be better suited for writing up the donation guidelines for the "Gifts" page. She will know whether or not to post the guidelines on the website or if she would prefer to be contacted directly for inquiries. Furthermore, your volunteer docents may have input on the most common questions visitors ask. You can use these to create a FAQ page that tells visitors to bring jackets to wear in the chilly gallery and advise them that you sell water in your small gift shop.

Not all pages need to written by different people, and some of your pages may even be collaborative. Generally, your "About Us" page will have more collaboration-friendly content because it might contain things like your mission and values or organization's history. Your "Hours and Information" page, on the other hand, can be written by one person and then checked by others for errors along with the rest of the site. Remember, regardless of who writes what, all pages and content should be submitted to the webmaster for finalization.

Once you have your page responsibilities agreed upon, develop a style guide. Following a style guide saves you time correcting styling inconsistencies and can actually make your collaborators feel more comfortable generating content on their own. Share the guide among all your collaborators. To simplify the process, you can start with one that is already written and adapt it to your purposes. Two great resources for developing a style guide are the *Chicago Manual of Style* and *The Elements of Style* by William Strunk, Jr. and E. B. White. Whether you start from scratch or adapt from an existing source, your style guide should address topics like:

- Whether you will use the Oxford comma[7]
- What abbreviations are appropriate for your site (e.g., MoMA or MOMA)
- What text is italicized versus bolded versus underlined
- What punctuation conventions you will follow
- What the overall voice for your text should be (e.g., will you be more friendly or more formal?)
- The format and style of headings and text
- Whether numbers are spelled out or written as numerals
- The capitalization and punctuation of lists

It bears noting that you should keep it simple—for this first step of content creation, keep text as plain as possible, as you will have to format all your text in the WYSIWYG editor when you place it. For the development process, stick with Times New Roman, a font native to every word processor. Do not worry about creating bullet points or double-spacing text just yet, as all that can be done once you insert the text into your website.[8]

When writing the text of your website, refer to your site goals often, always keeping your intended audience in mind. You may want to consult the section on Search Engine Optimization (SEO) in Chapter 2. This will help you identify keywords for each page to incorporate into your site content. Keep text in small paragraphs that are to the point and engaging. Your website should provide both quick answers and also detailed information (or instruction on finding more detailed answers) for those that want them. This means that key information should be concise and at the forefront of the text. More in-depth text belongs "deeper" in the website. For example, your main event pages, often your Calendar of Events, should list events by date, theme, and/or audience. An interested reader can then click on the event and be taken to a page with specific information about the event. You do not need to list every bit of information on the calendar, thus cluttering it up. Similarly, a page discussing your collections might give a brief overview of your object collection, archives, and current exhibitions. Deeper pages about each one of these will have lengthier lists, descriptions of specific strengths of your collection, or links to an online database. Essentially, the deeper the visitor goes into your site, the more information the visitor should find, and basics should be found prominently placed on top-level pages.

After you have a draft of all your pages, have everyone edit each other's work. If you are working mostly on your own, send your content around to as many readers as you can, but to at least three people. Beyond being able to catch errors, this helps unify the voice of the site. Either print out one copy of each page to pass around or distribute the documents electronically and use the Track Changes feature in your word processor—whichever your team feels more comfortable with. Review every page for content, spelling, grammar, flow, style, and anything else that comes up, using the checklist in Appendix B for each page. Incorporate the edits into your documents and get ready to start laying out your site. **Move to Chapters 2 through 6 to construct your site before beginning the review and testing phase and the website promotion that form the final steps in building your website.**

STEP 6: REVIEW AND TEST SITE

The penultimate step in preparing your website comes after you have put it all together in your WYSIWYG editor. Before beginning this step, you will have read through Chapter 2 on basic web design and laid out your website using information from Chapters 3 to 6 on WYSIWYG editors. You have added the written content, uploaded your photos, inserted your documents, and adjusted your fonts and colors. At long last, you are ready to review and test your website. Surprisingly, this may actually be the step that takes the longest, and is in many ways an ongoing task. Any time you add new content or significantly modify a page, you will want to have at least one person check it over on a separate computer for formatting or display issues and typos. Additionally, this, of all phases, is a step that needs to be done with a group of people. The good news is that this can—and should—be done by a variety of people on their own (and on their own devices). It is important that your website is reviewed on a number of different browsers and devices, and selecting a diverse group of reviewers will help you cast a wide net.

A month before you plan to finish your site, reach out to volunteers, interns, staff, family members, community members, and anyone else you think can give you helpful feedback about the functionality and content of your website. This group should include people who can view the site on smartphones, personal computers, and tablets; on Macintosh, Linux, and Windows-based computers; and on Google Chrome, Firefox, Safari, and Internet Explorer. If you know that visitors will be using another browser or device to access your website, seek out a way to test your website on that as well. Essentially, you want to verify that your site is accessible and functional to anyone who visits it and in whatever manner they visit it. The reviewers will be checking not only for functionality on devices, but also for grammatical edits, accessibility, and more. When reviewers agree to look over the site, send them a page-by-page review checklist, as seen in Appendix B. Every reviewer should check every page for edits and consistency, and using the checklist will give you easy-to-follow feedback that assures multiple reviews of each page. This part can take more time than expected, as the webmaster will be cross-referencing edits between each page. Plan to spend at least ten minutes per page to fix typos, but know that this may take up to three or four hours per page if you have a lot of content and/or feedback from your readers. You may want to provide reviewers with a guide to help them navigate your site, but ask them to find content on their own first if possible. That way, you can get an idea of your site's navigability.

Naturally, spelling and grammar edits are top of the list when thinking of the type of feedback you want from your reviewers. Just as you did with your content documents, you will want an in-house style guide, which can be used for more than just your website (e.g., letters, pamphlets, and other printed materials). You may need to adjust your style guide for the online review, as you will likely have added formatting and font stylizations to your text (e.g., you may now have bolded words to denote linked material). Just make sure that everyone reviewing and editing the site gets the same guidelines in the style guide. Any spelling, grammar, or text content edits should be made first in the word processing document you created in Step 5, saved with a new document title (e.g., if your original document was Home_Page.doc, the new one should be Home_Page_Edit_May_14_2014.doc), and then changed on your site. Anytime you update this kind of content, make a similar update to the document name. This way, if you need to reproduce a page or have accidentally deleted content, you always have the most recent version of your website's content saved on your computer and can easily replace it.

Reviewers should also check the quality of images and how they display on the page. Oftentimes, an image will not be sized correctly, causing the image to display larger than the screen so that the viewer has to scroll over to see it. Avoid this by following the graphic guidelines in Chapter 2. One such guideline is that images should be at least 72 PPI and not more than 300 PPI. This ensures that they are smooth and clear but do not cause overlong loading times for those with dial-up or otherwise slow connections. Your reviewers should be on the lookout for images that do not display correctly because of their physical or file sizes. They should also check for alt text on all images—descriptive text that allows accessibility features of different web browsers to "read" the images. Check this by hovering over an image on a page until a small line of text pops up, generally bearing the name of the image file or other description of the image content.

Checking links both between your pages and also to outside resources is extremely important, and should be done routinely, even after the website is finalized. Viewers will be frustrated by links that only reach dead-ends or 404 errors—they clicked on the link to find more information and instead found themselves on a blank page. Part of the monthly (or otherwise routine) updates to the website should be to check on important links.

If the website has online forms, such as those used to send a question to the visitor services coordinator to show interest in volunteering, reviewers should fill out a test submission on each form. Make sure that both *you* and also the *reviewer* receive confirmation of the form submission. Most WYSIWYG editors have the option to send form submissions to an email address or a cloud-hosted document (such as a Google Docs Spreadsheet). Determine who will check this in-basket for submissions and respond to them in a timely manner.

Embedded content, like YouTube videos or a Google Calendar, can be tricky to test, as you are dealing with two services, namely your website editor and the content host. The easiest way to test this content is by checking how it displays as soon as you link it. In two separate windows or tabs, open your editor and your website (where you have navigated to the page that will hold the embedded element). Once you embed the content, save/publish the changes. In the window that has your website open, refresh the page (Command + R or the refresh button). The element should update, letting you see if it is properly embedded. If, after review, it appears that you need to update the embedded content, you will need to log into the service that hosts the embedded content (rather than your WYSIWYG editor). If you have any outside accounts used to generate this embedded content, like Gmail (which includes YouTube and Google Calendar), Facebook, or Twitter, both these and your WYSIWYG editor account should all be linked to the email account you created in Step 1a.

STEP 7: PROMOTE AND UPDATE SITE

Many cultural institutions discover that the "if you build it, they will come" mantra is not inherently applicable to their physical sites. The same is true about a website; you still need to promote the newest addition to your institution. Put your new URL on business cards, postcards, email signature lines, and anything else you distribute to the public. Use search engines daily to find your institution and make sure your website appears on the first page of the search.[9] Look on Yahoo and Google Maps to verify that they have your business contact information and hours correct. If they do not, contact their

Help or Customer Service and make sure they properly link to your website.[10] Announce the new site in newsletters, at meetings, and in your museum. Ask your volunteers and employees to encourage visitors to access your collections, look up your hours and directions, or just generally find more information on the new site. Ring the bells far and wide, and be proud of all you have accomplished!

Work on your website does not stop after you have released the site to the public, however. During your site planning above, you should have created an update schedule. *Your site should be reviewed and, if necessary, updated at least twice per year.* If you have a blog, calendar of events, or other rotating information, it should be updated monthly to boost visibility and audience reach. Choose one day each month that you will remove old events and post new ones or write a short blog on what has happened at the museum the previous month. You can share blogging responsibilities among volunteers or staff members, as readers generally appreciate a variety of voices and viewpoints in the more informal setting of the blog. A classic blogging idea is a rotating "Day in the Life of a Museum Worker," where one post is from the curator, another from the director, another from the education coordinator, and so on. This lets your visitors get to know a different side of your organization, spreads the blogging workload around, and keeps drawing visitors back to your website—and therefore, hopefully, to your organization. Principally, what is important is creating a feasible editing and updating schedule—*and keeping to it.*

NOTES

1. Consider signing up for Google for nonprofits if you already own or plan to buy your own domain. Found at google.com/nonprofits, this program offers viable nonprofits specialized email addresses and access to many Google products for free.

2. "Ideal" does not mean "perfect," simply that the person is likely to visit or seek your organization out.

3. *Search Engine Optimization Guide*, Google, 2010, accessed February 21, 2015, http://static.googleusercontent.com/external_content/untrusted_dlcp/www.google.com/en/us/webmasters/docs/search-engine-optimization-starter-guide.pdf.

4. One route a lot of small businesses have begun taking is developing a logo using crowdsourced logo design. Sites like DesignCrowd, 99designs, and Freelancer let you submit a project to multiple designers all at once and then pick the best result. You describe your institution and a general idea of what you are looking for, any of their certified designers can design and submit a design, then you can choose the one you like most. DesignCrowd and 99designs are on the more expensive end, with design packages starting around $250 and above, but Freelancer lets you set whatever price you can afford and judge to be fair. The former two sites tend to pull in more

submissions because of the higher pay, but Freelancer has had many satisfied customers for a lot less—even as low as $10. Find links to these sites in the Additional Resources section at the back of the book.

5. Museum copyright is a much-debated issue. For more information on this subject, check out Marilyn E. Phelan, *Museum Law: A Guide for Officers, Directors, and Counsel*, 4th ed. (Lanham: Rowman & Littlefield Publishers, 2014).

6. In 2007, Microsoft introduced a new file format, the .docx, which cannot always be opened in previous versions of Word or on Mac computers. If you are using a Windows-based computer with Word 2007 or later, make sure that you save your files in compatibility mode—this ensures that all collaborators can open the documents. To save in compatibility mode, you will need to save your file as a .doc with no final "x." This can be done by selecting Save As, typing in the file name, selecting Word 97–2003 Document in the drop-down menu of document types, and clicking Save.

7. Also known as the serial comma, the Oxford comma is used after the final item in a list of three or more. A great discussion of this topic can be found in *Eats, Shoots & Leaves: The Zero Tolerance Approach to Punctuation* by Lynne Truss. Ultimately, the choice is up to you, but think about the difference between the following sentences:

I admire my parents, Superman, and Wonder Woman.
Wherein you admire four people: two parents and two superheroes.

I admire my parents, Superman and Wonder Woman.
Wherein it is unclear whether you admire the four people stated above or two people: your parents, who are Superman and Wonder Woman.

8. It is also worth noting that you do *not need* to use two spaces after a period. The internet is plagued with dozens of arguments back and forth about using two versus one space, but consider this: both the Chicago Manual of Style (CMS) and the Modern Language Association (MLA) support a single space in published material—which your website will be.

9. For more on how to do this, look to the section on SEO settings in Chapter 2.

10. Look at google.com/business and smallbusiness.yahoo.com/local-listings for more information on your free listing on each of the popular search sites.

Chapter 2

Designing Your Website

How you go about designing your site depends on which WYSIWYG platform you choose to use. The following section introduces some basic web design principles, including color matching and font selection, but the ultimate layout of your site will be subject to the limitations and abilities of your WYSIWYG editor. If you already know which editor you will be using, spend time experimenting with it to get to know the possibilities (or, if you choose to use a fairly complete template, look at the layout into which you will be fitting everything). If you do not know yet, look at page 34 and peruse Chapters 3–6 to get an idea of template layouts, fonts, colors, and overall flexibility each editor offers. Working through the first two sessions of each chapter may give you an idea of what WYSIWYG editor is right for your organization.

Unlike the process of developing content, design should not be done by committee. While the final design may be subject to group *approval*, having a single aesthetic taste unify the overall feel of the site streamlines the process and makes what is often the hardest-to-agree-upon aspect of the site less stressful to develop. The designer should work on the layout, colors, fonts, and similar elements with occasional input from others close to the process. If the group at large wants to participate in the design process, consider presenting them with two or three completed options to choose from for the final product. This gets everyone involved, but helps you avoid analyzing every element of the site via committee. One option is to lay out the same page (e.g., the home page) in two different designs using the guidelines below and then screenshot or print the designs for presentation to the committee.

Whether you have years of experience or no experience at all with design, coding, and content creation, the tremendous speed of technological development means that the rules of the game are always changing. Where once white space was forbidden and serif fonts were the law of the land, new viewing platforms and updated design techniques make options more flexible and more accessible to any would-be website designer. White space and color blocks can provide aesthetic relief in the online world of flashing media and noisy advertisements. Sans-serif fonts make for great body text and easy navigation of menus. No one can keep on top of all the changing trends, but this chapter lays out some timeless advice and some of the most important and practical design advice for creating sites on modern WYSIWYG editors.

BASIC SYSTEM REQUIREMENTS

These increased web design capabilities do mandate a few technological upgrades. Regardless of which computer and browser you end up using, always make sure that you have the most recent versions of Flash, Adobe Reader, and other software installed. There is no denying that the newer the computer and software, the faster and easier it will be to access the WYSIWYG editor. Desktops, as opposed to laptops, generally have bigger screens, which can make laying out and reviewing your website easier. However, the brand and form of computer matters less than the software versions you use and the speed of your internet connection. High-speed Wi-Fi or ethernet connections are ideal. Dial-up is sometimes too slow to prevent server timeouts on flashier sites.

Regularly updated browsers like Google Chrome and Firefox are best, as they quickly integrate bug fixes and software updates (they are also both free—and safe—to download.)[1] Safari is fairly quick to follow suit, but does occasionally fall behind in the web technology game. Internet Explorer, quite frankly, works poorly with many websites.[2] In fact, Microsoft is planning to discontinue Internet Explorer in the next few years and replace it with a brand-new browser.[3] Whatever technology you end up using, make sure that you have the most recent version of its software, and check for updates regularly.

WEBSITE STYLE

All pages of your site should follow the same style. This means restricting your colors, fonts, text styles, and layouts to no more than three each. The sections below offer some basic web design principles and guidelines, but keep in mind that your site will likely undergo changes as you add content and get a feel for how your site works. Divergent schools of design make it difficult to know which rules excel and which ones are just personal preference. That said, there are some generally agreed-upon principles—many even backed up by psychological studies—that can help guide beginning web developers.

Colors

Before you begin picking colors, review the color basics that follow to help you decide what colors and tones are right for your website. The color wheel, whose circular form was first designed by Isaac Newton in the seventeenth century,[4] looms large in any discussion of color. Use paletton.com to help you in your review of the following color basics: primary, secondary, and tertiary colors; warm and cool colors; color associations; and complementary, analogous, triadic, split-complementary, and tetradic color schemes.[5]

The color categories below serve as the basis for all color mixing, so it is important to familiarize yourself with the way the colors on the color wheel relate to each other. The first concept to master is primary colors, followed by their "offspring," secondary and tertiary colors.

- Primary colors: The three colors from which all other colors can be created are red, yellow, and blue.
- Secondary colors: The colors that are made by evenly mixing two colors are orange, green, and purple. *Red and yellow together make orange; yellow and blue make green; blue and red make purple.*
- Tertiary colors: The colors that can be made by mixing primary and secondary colors are red-orange, yellow-orange, yellow-green (lime green), blue-green (teal), blue-purple, red-purple (burgundy).

The color wheel can also be divided (roughly in half) into warm and cool colors. Vivid, warm colors like red, orange, and yellow convey energy and openness. Calm, cool colors include green, blue, and violet. White, black, and gray are not included in these categories, as they are considered neutral. There is no firm rule about which of these categories creates more favorable visuals online, but keep in mind that colors inspire various feelings in every viewer and carry a myriad of associations in different cultural contexts. For instance, blue is often considered a safe option for a diverse audience because it has positive associations in many cultures. Because of its popularity, it is quite prevalent in logos—think about how many logos you know of with a large amount of blue (Twitter, Facebook, WordPress, Major League Baseball, BMW, Hewlett-Packard, Gap, and various sundry more). Though you cannot predict every visitor's reaction to your website, examine the different color associations[6] listed below and mull over how they relate to your institution, goals, and overall feel of your site.

- Red: romance, adventure, luck, boldness, youth, passion, joy, celebration, anger, danger
- Orange: health, cheer, friendliness, confidence, excitement, warmth, courage, adventure, autumn, Halloween, energy, vitality, enthusiasm, mourning, gluttony
- Yellow: happiness, warmth, optimism, clarity, courage, cheerfulness, hospitality, money, success, illness, frustration, anger, mourning
- Green: peace, growth, health, luck, wealth, nature, strength, environmentalism, sexuality, jealousy
- Blue: dependability, professionalism, spirituality, serenity, peace, trustworthiness, loyalty, cleanliness, femininity, protection, sadness
- Purple: creativity, imagination, dignity, royalty, decadence, wealth, fame, virtue, honor, intellectualism, wisdom, exoticism, mourning
- Black: power, formality, sophistication, masculinity, wealth, prosperity, magic, mourning, evil
- White: purity, holiness, peace, innocence, coldness, sterility, blandness, death, mourning
- Grey: balance, neutrality, calmness
- Pink: love, femininity, romance, gentleness, youth, freshness, fun, calmness
- Brown: strength, reliability, warmth, comfort, security, nature

If choosing a color scheme with multiple colors, you will want to use colors that go well together because they act as color chords (also known as color harmonies). Consider the following chords when picking your color scheme:

- Complementary: Colors that are opposite each other on the color wheel
  These create a very vivid palette, though they are hard on the eye if used for the entire site. They are good to use when you want to call attention to something and make it stand out. Example: red and green.
- Split-complementary: One color and the two colors that are adjacent to its complement
  These color schemes also create a strong visual contrast like their cousin, complementary color schemes, but are often more harmonious. Example: green, red-orange, and red-purple (often called burgundy).
- Analogous: Colors that are next to each other on the color wheel
  Analogous color schemes are generally pleasing to the eye. You can easily incorporate a third analogous color for accentuating certain elements. Example: green and blue-green (often called teal) or green, blue-green, and yellow-green (often called lime green).
- Triadic: Three colors that are evenly spaced on the color wheel
  This is another very lively color scheme. One color should be the dominant color, and the other two used for calling attention to certain elements. Example: primarily blue with green and red accents.

- Tetradic: Four colors chosen from two complementary pairs
  This color scheme creates a bold palette. If warm and cool colors are balanced well, one color will dominate the other three but will not be the only noticeable color. Example: primarily blue with accents of red, orange, and green.

After perusing the color wheel, pick out different color combinations you feel appropriate for your website and your institution. For a visual tool you can use to explore color combinations that work well together, visit color. adobe.com.[7] All of the WYSIWYG editors discussed in this book include themes and/or color palettes to choose from, so unless you choose to edit the HTML or CSS of your site, you do not *have* to select your exact colors, only have an idea of the tone you wish to achieve. Some of the platforms, in addition to providing a color palette to choose from, do offer the ability to select specific colors using RGB and hex codes.[8] If you do choose to select specific colors and/or edit the code of your website, look to Chapter 7 to learn about web-safe colors and RGB and hexadecimal color codes.

Throughout, keep in mind that although color plays a major part in your website, your content should not be color-dependent. Some of your visitors may not actually be able to see the colors, as is the case for colorblind users or those using web readers for accessibility reasons. Certain browsers and devices do not support all colors, so stay away from designs that are all color (e.g., seven shades of green with no white on the page), have poorly contrasted colors (e.g., light blue on a dark blue background), or require that users follow colors rather than words (e.g., text that reads "Click on the red button below to learn more about volunteering here"). Poorly contrasted colors make it difficult for some users to read your website. To make your website easily readable, avoid dark backgrounds and colored body text. Rather, use light or neutral backgrounds wherever you have text, and only use colored text for headlines, titles, and other areas of emphasis. Generally, black and dark gray are best for all body text. If you set specific colors for your text, also set them for the background. Some users have default fonts and colors set on their browsers, so if you define the background, you have additional control over how your site is displayed when it is viewed on such a browser.

Fonts

When it comes to choosing your website's font(s), consistency is again the king. Whatever typeface(s) you decide on, make sure your style carries across all pages. There are two important rules for fonts on websites that you should keep in mind:

1. *Restrict yourself to no more than three typefaces.* If you choose a font family, such as Helvetica or Gill Sans, you have a variety of font style options (italic, bold, light, etc.) that can help you call out important features without distracting the eye with a mishmash of fonts. Unless you feel confident that an eclectic, playful, and spunky feel for your site portrays your institution accurately, stick to relatively few fonts to keep your visitors focused on the content and direct them to the information they seek. Font styles should also be kept in check, but as long as you stick to the same family of typefaces, you can vary text styles between headlines, body, captions, links, menu items, quotes, etc.
2. *Sans-serif fonts make your website more quickly accessible to visitors.* While serif fonts can lessen eye fatigue in traditional print, this does not necessarily mean much to websites.[9] Visitors do not read a website the way they read a book. Their eyes jump from the header to the page title and around succeeding paragraphs to find the information they seek, so there is no need to push their eye forward along the lines as book typefaces do.

Ultimately, you need to pick a typeface or font family that fits with the personality of your site and the image you want to portray. Many designers feel that sans-serif fonts feel "younger" or more modern. Others swear by Georgia as an eye-catching technique. Most WYSIWYG editors come with a basic fonts, like Arial, Helvetica, Times, and Georgia, in addition to their own array of fonts. Play around with your layout to see what fonts will simultaneously be readable and also able to express the feel of your organization.

As noted above, stick to black or dark gray for your body text. Colored headers and titles are perfectly fine, as is colored text for emphasis, provided that the color stands out from whatever background is behind it. Making the font too small renders it unintelligible; make it too large and there will not be room for anything else on the page. Engage multiple people in testing the readability of your font, making sure the color, size, and style are generally legible and not distracting.[10] The website should look interesting and engaging, but be readable and navigable above anything else.

Layout

Laying out content for the web has a surprising amount in common with designing for newspapers and magazines. The most important content should be at the top of the page, with no need for clicking or scrolling to locate the introduction paragraph, photo, or other main content.

In newspaper layouts, this is akin to "designing above the fold." Minimize horizontal scrolling (completely avoid it if you can). Downward scrolling is perfectly acceptable, but do not make pages seem vertically limitless. Keep heavier elements[11] to the outside, especially if you have a side menu on the left. This means putting photos on the top and in the upper right and text in the center, rather than menu-photo-text (the exception being blog entries). Think of it this way: if you are announcing a major fundraising event or the awarding of a grant to help rehouse your collections, you would not hide the announcement in the middle of the third page of your newsletter. It would have a big, bold headline on the top of the front page. Though recommended, your home page does not have to have announcements or rotating content front and center. Whatever you determine the main content of your home page to be, make it prominent and immediately visible.

Each and every page should have the title of your site *that links back to the home page* and a menu in the same location (be it top or side). The linked title makes it easy for visitors to navigate back to the home page no matter where they are on your site, and many viewers expect such a link to be there. Keeping the menu in the same location similarly avoids confusion and aids navigation. Most WYSIWYG editors automatically place your menu for you, so this is not generally an issue. Your website will ideally have no more than three or four page layouts across the whole site. Different pages have different needs (you would not design your photo blog the same way as your Donate Now page) but having a different layout for every single page adds an unnecessary element of chaos to your website that distracts viewers from their main purpose for visiting the site. Selecting a pre-made theme or template will help you minimize the number of layouts you use and add overall cohesiveness to your site. As you may have guessed by now, websites are no exception to the rule of three: whole sites and individual pages should have three or fewer main colors, fonts, and basic layouts.

In much the same way they read magazines, visitors are more likely to scan the page and jump from section to section than to read it thoroughly.[12] This means that blocks of text should be broken up into paragraphs fairly regularly and run no more than six or so inches across. Headlines and section titles that are bolded or in color aid viewers in quickly identifying the information they seek. If you try to lay out your page sans text, it may surprise you when you fill in the final content and are suddenly unable to see the section headlines or are overwhelmed with text. Using placeholder text is an easy way to assure that your layout is clean and attractive. To generate faux Latin text as a placeholder, visit lipsum.com.

Graphics

The images on your website are there for two reasons: to convey information about that page's subject and to add to the aesthetics. The former requires that the image be relevant and in your possession; if you have merely linked an image from another site, it will not convey much of anything to your visitor. The latter, however, has a bit more work involved. Not only must the image itself be in some way compelling, it must be the proper resolution and have appropriate dimensions.

Resolution for images is generally given in terms of PPI (pixels per inch) or DPI (dots per inch). These terms are often used interchangeably, but there is a difference. The former refers to the number of pixels in a given inch, though the size of the pixel itself is determined by the viewer's computer monitor.[13] The latter refers only to printer output—the density of ink dots on the page.[14] The images discussed in this book are intended for use on the web, and as such, the term PPI is used to describe the resolution of images, though your software program may use either term to refer to resolution. The term it uses depends on its sophistication, so you may have to experiment with image resolution to get the hang of what it means for your computer. The ideal web resolution for images is 72 PPI unless you are uploading scans or photographs of collections items (see Chapter 8 for more information on this process). When creating an image from scratch (via photography, scanning, or a graphic design program), 300 PPI is an acceptable starting point—it is best to start with a high-resolution image and alter it from there. See Chapter 8 for tips on preparing items for an online collections database, such as Omeka. With the possible exception of prominent images in a slideshow or banner, your final file should be 72 PPI. This allows for superior resolution for display on computers and smartphones but is not such a high-quality file that visitors can steal your images, especially if copyright is a concern for your institution. Additionally, smaller file sizes help your site load faster, avoiding issues caused by dial-up or other slow connections.

Most importantly, *images should not be in any way distorted*. Whatever the original dimensions of the image, you should maintain them in proportion as a strict rule. Stretch neither the width nor the height without ensuring the same adjustment to other dimensions. In a Word document, for example, the easiest way to do this is to adjust the image from a *corner* rather than from one side and then another. When it comes to website aesthetics, nothing is less attractive than a pixelated and very wide photograph of your board of directors sitting around a table.

All image files should be in JPEG (Joint Photographic Experts Group), TIFF (Tagged Image File Format), or PNG (Portable Network Graphics)

Table 2.1

	Size	Quality	Attributes	Ideal For
JPG	Small	Good	Reduces file size significantly; may eventually "decay" if resaved over and over	Most images
PNG	Medium	Good	Reduces files size somewhat; maintains transparent backgrounds	Graphics, such as logos created with transparent backgrounds
TIFF	Large	Excellent	Generally maintains transparent background; superior image quality	Feature images or those with lots of details

formats. Each file format has its own vices and virtues, discussed in relation to collections images in Chapter 8. Before you create and save your image, try to determine what use you will put the image to (e.g., a documentary photograph of an object for study purposes or a promotional image for education programs). In general, saving the majority of your images as jpeg (or jpg) files will save a lot of data space, making your website load faster and keeping you away from any data limits on your account.

Furthermore, all images should be saved with a clear and descriptive title. This serves multiple purposes. On the back end, saving images in a single folder with titles like "Volunteer Betty Burleigh Holding 1788 Madison Manuscript.jpg" makes the image easier to locate and identify than one named "DSC008372.JPG." On the front end, users who cannot view the image because of loading time or who are using web readers will be able to read the descriptive text (known as alt text) of the image and understand its content. The same rule goes for documents or other embedded content. Viewers who hover over an image or document with their mouse will see the alt text and understand the content even if they cannot view it (or if they can but you forgot to put a caption under the image). Many WYSIWYG editors offer a space to attach captions or alt text onto an image when you upload it; check each editor's guide for more information on this.

Multimedia

Multimedia, as the name implies, comes in many forms. Slideshows, videos, audio files, and interactive components can all be successfully deployed on your website if you bear a few things in mind. The first rule of multimedia on any website is that it should be a *choice* for the visitor to engage with it. A visitor does not want to navigate to your website and immediately be bombarded with music without access to a pause button or an auto-play video that slows down the page's loading time when all he wants to know is your address. If you have rare video footage from the archives or a narrated audio tour of the gallery on your website, by all means guide your visitors to the content, but then allow your visitors to *choose* to click the play button once their volume settings are adjusted and they know what it is they are about to access.

As with images and documents, multimedia files should have captions or descriptive alt text when possible. While many WYSIWYG editors have built-in visual slideshow capabilities, most do not have their own audio- or video-creation technology. This means that you will need to find or place your content on another site and/or create it using other software. Many museums and historical societies have recently found "1-Minute History" videos popular with their audiences, for example. Using a handheld video camera (or even quality smartphone), they create and edit a video and upload it to YouTube or Vimeo. From there, they embed the video on their website or link to it on the video-hosting site. This works well, as it saves storage space in the WYSIWYG editor and allows users to access the content through both the video-hosting platform and the institution's website.

While audio- and video-creation instruction is beyond the scope of this book, a few pieces of advice are in order. If you choose to generate your own content, approach the process much as you have done for creating your website. Plan ahead for your technology, content, and revision. Newer Macintosh and Windows-based computers come with audio- and video-editing software (GarageBand and iMovie for Macs, Music Maker Jam and Windows Movie Maker for Windows). Both are sufficient for simple audio and video editing—and even for some more complex manipulation and effects. To see an example of iMovie in action, visit sustainingplaces.com/watch/two-min-ute-techniques for numerous videos created by museum professionals and museum studies students. If you are linking to relevant material, make sure the video or audio file you link to or embed is from a trusted site and is actually what you think it is. Visitors will not appreciate being linked to untrustworthy sites or videos that are mislabeled and irrelevant. Regularly check in with your embedded and linked content to make sure the original content is still there.[15] Also consider providing a transcript or captions for videos so that deaf users or those who choose not to use volume can follow along with your multimedia components.

SEO Settings

Have you ever gone to the Google search engine looking for a product, business, or other information and received hundreds of search results, none of which are pertinent to your search? This is a common problem for websites, especially those that are new or less traveled. The difficulty occurs because the organizations those websites belong to may not have optimized their sites to be read by search engines like Google, Yahoo, and Bing using what are called SEO (Search Engine Optimization) settings. For instance, if a potential visitor does not already have the URL for the Missoula Tapestry Museum, his first move will likely be to search for "tapestry museum" or "tapestry museum Missoula" in Google. If the Missoula Tapestry Museum has put effort into its SEO settings, its website will probably be one of the first search results on the page. However, if the Missoula Tapestry Museum has neglected its SEO settings, its website may be three or four pages into the search results—or it may not show up at all.

The best way to make your website easy to find and to reach out to potential visitors who do not already know of your website is to spend time setting up your SEO and then submitting your website URL to three main search engines: Google, Yahoo, and Bing. To understand what these settings are and why they are important, first think about what happens when you use a search engine, such as Google. If you are looking for the Missoula Tapestry Museum, you will navigate to Google and type in the two to five words you think are most likely to return results that include the website you are looking for. To find the address of the museum, you type in "tapestry museum Missoula address" and click Search. Google then sends out the "Googlebot,"[16] which runs through thousands of websites looking for those four words. The more times those words appear on a given website and in that order, the higher up on the result list that website will be. Alternatively, perhaps you do *not* know specifically what you are looking for. You are just looking for museums to visit while in Missoula on vacation, so you type "museums Missoula family vacation." The process is the same. The search engine is not just looking at the visible text on each website, but also at alt text, links, page titles, file names, and much, much more. Think of the data search engines are looking for as SEO "points." The more relevant points your website has, the more "attractive" it is to search engines and thus the more likely it will show up in relevant searches.

Your website gains these points by having relevant and well-defined SEO data. In turn, this does a lot to increase the visibility of your site without costing money. In this sense SEO data is the "organic" visibility of your site— publicity you do not have to purchase. The areas of SEO data where you can earn the most points and that you have the most control over are your:

- (Meta) Keywords
- Site Description
- Site/Page Titles
- Alt text

- Links
- Regularly updated content, like blogs

Webmasters disagree about which of these data sets is most important (or if some of them are even helpful at all), but if done well, each set can really only help you drive interested parties to your site. Every WYSIWYG editor gives you different access to these SEO settings, but most of them will help you garner attention for your site by allowing you to edit the first two: keywords and site description. You always have control over the last three on the list above.

Meta keywords are, as they might suggest, twenty to thirty words or phrases that are very strongly associated with your site. For a museum, these keywords would comprise visitor information as well as artists, subjects, movements, or objects that are prominent in the collection. In the case of the Missoula Tapestry Museum, these might include tapestry, museum, Missoula, history, education, research, family activities, textiles, archives, exhibition, hands-on, weaving, looms, dyes, Unicorn Tapestries, Beauvais, Bayeux, arts and crafts, William Morris, and Le Corbusier.

Character numbers for SEO settings are sometimes limited, so use them wisely, avoiding what are called stop words: a, and, are, the, is, other, there, etc. These are words that do not add substance to a description—sure, they help you write complete sentences, but when a search engine looks for quick and detailed information about a website, these words do not reveal anything of interest. For a list of these stop words, look in the appendix or visit freethemuseum.net.

Any keywords you use must appear elsewhere on your site or they will not add to your SEO points. Search engines will ignore a keyword if it only appears once in the keyword section and nowhere else on the site or if you use the same word over and over. Both of these habits make it look like your site is "fishing" for hits without providing related content. For example, the Missoula Tapestry Museum needs to determine the final keywords for its website, and it has the following options:

- Missoula
- tapestry
- the Bayeux tapestry
- Adoration of the Magi tapestry
- Lady and the Unicorn tapestry
- museum
- art museum
- history
- tapestry history
- medieval history

- education
- elementary education
- education programs

Instead of listing each of these keywords and risk repeating the words tapestry, history, and education multiple times, the Missoula Tapestry Museum would list:

- Missoula
- tapestry
- Bayeux
- Adoration
- Magi
- Lady Unicorn
- museum
- art
- history
- medieval
- education
- elementary
- programs

This list eliminates stop words and the repetitive words because the Missoula Tapestry Museum webmaster knows that the search engines can pick up on each of these words and any of their potential combinations (e.g., education, programs, and education programs—three keywords for the price of two).

The site description should be two or three sentences long and give a concise but comprehensive summary of what the institution does or has. The description should use some of the most important keywords your site uses. For example, the Missoula Tapestry Museum would probably produce a site description such as: "The Missoula Tapestry Museum explores and celebrates the art and history of tapestry weaving. Our collections include reproductions of the famous Unicorn Tapestries and portions of the Bayeux Tapestry. We routinely feature family-friendly, hands-on education activities like tapestry weaving." Keep the site description around 150–200 characters so that search engines do not have to deal with extraneous information.

Site and page titles and descriptions are essentially shorter versions of your site description that are *specific* to that page. Each page should have a different description (and keywords) though it is perfectly acceptable to reuse words *if they are actually relevant.* You do not need to use complete sentences, and these titles should be fewer than seventy words. Again, use some of the keywords you have selected for the page in the page title. "Missoula

Tapestry Museum family calendar of events" makes a good page description. If the WYSIWYG editor does not give you access to individual page titles, you can create them by inserting invisible bits of code at the top of each page (see Chapter 7 for more details on this).

Regardless of what SEO settings a WYSIWYG editor allows you to control directly, you have the most control over the last three items on the list: alt text, links, and updated content. These three affect your SEO points directly, though they alone are insufficient to really push your website to the top of the search result list. As discussed earlier in this chapter, the alt text on your content, especially images, can play a big role in how usable your site is. Using intentional titling on all of your images aids both visitors and search engines in determining what content is on your page. Links include links both to and from your site. While you may not have control over who links to you, you certainly govern what sites your own website links to. These associated links are analyzed by search engines to help visitors find similar websites. If you can foster two-way links between your site and another local or topically related museum, both websites will see a boost in SEO points because each website gains credibility. This also means that you should avoid linking to irrelevant or disreputable sites, which is most likely to happen in blog posts where links are more casually inserted rather than seen as endorsement of a site.

The last way to gain SEO points is to regularly update your content. The easiest way to do this is to have a blog that you post to once per month. Search engines like updated content because it shows that the site is actively curated and therefore the information on it is more likely to be correct. Just think—if you came across a website selling laptops, but the page had not been updated since 2001, the chances of getting a reliable computer from the site might seem rather slim. If, however, the website was updated yesterday, you would feel more comfortable assuming that the prices are updated and the company will respond to your inquiry in a timely manner.

One final way to help potential visitors find you is to submit your site for indexing to the major search engines: Google, Yahoo, and Bing. When you give these search engines your URL, you are submitting a request that they send Googlebot (or its equivalent) to your site to analyze the SEO data you just edited. *After* making sure that your WYSIWYG editor settings allow your site to be found and indexed by search engines,[17] visit bing.com/toolbox/submit-site-url (for both Yahoo and Bing) and google.com/webmasters/tools. There, you will be prompted to enter the domain or home URL of the site you want indexed.

After you have entered your SEO information and submitted your site to search engines, it may take up to three months for your SEO settings to really take root and start returning results. While you wait for your website to appear on the first page of search results, you can help move it up the list by searching for the website on various search engines using some of the keywords you picked or the name of your institution. Once you find the correct URL—and without clicking on other links first—click on the link that leads to your website. Do this at least once a day and encourage other staff members or volunteers to do the same. This will prove to the search engines that your site is interesting to searchers and that the keywords you entered to find it should direct other visitors to the same place. Though editing your SEO settings might seem like it returns intangible benefits, the process is well worth the time. SEO is an important way to make your website more readable and attractive to search engines—making it more likely that those searching for your institution will find your website and the information they seek.

NOTES

1. Google Chrome: www.google.com/chrome and Firefox: https://www.mozilla.org/en-US/firefox/new.

2. Internet Explorer's shortcomings have been of note among the web design community for years. For more on this, see Nicholas C. Zakas, "It's Time to Stop Blaming Internet Explorer," July 12, 2012, accessed February 20, 2015, http://www.smashingmagazine.com/2012/07/12/its-time-to-stop-blaming-internet-explorer; Alex Charalambous, "Understanding How Internet Explorer Affects Website Design," March 18, 2014, accessed February 20, 2015, http://www.business2community.com/online-marketing/understanding-internet-explorer-affects-website-design-0814809; and "Internet Explorer in a Web Designer's Life—Problems and Solutions," *Design Your Way*, accessed February 20, 2015, http://www.designyourway.net/blog/resources/internet-explorer-in-a-web-designers-life-problems-and-solutions.

3. Sounak Mukhopadhyay, "Microsoft To Discontinue Internet Explorer, To Launch New Browser For Windows 10," *International Business Times*, March 18, 2015, http://www.ibtimes.com.au/microsoft-discontinue-internet-explorer-launch-new-browser-windows-10-1430604.

4. Institute for Dynamic Educational Advancement, "Newton and the Color Spectrum," *Color, Vision, & Art*, 2006, accessed February 23, 2015, http://www.webexhibits.org/colorart/bh.html.

5. Bonus review: tints are colors made lighter by adding white, shades are colors made darker by adding black, and tones are colors dulled by adding grey.

6. List compiled from: Patrick McNeil, *The Web Designer's Idea Book* (Cincinnati: F&W Publications, Inc., 2007), 115–70 and Cameron Chapman, "Color Theory for Designers, Part 1: The Meaning of Color," *Smashing Magazine*, January 28, 2010, accessed March 3, 2015, http://www.smashingmagazine.com/2010/01/28/color-theory-for-designers-part-1-the-meaning-of-color.

7. Other color exploration tools that help you find easy, attractive color palettes include colourlovers.com/palettes, color-hex.com/color-palettes/popular.php, paletton.com, color.hailpixel.com, and the Color Sphere! extension for Chrome.

8. A quick tool to convert colors from one color system to another is available at colorhexa.com.

9. Look to webdesignerdepot.com/2013/03/serif-vs-sans-the-final-battle for an excellent summary of the debate.

10. For more on testing your website for usability, see Chapter 6.

11. Examples of heavy content include big images, moving graphics, and large, bold text.

12. Jakob Nielsen, "How Little Do Users Read?" Nielsen Norman Group, May 6, 2008, accessed February 15, 2015, www.nngroup.com/articles/how-little-do-users-read.

13. Alex Bigman, "PPI vs. DPI: What's the Difference?" *99 Designs*, February 13, 2015, accessed March 31, 2015, 99designs.com/designer-blog/2013/02/26/ppi-vs-dpi-whats-the-difference/

14. Ibid. Visit andrewdaceyphotography.com/articles/dpi and helpx.adobe.com/photoshop/using/image-size-resolution.html for more information on DPI, PPI, and how they affect your images.

15. Review Chapter 1 for guidelines on setting up your update schedule.

16. *Search Engine Optimization Guide*, Google, 2010, accessed February 5, 2015, http://static.googleusercontent.com/media/www.google.com/en/us/webmasters/docs/search-engine-optimization-starter-guide.pdf.

17. See Chapters 3–6 for individual WYSIWYG instructions on finding this.

Part II

CRAFT YOUR WEBSITE

∽⊛

The guides in the following chapters aim to provide a basic introduction to the features of popular WYSIWYG editors Weebly, Wix, WordPress.com, and GoogleSites. The guides include basic instructions on how to use each editor so that you can determine if it is the right tool for you. As with all so-called "freemium" services,[1] these WYSIWYG editors offer free base packages, which are more than sufficient to develop a professional website, but some features are only available after upgrading. These upgraded features are sometimes mentioned but instructions are not always included in this guide. WYSIWYG platforms routinely add new features and update their editors, so images and details included in the following chapters may not always match new features. Visiting each editor's support center may answer additional questions you have about options and features available in each platform. Instructions for locating the help section are included at the end of each chapter. As always with WYSIWYG editors, remember that experimentation is the best way to get used to a platform. These editors have multitudinous components and capabilities, and experimenting with these to get used to the editor will acquaint you to your options much faster than the book alone.

Each platform guide is structured into website-building sessions. The sessions are designed to get you comfortable with the WYSIWYG editor and use what you learn to flesh out the rest of your site. Every session goes over different elements of creating a website on the selected platform. You can work through them in sequential order or, once you have the basics set up, jump to relevant topics and skip over irrelevant ones. To avoid repetition, sessions are written with the assumption that, while you may be skipping *between* the sessions, you are working *through an entire session* before moving on to a different session. Some sessions will be quick, taking ten or fifteen minutes. Others may take a few hours, depending on your speed and comfort level with the material. Do not feel rushed to move on to another session if you still want to experiment more with the material in an earlier session. When building your site, you have two basic options: build the framework (pages) for your entire site and fill in the content later, or build your site page-by-page, adding the elements you need on each page as you go. Either method is compatible with the session structure of the guides.

To help with the learning process, this book recommends creating a test site in one or more platforms. Each WYSIWYG editor allows you three to five free sites per account, so you do not have to worry about chipping away at your final site's data storage limits (and you can always delete test sites later). A test site will give you the freedom to explore each platform's capabilities and components without the worry of accidentally altering or deleting important information from your real site. By using a test site, you can practice adding different elements to a website, investigate different template and color options, and appraise each platform for its ease-of-use and compatibility with your institution's needs and abilities. The four WYSIWYG chapters

Table P.2

	Weebly	*Wix*	*WordPress*	*Google Sites*
Ease-of-Use	5	3	3	3
Flexibility	3	5	2	2
Support	3	3	4	2
Built-in Features (quality and quantity)	4	4	2–4*	2
Free Templates (quality and quantity)	5	5	4	3
URL Structure (free version)	5	3	4	2
Server Speed/Reliability	5	3	5	5
SEO Editing	4	5	N/A**	2
New Features (frequency of updates)	3	5	3	2
Data Space	Unlimited	500 MB	3 GB	100 MB
Good for . . .	Those with little or no web design experience who are comfortable doing small modifications to pre-built templates	Those with little to advanced web design experience who want ultimate flexibility in a website	Those whose website focus is mainly blog functions	Those who want simple sites and are comfortable with Google products

1 = Low; 5 = High
* Depends on theme.
** Built-in optimization

are arranged in order of the optimal mix of flexibility and ease of use. Once you feel comfortable with your selected WYSIWYG editor, you can begin your final site anew or, if you like what you created with the test site, adjust it to become your final product.

∽

The above ratings are all based on free packages (n.b., level of support is higher with paid packages).

NOTE

1. Freemium.org describes the term thusly: "A business model in which you give a core product away for free to a large group of users and sell premium products to a smaller fraction of this user base." *What is Freemium*, accessed February 15, 2015, http://www.freemium.org/what-is-freemium-2.

Chapter 3

Getting Your Website Started on Weebly

Weebly is a great WYSIWYG website creation tool. It gets along well with other applications, has a good support center, and comes stocked with a variety of basic templates that can be modified to fit the color scheme, font, and overall feel of the website you want. While you do not have complete freedom (e.g., you are restricted to a set of two to six colors for each theme and you must use Weebly's built-in fonts), there is plenty of room for customization within each template. In general, you have a fair amount of flexibility in available colors, fonts, and layouts without the hassle of making everything from scratch. If you are looking for a customizable, professional design for your website without having to define every component of your design, Weebly is the editor for you. While you construct your Weebly site, your edits are automatically saved, and the public will not see them until you choose to "publish" your site. The edits you make to colors, fonts, and content will appear to you as you edit, so you can tell right away if you are constructing the look you want for your site.

In the Weebly guide, you will find ten different website-building sessions. Each session goes over different elements of creating a website on Weebly, and you can work through them in sequential order or, once you have the basics set up, jump to relevant topics and skip over irrelevant ones. Some sessions will be quick, taking ten or fifteen minutes. Others may take a few hours, depending on your speed and comfort level with the material. Do not feel rushed to move on to another session if you still want to experiment more with the material in an earlier session. The material covered in each session is as follows:

- Session 1
  - Create an account
  - Choose a theme
  - Select or create a domain
  - Use the site planner
- Session 2
  - Add page(s)
  - Add or edit text
  - Change fonts
  - Delete or move an element
- Session 3
  - Add or edit images
  - Create a slideshow or gallery of images
  - Change theme and theme colors
  - Publish your site (make it visible to others on the web)
- Session 4
  - Add a divider or spacer
  - Add a column
  - Edit header
  - Insert or edit HTML
  - Embed a map
  - Embed a video
  - Embed a document or file
  - Create links to other pages or websites
- Session 5
  - Add a blog
  - Add a contact form or another type of form
  - Add a survey or poll
  - Add a forum
- Session 6
  - Hide page(s) from menu
  - Create a menu from scratch
  - Create or edit footer
  - Add social media buttons
- Session 7
  - Add a Google Calendar
  - Adjust general settings, including changing or adding a domain
  - Edit SEO settings
- Session 8
  - Create an online store
  - Adjust online store settings

- Sell memberships and accept donations online
- Session 9
  - Check and modify mobile site
- Session 10
  - Add Google AdSense
  - Check site stats
  - Run Google Analytics
  - Upgrade site

With the exception of Session 1, which starts from the weebly.com home page, all sessions start from the account home page:

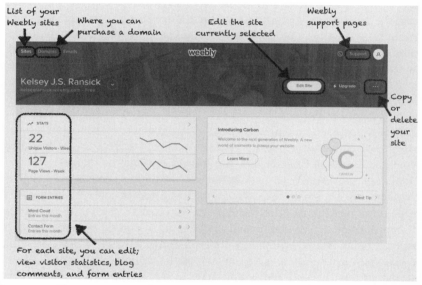

Figure 3.1   The new account home page. For information on updates to the Weebly platform, visit freethemuseum.net/weebly.

From here, you can edit your site, view basic statistics about who has visited your site and which pages are most popular, view comments on your blog (if you have one), view form entries (if you have forms on your site), copy your site for testing or other duplication purposes, or delete your site. Through this screen, you can also purchase or add domains, invite others to join you on Weebly, change your account settings, share your editing capabilities with an outside collaborator, and view support forums. When you sign into Weebly for subsequent sessions you will see the account home page first.

SESSION 1

Create Account

Signing up for a Weebly account is quite simple. You can sign up through Facebook or with an email account. Navigate to weebly.com/link/x5nQdP and enter your name, email address, and chosen password. Once you create an account, you will be asked to start your first website.

Choose Theme

As soon as you open a Weebly account, the platform will walk you through the process of selecting a site theme. Weebly will ask you a few questions about the purpose of your site to help it determine what themes to suggest. Generally, you will want to pick Site, unless you know you want to build only a blog or only an online store. Scroll through the proposed themes to find a few that you like. Hover over a theme to see what its built-in color options are. The colors available with each theme appear as small colored boxes when you hover over the template with your mouse. Some themes will have seven or eight options and some will have only one. To see how these color schemes would look on a given theme, click the colored square and see what changes—usually buttons, text, or background colors. Refer to the section on layout and design in Chapter 2 as you browse through the themes.

Picking a theme on Weebly does not lock you into a specific color scheme or content layout, but it can offer a quick and professional-looking overall design that saves lots of time. Weebly lets you transfer your content between different themes before you actually publish it, so you do not have to worry about not being able to switch to a different theme if you find you do not like the one you have selected. You can change the theme at any time with very little adjustment needed afterward. Keep in mind that if you like a theme but not its menu, the menu can be adjusted by following the instructions in Session 6. Once you see a theme you want to experiment with, click the Choose button that pops up over it. The screen will then open up your editor home page, which you will use in later sessions.

Select or Create a Domain

If you just finished selecting your theme, you will be at the editor home page and a box will pop up prompting you to select your domain. You have three choices: use a subdomain of Weebly (e.g., kelseyransick.weebly.com), register a new domain (e.g., kelseyransick.com purchased through Weebly), or connect a domain you already own (e.g., kelseyransick.com purchased through GoDaddy). If you choose the second or third options, Weebly will walk you through purchasing or connecting your domain. If you do not already own and do not plan to purchase a domain, the first option is for you. Weebly offers simple subdomains for its customers using the free package, so this is an altogether expedient option. Moreover, if you are not sure yet which editor you want to use, this first option is best for creating a test site, which you can always rename later.

Weebly's Website Planner

Weebly offers a free website planner, and whether or not you follow the website planning guide in this book, the website planner is a good way to electronically keep track of your site goals, audience conclusions, and other planning information. Weebly's website planner is simple and takes you through all the steps of focusing your website for your purpose and audience and making sure you meet your site goals. You can, of course, be more in-depth than the site planner suggests, but most of that planning will take place offline. To access the site planner, open your website up in the editor by clicking on either the site title or the Edit button next to the site title on your account home page. Once in the editor, find the question mark at the top of the page, click on it, and then click on the Site Planner menu option. Weebly will then guide you through the process of identifying goals and target audiences for your site, give you design tips, and help you select and customize a theme. You do not have to use the planner, especially if you feel confident that you already know what your site should look like and what its purpose should be.

SESSION 2

When you are ready to start building your site, navigate to the editor by clicking the Edit button next to the title of your site on the account home page. As you can see in Figure 3.2, the left side has an editing panel from which you can select text, images, and other elements to add to your site. The top bar has your editing tabs from which you can change the look of your site, add pages, set up your store, and adjust settings. The largest portion of the screen is taken up by the actual WYSIWYG editor. Sans a few administrative pieces, this is what your visitors will see when they come to your website. The template you select will have a number of pre-made items, such as images, text boxes, and pages that you can see in the WYSIWYG editor. Regardless of which template you pick, it will have at least one page to begin with (the home page) and possibly a few other preset pages.

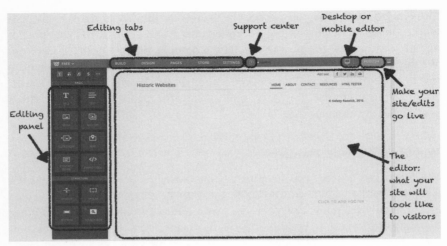

Figure 3.2   The Weebly editor

Add Page(s)

One of the advantages of using Weebly is that there are built-in page templates in each design. When you are ready to add pages to your website, click on the Pages tab in the top bar. This will open up the page options, seen in Figure 3.3.

On the left is a list of your pages in menu form. On the right are specific page options for the selected page. To add a new page, click the + Add button on the left and select what type of page it will be: Standard, Blog, Store, [Store] Category, [Store] Product, or External (a link to another site). Most likely, the majority of the pages you add will be standard pages (the other pages are covered in later sessions). Both the landing page and header pages are standard home page designs. When using pages with the built-in header function, you can upload, edit, and save an image to use on just that page or throughout the site. When you add a header image, Weebly will give you the option of saving it to the current page only or to all header pages on your site. The short header is just a cropped version of the tall header image, though again, you can save any header to a single page or to all of the pages that use a header.

For now, select Standard Page. Your new page will appear at the bottom of the list. This list controls the display of items in your final website menu. Any new pages you add will automatically be added to this section, where you can rearrange their menu order by dragging the "bar" of that page up, down, or over. Dragging a page further up the list will make it appear further to the left in a top menu and further toward the top in a left-hand menu. Dragging the page underneath another page and to the right makes it a subpage, in

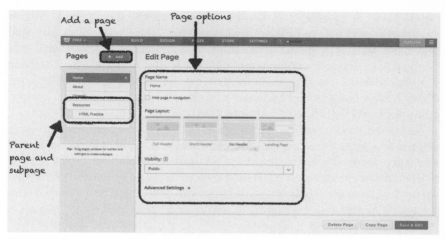

Figure 3.3

which case visitors will see it as a drop-down menu item underneath the parent page. You can have multiple layers of pages, so you can have top-menu items, subpages, sub-subpages, and so on. Rearrange the pages you have until they are in the order you want. Once you are satisfied with its menu placement, title your page and select a page layout. You can add all your pages now if you are so inclined, or wait until you have built up the existing pages more. For each page, you can choose to protect it with a password (so only those with a password can access it), hide it from the navigation menu, copy the page (if you are doing multiple pages with the same or similar format or content) or delete the page.

Add or Edit Text

The next step is to add text to your page and edit it. From the Pages tab, click on the page you want to edit and click Save & Edit and this should bring you back to the editor home page. Some of the original pages may have text on them already, generally in the form of a sample "About Us" text block or site title. To edit existing text, simply click on the text. Just like in a word processing document, a flashing cursor will appear and you can delete old text or type new text. To add new text, you will need a Text Element.

In Weebly, an Element is any editable item on your web page. This includes text, images, columns, galleries, and more. Any Element in the Build panel that has a star on it indicates that it is only available with an upgraded account. These are generally more advanced Elements that most sites will not need but are a nice bonus if you plan to upgrade your site anyway. The Build panel should be open. If it is not, move your cursor to the left-hand side of the window and the Build panel will pop open. Under this panel, you will find Basic Elements like text, images, maps, and contact forms; Structural Elements like dividers, columns, and buttons; Media Elements like YouTube video embedding, Flash, and downloadable documents; Commerce Elements like products and Google AdSense; and other Elements like block quotes, customizable HTML boxes, polls, and forums.

Below the header area of your website, there is a small grayed-out image that reads "Drag Elements Here." This is where you can start to add your own Elements, be they text, images, maps, or something else entirely. Click on the Title Element and drag it into that area, releasing the mouse. Notice that when you add a new Element, a small blue line will appear to indicate where the new Element will be placed. Keep in mind that in Weebly, Elements automatically move to the most upwardly left position free. Occasionally, you will see that the line appears on the side of an already existing Element, rather than above or below it. This will create columns on your page (the first Element will be on one side and the new Element will be on the other). Session 4 will discuss columns and dividers in more detail, but for now, keep things simple by trying to place everything above or below existing Elements rather than alongside them.

Work on adding a few of these Text Elements to your site. For now, keep it simple and concentrate more on the layout than the content. One excellent tip for making this easier is to visit lipsum.com to generate a great faux Latin text as a placeholder. This will fill your text box to give you a sense of the text's visual effects, but will not distract you with its content. If there are existing Text Elements you want to edit, such as the site title, click on them and edit them as well.

Change Fonts or Set Default Fonts

When it comes to changing the font of your text, you have two options: you can change each block of text or string of words individually or, ideally, set different styles for headers, body text, and other types of text. The former option will come in handy if you need to emphasize a single word to indicate that it is a link or italicize the name of a book. The latter will, just like in a Microsoft Word document, update *all* instances of that type of text. For instance, if you want all the body text on your website to be Helvetica 12 pt. black and all your paragraph headings to be Helvetica 16 pt. blue, you can use the information in this session to change them all in one fell swoop. To change individual sections of text, click on the Text Element that contains the text you want to edit. When you click in the box, a black row of buttons will appear that has a number of commands on it. In order, these commands are: Bold (**B**),

Italicize (*I*), Underline (<u>U</u>), Increase Size (+), Decrease Size (–), Change Text Color (<u>A</u>), Create Hyperlink, Align/Justify, Create Bullets, Create List, Remove Formatting (T_x), Undo, and Redo. Highlight the word or words you need, and click on the appropriate button.

Changing the style of different types of text is best done when you have a fair amount of text (whether real content or placeholder text) on the site but are not all the way finished. Sometimes fonts look really nice in the sample and are then almost unreadable in a block of text, so waiting until you have substantial blocks of text to test a font out on your site will help you avoid formatting issues later on. To adjust these, navigate to the Design tab. In the left sidebar, click on the Change Fonts button. This will pull up all the different types of text you can edit. Hovering over a text type will highlight any instances of that text on the current page of the WYSIWYG editor. Clicking on a text type will open up a menu of options for setting the font of that text type.

Delete or Move Elements

If you have added an Element that you no longer want or inadvertently put in the wrong place, you can move or delete it. Click anywhere outside the Element you want to move or delete (you cannot do either while your cursor is *in* the Element). Then, hover over the Element until you see the light blue outline appear, complete with the arrow and X symbols mentioned in Figure 3.4. When clicked, the arrow on the left allows you to move or copy the Element to another page. The X on the right deletes the Element (you will have to confirm your deletion). The spotted rectangle on the top of the box in the middle acts as a handle for the Element, so you can click and drag it to a new position on the page.

Weebly Tip #1: When adding an element to a page, a blue line appears as you drag the element around the editor. The line indicates where the element will land. The line always adjusts to the full width of the page or column. The element will automatically adjust to the full length of content; if you want to lengthen the space before or after an element, add a spacer (or hard returns within a text element). The arrow on the left of the box will give you the option to copy or move the element to another page. The X on the right side of the box will delete the element.

Figure 3.4

SESSION 3

Add or Edit Image

Navigate to the editor by clicking the Edit button next to the title of your site on the account home page. The first step in this session is to add an Image Element. From the Basic Element section in the Build Panel, drag an Image Element into the editor. Click on the Upload Image graphic that appears in the new Element. From here, you have four options: upload a new image from your computer, search within the Weebly database, choose from "favorited" images within the Weebly database, or grab an image from elsewhere on the web.[1] Most often, you will use the first option, but should you want to use an image from Weebly, you can choose from lower-quality free images or purchase a professional image from Weebly for five dollars. If you look through these images, you can add them as favorites to come back to later. If you choose the last option, to link an image from elsewhere on the web, recall from Chapter 2 that this can be tricky. If you do not have the image file in your possession, your chosen image might be deleted or moved without you noticing, thus leaving a hole or error message on your page. However, you might also pursue this option if you plan to use the same photo repeatedly on your site. When you add an image to your website, it does not go into a gallery that all your Image Elements can easily access. In other words, if you want to use the same image twice, you will need to either upload it in each place you want to use it or use this linked feature, finding the URL for your image after your site has been published and then pasting it into this box.[2]

To add your own image, click on the large green button and find where the image is stored on your computer. Weebly will upload the file and the image will appear once that is complete. Once an image is added, you can edit it by clicking on the image. A gray box will appear, and from here you can edit the image, change the alignment of the image, turn on the light-box,[3] make the image a link to another web page, create spacing margins around the image, add a caption, and add alt text. Editing the image gives you the opportunity to crop or rotate it, change the opacity, and add effects. Remember to always add descriptive alt text to your images to boost your SEO points and to help those with vision impairment or slower loading times decipher what the image is. Visit Chapter 2 to review the importance of these alt text uses.

There are two types of Image Elements: those that are added to the editor and can be moved and manipulated, and those in headers that are permanent (because they are built into the page layout template you chose when adding the page). To change the former, click on the image to change it through editing eebly Tip #2: One of the great things about Weebly is that you can navigate through the website while editing by clicking directly on the elements on the page.

or replacement. To change the latter, hover over the image until an orange Edit Image button pops up. This will take you to the image editing page, where you can click the green Add Image button to upload one of your own images or edit the existing image. Once you finish editing or adding an image to the header, Weebly will ask if you want to save the image to all pages or just this page. If you choose to save it to all pages, the same image will appear on all pages on the site that have a header.

Create Slideshow or Gallery of Images

Using a Gallery Element allows you to post a series of still pictures across or down a web page. After adding a Gallery Element, click on the Element to upload your images. Once uploaded, they will appear in a random combination of rows and columns, depending on the size of your Element and the number of images. If you click in the Gallery Element, you will see that you can add additional images, change the number of columns from two to six, change the gallery spacing, set when the captions appear for each image, and change the cropping and borders of the images in your slideshow. On top of each image, there are buttons for making an image into a link (useful if you are using a gallery to display shop items or collections items that have their own page elsewhere on the site, for example), entering a caption, or removing the image.

The Slideshow Element presents photos in an automatic slideshow in a number of different formats. Drag a Slideshow Element into the editor. You will then be prompted to choose a layout for your slideshow and add your photos. After the images are uploaded, you will see the same link, caption, and delete options as you did with the gallery. You can rearrange the order by dragging images to the desired position. Once you are satisfied with the images (which you can always link, caption, or delete later), click save and check to make sure that the images are displaying the way you want them. If you click on the Slideshow Element, you will see that you can return to the slideshow image editing page, change the slide transition style, alter the navigation for visitors who want to skip through images, set the speed at which images transition, alter the spacing and caption display of images, and determine whether images will automatically advance or if visitors will be able to start, pause, and skip through them.

Change Theme or Theme Colors

If the template you chose comes with multiple color schemes and you have decided that you want to try a new one on for size, click on the Design tab. This will open up the Design Options panel, where you can click on any of the other color options to see how they look on the site. Some themes will not have many (or any) options, but most will have a few. Some themes have subtle color components, such as a line in the menu under the current page, but others will have entire backgrounds that change with the color selection. Experimenting is the best way to find out what each of these colors can do for your site. If, after working with your theme for a while, you decide that you would prefer a different theme, the Design Options panel also holds the Change Theme option. When changing themes, any content you already entered on your site will transfer, though you may need to rearrange or adjust the layout after the new theme is selected.

Publish Your Site

Weebly auto-saves your work every minute or so, which means there is no need to back up your work. Saving, however is different than publishing your site. When you save your site, only you can view the latest version through your site editor. When you *publish* a site, it makes it visible to the world. In other words, no one can navigate to a URL on your site until it is published and no one will see edits you make on an already available site until you publish those changes. Once you click Publish, if you have not already chosen a site URL, Weebly will prompt you to choose one, encourage you to purchase a custom domain, and post your finished work to Facebook and/or Twitter. To unpublish a site, should you decide you are not ready to share the final product with the public, click on the Settings tab. Scroll to the bottom, where you will see an option to unpublish the site.

When you publish your site, verify that it is open to search engines. One of the best ways to do this is to submit your site to Google Webmaster Tools. This program, found at google.com/webmasters/tools, will help ensure that your site is indexed more regularly so that searchers are more likely to find your site through a Google search. This site will walk you through the process of submitting your site for indexing. You will need a Google account. As you work through the process, make sure you select Alternate Methods to produce an HTML tag that you can then paste into your Weebly site. Copy the HTML code that Google provides and return to your Weebly editor. Under

Settings → SEO, paste the copied code into the header box. Republish your site and wait a few minutes. Return to Google Webmaster Tools and click on Verify to see if your site has been successfully linked. You can also click Continue to submit your sitemap and boost your SEO even further. Weebly automatically creates a sitemap on your behalf, found at either http://*your-site*.weebly.com/sitemap.xml (if using a Weebly subdomain) or http://www.*yoursite*.org/sitemap.xml (if using your own purchased domain). Click on the Sitemaps bar and enter sitemap.xml at the end of the URL Google provides (which should match your domain name).

SESSION 4

Add Divider or Spacer

If you want to create space on the top or sides, you will need to insert a Spacer Element. The spacer has no visual characteristics of its own, so if your background is blue, there will be a blue space on the page; likewise, if the background is white, visitors will see white space. To begin, enter the editor by clicking Edit on the account home page. Under the Structure Elements section, grab a Spacer Element and drag it to where it belongs on the page. Once it is there, you can adjust its height by dragging the thick blue line that appears at the bottom of the Element box when you hover over the spacer. While the spacer appears slightly gray to you, your visitors will see nothing but the empty space.

Inserting a divider follows much the same process. Dividers are thin gray lines that can be used to separate page sections. Once you drag the divider to the appropriate location on the page, click on it to see your editing options. While you cannot change the thickness of the divider, you can increase or decrease the padding above and below the divider and adjust the width of the divider. This last option is useful if you plan to use the divider to indicate a slight page break (as in the chapter breaks one sees in books) rather than separating whole sections of the page. Should you want a thicker divider, consider inserting a thick line as an image.

Add Column

While dividers only appear horizontally (and therefore should be used above and below Elements), spacers can be placed above, below, or to the side of one or more Elements using columns. To add columns to a page, drag two or more Elements onto the page and arrange them left-to-right, using the blue line that indicates an Element's placement as a guide for when items will be next to each other, as opposed to above or below each other. The editor will automatically create these columns, and you can drag a column line left or right to resize each column as necessary. These columns can get tricky if you plan to place some Elements on a page side-by-side and other Elements full-width across the same page. Keep an eye on the blue line—if the line only appears across part of the page, the Element will be placed in a column. If the line appears across the full width of the editable space, the Element will be as wide as the page. Using spacers, you can also implement empty columns as wide or thin as you need if you know you want blank space to the side of an Element but have nothing to put in that space.

Edit Header

All Weebly templates have a spot for your site title, logo, or both on every page. Most have a spot for a header image. To edit the site title or insert a logo, hover over the default site title, "My Site." You will see three options appear: Off, Text, and Logo. With the first, you can remove the site title from your website altogether (not recommended unless you will be reinserting the site title elsewhere for design reasons). To edit the site title as just text, click on the words and type in your new title, which will appear on every page. Should you want to use a logo either on its own or in addition to text, select the Logo option. Upload your logo, keeping in mind that it should be of high resolution but not with overly large dimensions. Once the logo is uploaded, hover over it until the options appear again, and click Edit. From here, you can edit the image and add your site title in. Click on the Add Text option and add your site title accordingly. You can rearrange the logo and text within the header so that they are positioned wherever you need them, but be aware that they will be in those same positions on every page.

Ⓦeebly Tip #3: All Weebly site titles or logos made using this feature automatically link back to the home page—a significant bonus, as most visitors expect this to be the case.

Figure 3.6

Create Links

Hyperlinks allow visitors to move between pages and to other web resources by clicking on text or images. Weebly makes creating hyperlinks relatively easy and seamless. First, you will need to create a linked image. Once you have added an image, as in Session 3, click on the image to bring up the editing bar. Click on the Link option and choose the appropriate action. Your link will be active once your site is published. Weebly includes a font style for linked text, but you may want to add additional emphasis, so consider bolding or colorizing linked text (just be consistent). This will make the link stand out from the rest of the text so visitors know they can click on it to move to new content. To create hyperlinks using text—called hyper-text—highlight the word or words you want to use as a link (remember that for SEO points, you should use the descriptive words, rather than a generic "Click here"). Click the link button and choose where the link will go: to a website URL (generally of an outside website), to an internal page (on your website), to a downloadable file, or to an email address. In most cases, you will want to have links to outside websites open in a new window so that visitors can easily find your website again by closing the window. When linking to your own site, this is not necessary. Linking to a store page comes into play if you have a gallery of products and you want visitors to be able to click on an image for more details, which is often the case if you do not like the built-in storefront or have not upgraded to a business plan. Linking to an email address will provide visitors with an easy way to contact you, and clicking on such a link often automatically opens up whatever email pro-gram the visitor's computer uses. One way to avoid accidentally launching the visitor's email program is to never use "hidden" email addresses. If you write: "Contact our Visitor Services Coordinator for more information," and use the words "Visitor Services Coordinator" as the hypertext, this is a hid-den email address. This can be useful for those using native email programs on their computers, but is frustrating for those who just want to know what the email address of the Visitor Services Coordinator is. To appeal to both parties, use this instead: "Contact our Visitor Services Coordinator at vsc@ tapestrymuseum.org for more information," and make vsc@tapestrymu-seum.org the hypertext.

Insert or Edit HTML

Whether or not you intend to write HTML code, the Embed Code Element can be very useful for a Weebly webmaster. You might use it to insert SEO code or you might just want to use Yahoo Maps on your site instead of Google Maps. Whatever the reason, it all starts by dragging the Embed Code Element into your editor. When you click on it, a settings bar will pop up. Click the Edit button to open up HTML editing capabilities for the Element. Note that when you edit this HTML code, *it will only affect content in the Embed Code Element*, not the entire page. If you are inserting prewritten code for a map, video, or other embedded content, continue on to the rest of the session. If you plan to write bits of code for an Embed Code Element, this is discussed briefly below; visit Chapter 7 for more details on using HTML in your site.

In general, you will not need to do any HTML or CSS editing. However, if you feel comfortable editing fonts, colors, or more using coding, Weebly offers a way to edit your site using these languages. You can edit the CSS for the site, create a new page layout template, or export a theme (for use on other websites or for reference in case you ever need to go back to a past design) by clicking on the Design tab and then the Edit HTML/CSS button in the Design panel. The HTML/CSS editor provides both a coding screen and a visual screen, so if you have experience with Dreamweaver, this will look familiar to you. If you know exactly what colors you want and want to take a gander at editing the HTML or CSS of your site, this is the place to do it—just click on the gray Edit HTML/CSS button at the bottom of the editing panel. This menu allows you to edit the overall CSS for the site, create a new page layout template, or export a theme for use on other websites or for reference in case you ever need to go back to a past design. The HTML/CSS editor provides both a coding screen and a visual screen, so if you have experience with Dreamweaver, this will look familiar to you. In most cases, you do not have to worry about this function unless need to add outside components to your site and you feel comfortable editing HTML or CSS. Generally, all the editing you need to do can be accomplished through the Weebly site editor.

Embed Map

Weebly has an easy-to-use Map Element, perfect for embedding a Google Map that shows your institution's location. To begin, drag the Map Element into the editor to the desired location. Click on the map (automatically pinned to downtown San Francisco) and you will see the editing bar pop up. From here, you can input your organization's address so that visitors will see your location and be able to zoom in and out as with a regular Google Map. You can also set the automatic zoom distance, where one is zoomed out to see all of Earth and seventeen is close enough to see the individual buildings. You can also edit the dimensions and alignment of the map to accommodate your desired layout and adjust spacing and other display settings. If you want to use another map service (like MapQuest) or show driving directions (as between two of your institution's locations), you will need to construct the map according to that platform's instructions. Once you are finished, you can copy and paste the code to embed a map on your site into the Embed Code Element discussed above.

Embed Video

You can upload new videos or link to existing videos elsewhere on the web in two ways. Weebly offers a video-hosting service, but it is only available with a paid upgrade. If you plan to upgrade to Weebly Pro, this video hosting capability is very useful because it provides unbranded hosting (no YouTube advertisements or logos). However, it is still possible to embed a video on a free Weebly site by using the YouTube or Embed Code Elements. YouTube offers free video hosting with any Gmail account, so you can take advantage of this if you are creating your own media, or use videos that others have created that are relevant to your institution.[4] To embed a YouTube video, add the YouTube Element to your editor. Navigate to the YouTube video and copy its URL. Back in Weebly, click on the Element and paste the URL into the settings box that pops up. From there, you can also adjust alignment, spacing, and video size. If you choose to use another video service, such as Vimeo, you will need to find the embed code for the video. On Vimeo, this is the paper airplane graphic on the upper right of the video. If you want to adjust the video size, control options, or adjust other settings for the video before you embed it, click the More or Show Options buttons. Though under the extra options you may be able to remove the volume and other controls, most visitors will want to have option to adjust volume and video size. Including these controls is a good idea.

Return to Weebly and paste the code into the Embed Code Element. Once pasted, click anywhere on the page outside the Element. Your video should appear soon, and you can click on the play button right away to make sure it has embedded correctly.

Embed Document or File

Making files accessible to your visitors can take one of two forms: an embedded document that shows up directly on the web page or a downloadable document. Embedded documents, as opposed to downloadable documents,

Figure 3.7   YouTube and Vimeo embedding

are good for when you want visitors to see the content of a document directly on the page. For embedding a document on the page, Weebly uses a service called Scribd.[5] The service embeds most document types,[6] but they will be displayed as images and cannot be edited by visitors. To access this, drag a Document Element (not the File Element) into the editor and click on it to upload your file. After it uploads, you can change the display height, though visitors may still have to scroll to see the whole document.

A downloadable document can be almost any file type—mp3, jpeg, pdf, Word document, Excel sheet, ZIP file, and more. To add a file, drag the File Element (not the Document Element) into the editor. Upload your file and assign an alignment and file name. Another option to insert a downloadable document is by creating a text hyperlink—a bit of text that acts as a download button or link, also known as hypertext. For example, if you want visitors to have access to your collections policy, you might type: "You can download a copy of the Missoula Tapestry Museum Collections Policy to learn more about our mission and scope of collections." You want visitors to be able to click on the words "Missoula Tapestry Museum Collections Policy" and download the document. To do this, highlight the word or words you want visitors to click on and click the link button in the editing bar that pops up. This will give you the option to link to a file stored in your "file cabinet" or upload a new file. For advice on creating and editing hypertext, move to the next step.

SESSION 5

Add Blog

Adding a blog to your Weebly site is a great way to make easy, regular updates to your website. The platform has a built-in blog function that is actually part of your site—not a separate blog, nor the whole focus of your site. Entries can be back-dated, include an option for allowing comments or replies, and allow for archives and categories. To add a blog, click on the Edit button on the account home page to enter the editor. Go to the Pages tab and add a page, this time selecting Blog Page. Set up your blog page layout and settings, and then click Save & Edit. This will take you to your blog home page.

Before adding blog entries, adjust your "About" section. When you are ready, click on the New Post button in the lower right. This will open up a new single post that you can edit much as you would any other page on your site. You can add text, images, maps, dividers, buttons, YouTube videos, and more, just like on the other pages you have created.

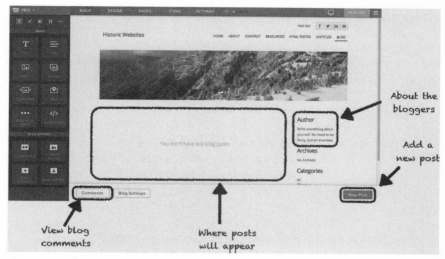

Figure 3.8   The Weebly blog home page

Name your post and then add text, images, or whatever else you might like to it. If you want the time stamp on your post to be on a different day, click on the date below the post name and select the appropriate day. You can also save your entry and come back to it for editing or posting later. If you want to add a category, click on the Post Options button in the Build panel. Click Add Categories to assign one or more categories to this specific post. This is important for boosting your SEO points. From this panel, you can also change comment options (i.e., auto-accept, require approval, or remove the comment option altogether) and edit SEO settings for this individual post. When you have your post the way you want it, click on the Post button in the upper right-hand corner of the editor. If at any time you need to edit a blog post, start from your blog home page. Click on the entry to be edited so that the individual post opens back up for editing. Edit the post and click Update in the upper right-hand corner when you are ready to repost it.

To monitor comments on your blog, return to the blog home page and click on the Comments button at the bottom of the editor. Here, you can see recent comments and approve pending comments, as well as delete or mark comments as spam so that their posters cannot return and post similar spam. Clicking the Blog Settings button next to this will open up the Settings tab. If you need to limit the number of posts that appear on your blog page, establish sharing options (to give people an easy way to brag about you on Facebook or Twitter, for example), set parameters for commenters, or modify the date and time display format, this is the panel to do it from.

Many institutions that maintain blogs want to keep an updated feed of blog activity on their home page so visitors can see announcements about the museum or read about a recent museum event. Before you set this up, your site will need to be published, even if it is hidden to other visitors. This is so that the RSS feed reader can find the page is it supposed to be drawing information from. You will need to find the URL of your blog page, so navigate to the blog page on the *published* site. At the end of the URL, without deleting any of the text that is already there, type in */feed* and hit the return key. This should take you to a page of nothing but strange-looking text, possibly with the message: "This XML file does not appear to have any style information associated with it. The document tree is shown below." If you see this message, you are on the right track. The text you see is called XML, which is a language computers use to send data to one another, and it is discussed further in Chapter 7. For now, just copy the new URL, which should be something like http://missoulatapestrymuseum.weebly.com/blog/feed.

Next, set up your feed reader. Return to your editor and navigate to the home page (or whatever page you want the feed to be on). Under the More section of the Build panel, select the Feed Reader Element. Move it to the appropriate location on your page, generally on the right-hand side to act as a sidebar. Click on the top of the sample RSS feed that populates the Element. This will open up a settings bar. Paste the copied URL into the Feed Address field and adjust the dimensions, position, spacing, text length, and the number of items to display as needed. You should now see the first post or posts that you published above. As you add new posts, the feed reader will rotate content in and out so visitors will always see your newest content first.

Add Contact or Other Form

Weebly has a number of different prebuilt forms that you can implement on your site, including a contact form, RSVP form, and booking form. Any of them can be adapted to many different uses, though the prebuilt forms are convenient if you are trying to keep things simple or are on a deadline. For instance, when you drag the Contact Form Element into the editor, it is automatically set with Name, Email, and Comment fields. If these are the only fields you need, there is no need to edit. If, however, you want to add a form title or change the fields, click on the Form Element. Once inside, you can click on individual parts to edit them. Clicking on the top line allows you to edit the form title. Clicking on any of the form fields opens up the editing box, where you can rename the field to anything you want, declare whether the field is required for submission, adjust spacing, and type instructions for visitors. Instructions appear as light words in the text box that disappear when the box is clicked on for form submission. In a field labeled "Preferred dates" your instructions might read: "Please list at least two date options for your rental in case one of them is already reserved." You can delete unnecessary fields by hovering over them and clicking the X in the upper right-hand corner. Once you are in the Form Element, you will notice that the Build panel has new components. These are other fields and Structure Elements you can add to the form, including drop-down boxes, a phone number field, images, and more.

When you finish editing your form, and before you save and exit it, click on the Form Options button in the upper right-hand corner. This will open up the form's settings box. It is important to set the email address to which form submissions will be sent. By default, this will be the email you used to sign up for your Weebly account. You can also view entries from your account home page by clicking on the More button next to your site title, but the email notification is a convenient way to keep abreast of new entries as they come in.

The confirmation that visitors see when they submit the form is another important setting to review before saving. There is a default and generic thank-you message, but you may want to customize this to your site. For example, if your sole employee is only in the office two days a week, it is a good idea to notify your visitors that their inquiries will be answered within the week but they may not hear back right away. Alternatively, you might want to redirect your visitors to a different page once they submit a form, as in the case for an event registration that they then have to pay for. To set this up, copy the URL of the page you want them to be directed to after they submit the form. Under confirmation options, click the Link option and paste the URL.

Add Survey or Poll

The Survey Element works just like any other Form Element. There are some preset fields to start off with, but you can delete, edit, or add to any of these. Drag the Survey Element into the editor and click on a field to edit it. Change the fields as necessary, setting field titles and requirements for each as you go. Click on the Form Options button to set the survey name, submission notification email, and confirmation message. Remember that you can view the results from your account home page under the More button next to the site title.

The third-party service Weebly uses for polls is called PollDaddy. Drag a Poll Element into your editor and click on the sample poll button and then Edit Poll button to get started. To use the service, PollDaddy requires a (free) account, which will be automatically created for you if you click the new user button. Click "Create a New Poll" and type in the poll question at the top. Type in the potential answers, deleting any unnecessary fields by clicking the red buttons. If you need more than the default number of answer fields, click one of the green buttons. To reorder the answers, use the small blue arrow buttons on the left side of the answer fields. Set the poll options on the right depending on whether you want to have a write-in field, let visitors select more than one answer, block repeat voters, or show the poll results. When finished, click the Save Poll button. You will then the prompted to select a layout style for the poll. PollDaddy has twenty built-in styles you can choose from, but you can style your own using CSS if you have a specific look in mind. Once you select a style, click Save Poll again, followed by the Add to Page button. Your poll will appear in the editor shortly after. To edit it again, just click on the Poll Element and click Edit Poll. You can change the settings of your PollDaddy account by entering the service through your existing poll and clicking the Settings tab. To see the results of your poll, click on any Poll Element, click on Edit Poll, and click on the small bar graph icon next to the poll you wish to review.

Add Forum

Including a forum on your website can be a great way to get community members involved in discussions about your collection or events. Weebly uses the third-party service Tal.ki for their built-in Forums Element.[7] Though a great tool for small forums, the free Tal.ki account has some limitations. With your free account, anyone can use your forum, and Tal.ki does not offer spam protection, so you will need to monitor your forum closely for junk comments.[8] Though you are limited to five subforums total (not per category), you can always upgrade your Tal.ki account to accommodate a particularly talkative community. There are a few other data limitations on a free Tal.ki account, but unless your community is regularly active, this will not pose too much of a problem because you can always delete unused threads and subforums. Drag the Forums Element into the editor. Tal.ki automatically creates a profile for you and adds you as the first community member. There are no boxes that pop up when you click on the Forums Element; instead, click directly on the content to edit the admin profile, view members, and manage settings. Navigate to the Forum Admin menu to change the forum name and description, control how users log in (e.g., via Facebook or Google), and configure the forum topics. To access these settings in the future, you can log in to Tal.ki directly or from the Forums Element in Weebly.

SESSION 6

Hide Page(s) From Menu

Occasionally, you may want to hide certain pages from the menu. This can be to reduce the complexity of the menu or to keep visitors from finding content without the direct URL. A common reason is that the webmaster wants a side-bar menu when the template has a top menu, or vice versa, which is discussed below. Whatever the reason, hiding a page is easily done. Open up your editor by clicking the Edit button next to your site on the account home page. Click on the Pages tab and select from the left-hand menu the page to be hidden. Under the page-editing options, check the box next to "Hide page in navigation" just underneath the page title. A small icon depicting a crossed-out eye will appear next to the page title in the left-hand menu. Once you click Save & Edit, the page will no longer appear in the published menu.

Create Menu From Scratch

For some themes, you might love the design but not want the default menu location. The best way to adjust this is to hide all the pages from your navigation according to the steps mentioned above (and remember to hide any new pages you add in the future) and then create your own menu to put on each page. There are three shortcomings with this method, though they are not particularly egregious. First, unlike with the built-in menu, your constructed menu will not be animated (i.e., when you roll over a page in the menu, no subpages will appear). Because of this, your subpages will either need to be permanently visible in the menu or not present at all, though you can easily indent subpages or change their style to donate that they are subpages. Additionally, when using this method, some themes will still have space allotted for the menu, and thus your header may seem larger than you would like. Other themes adapt to a lack of menu. Lastly, *you will need to update the menu on each page whenever you make an edit, rather than just changing the order of your pages in the Pages tab.* If you truly do not like the native menu placement but really want to use the overall theme, this method is quite feasible.[9]

Overall, the process is a great workaround for a theme's unwanted native menu placement. The process can take a while, as you will need to double-check menu consistency on all pages, but you will only have to set the menu up once and then make minor adjustments as you add or delete pages on your site. To set your own menu up, navigate to the Pages tab and click on each page's "bar" to check the "Hide in navigation menu" box. You do not need to click Save & Edit on each page after doing this. Any page that is hidden from the menu will have a crossed out eye icon next to it in the menu sidebar. You can then create your own sidebar or top menu.

To create a sidebar menu, drag a Text Element into the editor—note that this will mean every page has at least two columns, one for the menu and one for any other content. In the text box, type in the text of your menu with each page on a different line, such as:

Home
About
Contact
FAQs

If you have Elements to the right, adjust the size of your columns to fit your menu by sliding the gray marker between columns to the right or left. Then, highlight each line of text destined to be a menu item and click on the link symbol in your text editor. Select the correct page for the link and then repeat this for all items in the new menu. Once you have all the menu items properly linked, click outside the Text Element and hover over it to bring up the thin blue box and moving options. Click on the arrow in the upper left-hand corner, then click the copy tab and copy the Element to the next page on the list. Repeat this for every page on the site. Before finalizing your site, double-check that each text item's link copied appropriately.

To create a top bar menu, drag as many Button Elements as you have menu items into the editor across the top of your page. The columns will automatically be created to evenly space the buttons. In some designs, you may want to use a Divider Element underneath the row of buttons to make them look more like a traditional menu. Take into account the fact that if you have any pages with the Tall Header, Short Header, or Landing Page layouts, your button menu will appear *below* these visual components, not at the very top like on a No Header page. Click on each button in turn to rename it (by clicking on the text and typing the page name), set the button style (you have a choice of four), and set the page link. Unlike with a sidebar menu, you will have to copy *each* button to *each* page, making this method a little more involved. If you really want a top menu where there is none, the process is worth the effort. As with any link you make, verify that the links remain attached and active before sharing your site with others.

Create or Edit Footer

A footer is an excellent place to display your hours, address, and contact information so that it is easily and immediately accessible on every page. Editing the built-in footer in Weebly is only possible with an upgraded account, but you can work around this by creating your own footer on each page. As with any workaround, there will be a few compromises, and you may find you have more space at the bottom of your website than you might like. However, a bit of extra space at the bottom of a website is perfectly acceptable. To create your own footer, drag a Text Element or Elements into the editor. Add your text, logo, map, or other information. Once you are satisfied with the content in your built footer, click outside the Element, hover

over it, and click the arrow that appears in the upper left-hand corner. Click the copy tab and select the next page on the list. Repeat this for every footer Element and page on your site. *Remember that if you edit the footer, you will need to update the content on every page, not just one.*

Add or Edit Social Media Buttons

Most Weebly templates come with social buttons (e.g., quick links to a Facebook page or Twitter account) already in place. If you like the options and placement, all you have to do is link them to your respective accounts. Locate and hover over the buttons, generally near the top or bottom of your site in the header or footer. Use the menu that pops up to add the URLs of the social media platform your organization uses. Click the small X on the right of a social media platform bar to delete it from the menu. Alternatively, click on Add More to see other social media platform linking options.

SESSION 7

Add Google Calendar

In order to add a Google Calendar to your website, you will need a Google account. If you already have one, simply make sure you are signed in and navigate to google.com/calendar. If you do not already have an account, sign up for one at accounts.google.com, then visit google.com/calendar. If you have a list of events to add, go ahead and add them to the calendar now or add a sample event to get started. There are three ways to add an event:

• Click the Create button in the upper left-hand corner and edit the event date, time, and other details from there.
• Navigate to the day and time of the event, click directly on the calendar and drag the box that appears to the correct date and time, then click on the box to edit the details.
• Click anywhere on the calendar itself at any time and adjust the event date, time, and other details from there.

As you add events, you will have the option to create color-coded "subcalendars." For example, you might have an overall institutional calendar, and within that have sub-calendars for education, development, and exhibition events.

Once you have events on your calendar and are ready to embed it, you will need to make your calendar public so that visitors can see the events. If you have internal events or an internal subcalendar that you do not want to share publicly, you can still add them to the calendar but hide them by editing individual events or deselecting the sub-calendar in the next step. To make a calendar visible, click on the arrow next to its name when you hover over it in the calendar list. Click on Share this Calendar and tick the box next to "Make this calendar public." Do this for each calendar you want to make public. Then, click on the arrow next to "My calendars" and select Settings. Click on the name of one of the calendars you want to share in the list that appears. In the Embed This Calendar section, click on "Customize the color, size, and other options." The main section of the page shows you how the calendar will display. If you are happy with it, copy the HTML code at the top of the page. If you want to include additional calendars or change the look, use the menu of options on the left side of the page to modify your calendar until you are satisfied with it, including adding a Calendar Title. Once you are ready to embed it, click Update HTML at the top of the page and copy the newly generated HTML code.

Return to Weebly. From your account home page, launch the editor by clicking Edit next to your site name. Add an Embed Code Element to the appropriate location for your calendar. Double-click on it to edit the code, and paste in your Google Calendar code. Verify that it displays the way you expect it to, and publish your changes. After adding your calendar to your website, any changes you make on the calendar (e.g., adding, deleting, or editing events) will be automatically reflected in the calendar on your site.

Change or Add Domain

Open up the Settings tab. The first item is your side address (your domain). If you have not already selected one or you want to purchase or add a domain, click the Change button. Here, you will see the domain name options presented to you when you first began your site: Use a Subdomain of Weebly, Register a New Domain, or Connect a Domain You Already Own. Whichever one you select, Weebly will walk you through the domain setup. Bear in mind that if you purchase a domain from anyone other than Weebly, you will still have to purchase a Weebly upgrade package to connect that domain. Purchasing your domain directly from Weebly eliminates this double purchase, but the domain prices can be higher than with other domain services like GoDaddy or Namecheap.

Adjust General Settings

This section will work a little differently than those mentioned earlier. Instead of taking you through a specific process, it will methodically review the most important site settings, giving advice and tips on optimizing your site. Not all settings are covered, just the most relevant and impactful ones for a museum or historic site using the free Weebly package. There are a number of features in the Settings tab that you will not be able to access unless you upgrade to a paid plan, but your site will still be quite functional and attractive even without an upgrade.

- General → Site Title: Having your site title at the top of every page is, hands down, a great idea.
- General → Navigation: Menus look most attractive when they are simple and evenly spaced. Check the box that groups excess pages under "More" in the menu, or run the risk of overcrowding your menu or accidentally hiding some of your content.
- General → Facebook Sharing: If you plan to link your website to your institution's Facebook page (which allows visitors to easily navigate to your Facebook page or Facebook store), set it up here.
- General → Archive: Every few months, email yourself a ZIP archive of your site. If something happens and your site is deleted or if you plan to move your site content to a new platform, this feature will save your site data and files to make rebuilding or transiting easier.
- General → Unpublish: If your site is still under construction or needs to be taken down for maintenance (the latter is not recommended—just put up a "temporarily closed" sign on your home page) you can unpublish it. Your account will retain all your site information; it will just remove the domain from public access until you publish again.
- SEO: These settings will be covered after the rest of the site settings, due to complexity.
- Editors: If you want more than one person to be able to log in to your Weebly site and edit it (if you have multiple bloggers, for example), you can add them using their email addresses. With the free version, you will not be able to restrict other editors to Author or Dashboard Only privileges, only Admin (full-access) privileges.
- Members: This capability is only available with a package upgrade. If you have a museum membership or community group with the perk of online access, you can manage individual members and groups here.
- Store: These settings are covered in Session 8.
- Blog: These settings are covered in Session 5.

Edit SEO

Before editing your SEO settings, review Chapter 2 for SEO best practices. There are four areas on Weebly where you can directly edit your SEO settings: the storefront, individual pages, blog posts, and overall site settings. SEO settings for the store, covered in Session 8, are found in Advanced

Options on the Storefront menu page under the Store tab. To edit SEO for individual pages, navigate to the Pages tab and click on each page in turn. Under Advanced Settings, you will find fields for the page title, page description, meta-keywords, footer code, and header code. To edit the SEO for blog posts, navigate to the blog and click on a blog post. Click on the Post Options button in the Build panel, and from there, click on Advanced. This will open up fields for you to insert the SEO post title and description. The final SEO editing area is under the Settings tab. These fields apply to your entire site, rather than specific pages or posts, so the content you use here should be of a wider scope. Click on the SEO menu on the left-hand side, where you will see fields to edit the site description, meta-keywords, footer code, and header code. If you choose to use Google Analytics, discussed in Session 10, this is where you will place the Google Analytics code.

SESSION 8

Create Online Store

An online store on your site is a convenient way to give your visitors access to buying memberships, making program reservations, or purchasing products from your gift store. If you plan to sell items on your website, Weebly has a good built-in store page and eCommerce system. You can create a single store page, feature individual products on different pages, or a mix of both. To get started, build your products first, before setting up a store page, storefront, or featured products. From your account home page, click on Edit to enter the editor. Clicking on the Store tab brings you to your store dashboard. From here, you can add products to your store, add store details (such as what information will appear on invoices to your customers), and set up your payment processing system. Weebly has a four-step setup checklist to help you get started: Add a Store Page (optional), Add Products, Add Store Information (contact details for invoices), and Accept Payments. If you have not already added a store page to your site, click the Add button next to the first step in the store dashboard. This will take you to the Pages tab, whence you can add a store page.

Adding products to your store is relatively simple. As you add products to your store, ask yourself or your team a few questions: Is this product worth selling online, or will it cost more to process the transaction and ship it than the buyer will pay to get it? Do we want to have a minimum purchase amount to ensure that we do not lose money on processing fees? There are a number of reasons to be choosy when it comes to selecting items for your online gift store. For instance, if you use the free Weebly package, you are limited to five items in your shop. On your store dashboard, click on the Add button to the right of the second step. This takes you to the products list. Click on the blue Add Product button at the top of the page to add your first item. Name your item, write a short description for it, list a price, enter weight information (if basing your shipping off the final weight of the products purchased), and upload an image. With a business upgrade, Weebly can track your inventory and charge sales tax. *If you do not plan to upgrade your package, be sure to include sales tax in the price of your item.*

If you need to include more items than your package allows, you may be able to group like items together and use the Multiple Options component to specify different items. For instance, if you work at the Missoula Tapestry Museum, which sells both postcards and greeting cards, you can group these together. To do this, create a product named Postcards & Greeting Cards. In the description, write out what the full options are, such as "Cards come in packs of ten, and postcards come in a mixed pack of 10." Under Multiple Options, add the option title Select Item. Then, under Option Choices, add the following separated by commas or by a return: Mixed Postcards, Tapestry Greeting Card, Gallery Greeting Card, Flower Greeting Card. After each option is added, it should convert to its own "box" so you can tell what each option is. If one of the boxes under Option Choices contains two names or looks incorrect, it may be that two options were added. Click behind the incorrect box, press the backspace key twice to fully delete the option, and reenter the correct option name, making sure you hit return or enter a comma immediately after each individual option (no space necessary). Finally, select the Input Type. Visitors will only be given these multiple-choice options if they are accessing the store through a storefront. Individual Product Elements can only feature one of these options. If you plan to display some but not all your products in a storefront, you can hide individual items by unchecking the box next to Storefront at the bottom of the page. These items will still be accessible via Product Elements and your store dashboard.

Add the rest of your products to the store before adjusting your settings and editing your storefront. On the Storefront menu, you can choose which products appear in your storefront, determine the page display, and edit SEO settings for the store. Be sure to save your changes using the green Update Changes button in the lower right-hand corner. Once your products are added, you can group them into categories (e.g., holiday items, sale items, games, books) to make it easier for customers to search through them. This will also come in handy if you plan to sell memberships or event tickets through your online store. More information on memberships is included later in this session. For now, click the blue Add Category button in the upper right-hand corner. Type in the name of the category and select which products belong in it. You can upload an image for the category and change the page layout and SEO settings if you know this category will have its own page on your website. For instance, you may want to sell educational toys on your Education page and memberships on your Membership page.

Under the Orders menu, you can see a list of past orders, along with their status and other details. After you have your first order, you can begin managing your orders here by marking them as shipped, contacting customers about order details or missing information, and exporting your emails to a revenue-tracking program like Excel.

Adjust Online Store Settings

As with the general site settings mentioned earlier, the online store settings are not all included in the free package, so they will not all be addressed. For example, settings for shipping and taxes are only editable with an upgrade to the Business Package or higher. You can also just figure these costs into your product listing. Settings you should be aware of include:

- Store → General
  - Currency and Weight Unit are determined by your location.
  - Store Mode indicates whether visitors buy items all at once (Add to Cart) or one-by-one (Buy Now).
  - *Make sure you fill out your store information so that invoices and receipts can be sent to your customers.*
  - Your shipping and return policies provide important information to your customers about the turnaround time on their orders, their options for returning unwanted merchandise, and any effect the cost of shipping will have on their order. Any details you enter here will be given to your customer at checkout, on their receipt, or both.
  - If you want your customer to have the option of including a note with special requests or order details, slide the Note to Seller switch to On.
- Store → Checkout: This is where you will select which payment processor you will use. You can choose between: Weebly (via Stripe), Square, Authorize.net, and PayPal. As Weebly's preferred partner, only Stripe is available with the free Weebly package. The nice part about this is that Weebly's designers have made the Stripe checkout integrate seamlessly with your store. Visitors will never have to leave your site or create another account to check out. You pay for this integration—literally—with a 3 percent merchant fee to Weebly *in addition* to the Stripe fee of 2.9 percent + $0.30 per transaction. You may want to take these fees into consideration when determining the type and price of items for sale on your site. For information on using PayPal to collection donations and sell items, see the last section in this session.

- Store → Display: From here, you can edit the look of your store page. You can adjust the number of columns and products displayed, change the image display and layout, and select the way items are displayed when browsed using category groupings.
- Store → Shipping: You will need to purchase a business upgrade to set shipping rates. Without the upgrade, consider including the cost of shipping in the item prices.
- Store → Taxes: You will need to purchase a business upgrade to set tax rules. Or, if your state has sales tax, just include the tax in your item prices.
- Store → Emails: You can send customized emails to your customers as confirmation of their activity. There are order confirmation, download confirmation (for digital content), shipping confirmation, refund confirmation, and order cancellation emails. Click on each email type to customize the emails for your site. You can only adjust the header and footer, as the middle content is populated with specific order information.
- Store → Advanced: If you have a Google Analytics Tracking ID, insert it here.

Sell Memberships and Accept Donations Online

If you plan to accept donations or make membership purchases available through your website, you have two options: create donation or item buttons through an outside merchant, such as PayPal, or treat donations and membership packages as store items and include them in your list of products. If you go this last route, the memberships will essentially be sold as a gift shop item because they will be processed as an order for a tangible good. However, your visitors will never know that the difference if you set up separate categories for these items. Create at least two categories in your store (separate for Memberships, Donate, and Gift Store items) so that visitors can then visit the storefront and decide where to go from there based on what they want to do. Add each membership or donation as its own item, as they will be different prices, then add Membership or Donation to the category list. Assign the membership and donation items to the correct category and save it. If you have an online gift shop *and* you accept donation or membership payments online, consider creating a second store page (titled Memberships or something to that effect) for your nontangible items. In the storefront on these pages, include only the membership or donation items. Note that donations made through this method must be fixed amounts—donors will not be able to set their own donation amount.

Using PayPal to set up membership fees and donations has its benefits. Perhaps most importantly, PayPal has a lower fee rate (2.9 percent + $0.30 per transaction) which is lower for certified nonprofits. You will need to sign up for a business account with PayPal, making sure to indicate your nonprofit status.[10] For those users who have nonprofit status, PayPal offers buttons to collect donations right on your website. *This option is not available for personal or business accounts that do not have their 501(c)(3) status verified, so make sure that you indicate your nonprofit status when you sign up for your account.*[11] If you do not already have an account, make sure you indicate if you have nonprofit status (so you can qualify lower processing fees) and that you select "Option B: Create payment buttons using HTML" when signing up for an account and are asked how you want to use PayPal to accept money. You can set up donation buttons so that donors can set specific amounts for their donation or even establish recurring donations. Be sure to set up each button so that it collects contact information for donors and new members. This way, if visitors fail to enter their information elsewhere, you will at least have a record in your PayPal account of how to contact them. Use the sections below as examples to learn how to accept donations and add both individual items (a Buy Now button) and sell multiple items at once (an Add to Cart button).

Next, log into your PayPal account and navigate to the button editing section (Tools → PayPal Buttons). On the right side of the My Saved Buttons home page, click Create New Button. Use the drop-down menu to select Donations. Add the name of your organization, then click the arrow next to Customize Text or Appearance. You can use the default PayPal button or upload your own image, though the second requires that you upload the image elsewhere on the web (on your site, for instance) and copy and paste the image URL into PayPal. If you use the PayPal image, you can change the size of the button and decide whether the accepted credit card logos are displayed. The sample button to the right will reflect the changes you make. Under Contribution Amount, you can allow visitors to select their own donation amount or you can set a fixed donation amount. You may want to look at the settings available in Step 3, namely the option to collect the customer's shipping address and the option to reroute to a URL after a payment has gone through. The first section determines whether your customer can write you a note (such as whom the donation was made in honor of). The next section allows you to collect your customer's address (in case you need to send them a thank you or other promotional materials). The third section allows you to input a URL to take customers to after they have either canceled a checkout or completed a successful checkout (e.g., a thank you page or a form to fill out in case you need to collect more information). Depending on how you plan to process memberships and donations, you may need to set up this redirect URL for donors or members to enter additional information. If you are comfortable contacting new members and donors separately through email or post, the information you collect through PayPal may be sufficient. When you see you have a new transaction, you can find the purchaser's contact information in the order details.

Alternatively, you may want to direct members and donors to a contact form immediately after they complete their transaction. If this is the case, first set up the page you want visitors to be redirected to. This will most likely be back on your website, where you can insert a contact form and write instructions for completing their membership registration using the information in Session 5. Once you have the page in place, copy the URL (from the *published* site, not from within the Weebly editor). In Step 3 of setting up a button, check the box next to "Take customers to this URL when they finish their checkout." Paste the URL into the field below that, and verify that you did not tick the box for "Take customers to this URL when they *cancel* their checkout." Occasionally, visitors will fail to complete this step in the registration process, whether because they navigate away from the page or their computer fails. Capturing their contact information through the PayPal payment will make reconciling your records much easier.

The final step is to embed your PayPal buttons on your website. Once you have these settings adjusted to your satisfaction, click Create Button. On the next page, you will see a field with HTML code. You will see a preview of your button next to a box with automatically generated HTML code for your website. Click anywhere in the box so that all the text within is highlighted. Copy the code and return to Weebly. Drag an Embed Code Element into the editor and paste the button code. Click outside the Element to see the button appear. Repeat the process for as many buttons as you need; you can add the same button more than once to your website.

SESSION 9

Check and Modify Mobile Site

Allowing smartphone-wielding visitors to view the site with a layout specifically made for mobile devices is absolutely necessary. Equally necessary is the option to switch back to the full (or desktop) view if desired. Some visitors will prefer the mobile version of a website because it generally comes with a simplified layout and faster loading times. Others will find that certain Elements do not load correctly in the mobile view and will therefore need to toggle to the full-site version to see desired content. The good news is that you only have to create one website; Weebly automatically converts your site to a mobile-optimized view. It is imperative that you review the mobile version to check for any formatting gone askew or Elements missing, but the conversion is generally smooth. Any content edits that you make, including

Element or text changes, are automatically synced between the sites. This does *not* include changes in theme (such as changing theme colors or even entire themes), so you can have different looks for both of your site versions. There are fewer mobile themes, but that is inconsequential, as your sites should be aesthetically cohesive anyway.

To begin reviewing your mobile site, click on the Edit button on your account home page and enter the mobile viewer. On the top bar, right next to the Publish button, there are two small icons, one for a desktop computer and one for a mobile phone. The first view is the default; it is what you have been working in all through this chapter. The second is for adjusting your mobile-optimized site that includes all the information and content from your first site. Click on the mobile view. On the left of the screen, your build panel should look the same. On the right, you should see an additional mobile panel. This panel includes options for changing your mobile theme or color scheme and removing certain Elements, such as header images and social icons.[12]

Review your mobile site by navigating to each page, checking for overlapping Elements, strange formatting, images that do not appear, and other items that need fixing. In general, there should not be much to correct—Weebly rearranges your material into a mobile-friendly version fairly seamlessly. Remember that any *content* you change in the mobile view will be changed in the full-site version as well, so you should make sure that you are not deleting or adding anything to the mobile site that you do not also want changed on the full site. To check whether your pages pass the Google Mobile-Friendly Test, copy the page URL and paste it into the field found at google.com/webmasters/tools/mobile-friendly. As discussed in Chapter 2, the review is part of the final steps of website development and should be done again on a physical smartphone or tablet, not just on the mobile editor.

SESSION 10

Add Google AdSense

Google AdSense is a product that Google uses in cooperation with other businesses so that websites can generate income by showing ads to viewers. Essentially, you can place a Google AdSense Element anywhere on your website, viewers will see personalized and targeted advertisements, and the advertiser will pay you a certain amount of money for each view or click an ad receives. You will not be able to control what ads your visitors see, but you can control the size and location of the ads. Ads are generally selected based on visitors' cookies and browsing history, so you cannot directly control what is advertised on your site. If you feel up for having advertising on your site, then this is an easy and clean way to do it.

Do not attempt to place Google AdSense on your site before it is filled with content and published. Google may reject your request, as a blank site will not generate revenue. To use this service on a Weebly site, Google AdSense requires that you register through Weebly. Enter the Weebly editor by clicking the Edit button on the home page of your account. Navigate to the page where you want to place Google AdSense and drag a Google AdSense Element into the editor. When you do this, Weebly will prompt you to sign up for Google AdSense by clicking on the button that says "Authorize Weebly." You should link the new account to your single-stream email, especially if it is a Gmail account. Read over the legal requirements carefully. Enter your contact information to complete your Google AdSense application. Once your application is approved, Google will notify you, and give you further information on maintaining the service on your site. If you are rejected, wait for a few weeks while you add more content and boost the visibility of your site, then reapply. In the meantime, add Google AdSense Elements to your site wherever you want them—the bottom row or the side, one ad per page or just one ad on one page of your site. Google may not display ads in all of these locations at once, but by having them placed, you at least give Google the option if your site becomes particularly good at generating revenue through advertising.

Check Site Stats

Part of maintaining an active online presence is understanding how your audience receives your content. This means checking visitor statistics at least once per month. Weebly makes this easy by providing basic site stats with even the free package. You can see the number of unique visitors and the number of page views over a thirty-day period by clicking the Stats button on your account home page or the small button of three white lines in the upper right-hand corner of your site editor and then "Site Stats." The page you see next will have a line graph detailing the number of separate IP addresses that accessed your site on a given day, as well as the number of pages viewed on your site each day. For example, hovering over July 31, you might see that you had seventeen site views. When you click on "Unique Visitors," you see that you had seven unique visitors on that same day. This means that between the seven visitors to your website, they viewed seventeen of your pages. These could be all the same pages (as most visitors will visit at least your home page and move to other pages as befit their needs) or they could all be different pages. To get more detailed information, you need an upgraded Weebly package.

Run Google Analytics

Another option for getting more detailed site stats is to use Google Analytics, another free service from Google. Google Analytics is used to see where your visitors come from, what pages they visit, and what their demographics are. To get started, visit google.com/analytics. Once you have your Tracking ID, navigate to the Settings tab of your editor. Then, click on the SEO menu and scroll to the Header Code box. Google Analytics should supply you with a code to copy and paste into this box. If you plan to sell items on your website, make sure to enable eCommerce tracking in your Google Analytics account and then enter your Google Analytics Tracking ID into the Advanced settings menu under your Store tab. Log into your Google Analytics account to view the detailed site stats Google tracks.

Upgrade Site

At some point in your webmaster duties, you may decide that you want to upgrade your Weebly account to a Starter, Pro, or Business account. While there are only a few discrete ads for Weebly in the footer area of your free site, there are a number of other reasons you might want to upgrade. While you build your site, you notice that some of the features in your Build panel and elsewhere have a small star on them. This indicates that the feature is only available with an upgrade. For a full list of what each package offers, click on the drop-down menu in the upper left-hand corner of your editor that says, "Free" and then click "Compare Plans." The price for each upgrade depends on how long you purchase your plan for (e.g., the price per month for a six-month agreement will be higher than that for a two-year agreement). The cost for *one year* of registration, along with the most common reasons to upgrade, is as follows:

- Starter ($4.08/month): Customizable domain name (URL), expanded site stats, premium support, ten shop items
- Pro ($8.25/month): Customizable domain name (URL), expanded site stats, premium support, expanded professional multimedia features, site search, password protection, twenty-five shop items
- Business ($24.92/month): Customizable domain name (URL), expanded site stats, premium support, expanded professional multimedia features, site search, password protection, eCommerce system, unlimited shop items

To purchase an upgrade, navigate to your account home page. Underneath the URL for your site, click on the Upgrade link and select the plan that works best for you. You will need a debit or credit card to complete the transaction.

Once complete, your site will automatically have access to all the features included in your new package. You will need to renew the package upgrade when your term is over or your account will revert you back to the free package.

☙

As you build your site, feel free to experiment with different Elements. You can save your site over and over again, only publishing for the public after you are satisfied with the changes. Take time to browse through the different Elements you can add to your site, especially if you need to add special features like scheduling services or a member login. To view the Weebly help pages, visit help.weebly.com. Find updated Weebly information at freethemuseum.net/weebly.

NOTES

1. Review the image size and copyright info mentioned in Chapter 2.

2. If you need to find the URL of an image on the web, right-click on the image and select "Open Image in New Tab." Then, copy the URL in your address bar. You will not be able to do this for your Weebly site until it is published, as it will be by the end of this session.

3. The lightbox function allows users to click on an image to view it with its original size dimensions in a pop-up window. This is especially useful for high-resolution landscape images or collection images, as visitors can look at the image much closer than if it only resides on the page in one size. Note that you cannot use the lightbox function if you edit the image on Weebly—this is because the image resolution or dimensions are automatically changed by the Weebly image editor and thus your image will no longer benefit from being enlarged by the lightbox.

4. Even though visitors can follow embedded content to its source, it is, of course, always a good idea to give credit directly on your page for any embedded content that is not yours (apart from Google Maps, Google Calendars, etc.).

5. You do not need to create a new account or engage with Scribd in any way, as Weebly has integrated the service into its platform. Your final page, however, will have the Scribd logo visible next to the embedded document.

6. Including DOC, DOCX, EPUB, KEY, ODG, ODP, ODS, ODT, PDF, PPS, PPSX, PPT, PPTX, PS, RTF, SXC, SXD, SXI, SXW, TXT, XLS, and XLSX.

7. If you know you need a larger forum but want to find a free and almost unlimited one, look at Nabble.com, which offers free and embeddable forums, mailing lists, and more.

8. You can also ban any spammers or abusive members that appear later on.

9. Visit kelseyransick.weebly.com for an example of a "crafted" side menu that is created in a theme that originally had a top menu.

10. Only verified nonprofits can withdraw the funds they collect using donate buttons, as PayPal may choose to charge a lower fee for these transactions, thus giving the receiving nonprofit more of the donation.

11. PayPal's terms note that the donation button is strictly "intended for fundraising. If you are not raising money for a cause, please choose another option. Nonprofits must verify their status to withdraw donations they receive. Users that are not verified nonprofits must demonstrate how their donations will be used, once they raise more than $10,000 USD."

12. At the very bottom, you will see the option to switch between Apple (iPad and iPhone) view and Android view. These should display the same, so there is no need to check both versions.

Chapter 4

Getting Your Website Started on Wix

Wix is a very flexible WYWISWG tool with a wide variety of "widgets" or apps that tie in with your site. You can embed your Google Calendar, allow visitors to search your site, insert a live chat box, or let visitors sign up for your MailChimp newsletter—all right from your website. Wix has a fairly extensive support center, though it occasionally assumes more technical knowledge than other WYSIWYG support centers do. You can pick from a large number of templates or start with a blank page and add in any colors, layouts, and elements you want, including embedded HTML and documents. While you are limited to Wix's set of fonts, the selection is quite extensive, and you are sure to find one that suits your needs. If you want to almost have complete control over your website's look and are prepared to develop such a look, then Wix is the best choice for your website.

As with other guides in this book, this section should give you a good starting point on your website, but is not intended to be all-inclusive. This guide will provide an introduction to Wix's basic features—enough to get you set up with a professional-looking website without the hassle and expense of using an outside web designer. Most of the "apps" available through Wix have a free version with limited but sufficient functionality for basic operation, as well as a paid upgraded version with more storage, more complex functions, or a greater number of templates. These are great if you have a specific need, such as using an online scheduling calendar for tours or rentals, but subscriptions to these services can add up quickly if you want to use a lot of apps. If you think you will be using Wix as your editor, look through the apps before finalizing your sitemap and page layouts so that you can plan for apps or any workarounds necessary to incorporate them. One of the best features of Wix is that your site will not be visible to the public while you work on it until you choose to "publish" it. This means that you can set up and publish a "Coming soon!" page for your visitors to see and use the next few weeks to fully construct your website, all the while comfortable in the knowledge that your edits are routinely saved and will be made available to the public at a time of your choosing. Feel free to experiment! With an online WYSIWYG editor like Wix, you can see the results of your experimentation instantaneously as you make changes.

The Wix guide has ten different website-building sessions. Each session goes over different elements of creating a website on Wix, and you can work through them in sequential order or, once you have the basics set up, jump to relevant topics and skip over irrelevant ones. Some sessions will be quick, taking ten or fifteen minutes. Others may take a few hours, depending on your speed and comfort level with the material. Do not feel rushed to move on to another session if you still want to experiment more with the material in an earlier session. The material covered in each session is as follows:

- Session 1
  - Create an account
  - Choose a theme
  - Select or create a domain (for placeholder URLs or free sites)
- Session 2
  - Add and edit text
  - Delete or move Elements
  - Set default fonts and colors
  - Add page(s)
- Session 3
  - Add or edit images
  - Create a slideshow or gallery of images
  - Edit header and footer
- Session 4
  - Add a button
  - Add a forum
  - Add a poll, survey, or form
  - Add a shape or line
- Session 5
  - Add a menu
  - Hide pages from a menu
  - Publish your site (make it visible to others on the web)
- Session 6
  - Create links
  - Add a calendar
  - Use HTML to embed a document, video, or map

- Session 7
  - Add a blog
  - Add or edit social media buttons
- Session 8
  - Adjust general settings
  - Edit SEO settings
  - Run statistics
- Session 9
  - Create an online store
  - Sell memberships and accept donations online
- Session 10
  - Check and modify mobile site
  - Add Google AdSense
  - Upgrade site, including changing or adding a domain

With the exception of Session 1, which starts from the Wix.com home page, and Session 2, which starts from the account home page, all sessions start from the editor home page.

SESSION 1

Create Account

Once you have navigated to Wix.com and selected the option to create an account, sign up using Facebook, Google+,[1] or your single-stream email account. As soon as you complete the sign-up process, Wix will prompt you to select a theme.

Choose Theme

When using Wix, you cannot easily switch between templates once you have begun entering information on your site. If you select a template, add information, and decide later that you want to change the template, you will have to create a new site and reenter all the information. As such, it is wise to be fairly certain you like the general design before uploading photos and inserting a significant amount of content. To get started, click on the "View All Templates" link at the bottom of the Welcome page to begin browsing templates by category. Be aware that aside from the Online Store, Blog, and One-Pager categories, almost any template can work for any genre of website. The categories are there to help users visualize their own content on a website already incorporating similar images and content, but any image

Figure 4.1   The Wix editor home page

or feature can be replaced if necessary. Note that though most templates are free, some must be purchased.[2] Refer to the section on layout and design in Chapter 2 as you browse through the themes. If you want to explore what a template looks like to a visitor, click on View underneath the template. This opens up the template in a new window or tab where you can click through the site and get to know its built-in look and feel. Should you want to keep browsing templates, close the window or tab and return to the template-selection page. If none of the templates suit your purpose, consider selecting a blank template and building your site exactly the way you like it. This will mean a slightly longer site-construction time, but also give you ultimate flexibility. Once you have found the template you like, click Edit (underneath the template on the template-selection page) or Edit This Site (at the top of the template-testing page). This will bring you to your editor home page (Figure 4.1).

Select or Create Domain

Once you enter the Wix editor, an intro video will start to play, which you can watch to get a quick tour of the editor. Once you start editing, Wix will ask you to create a domain for your site—even if it is just a temporary one. Wix wants you to get started on your site right away, rather than worry about connecting domains before you get to know the platform, so enter a name (or placeholder, if you plan to connect a purchased domain later).[3]

SESSION 2

From your account home page, click on Edit Site next to the name of your website. This will bring you to the editor home page. Sans a few administrative pieces, this is what your visitors will see when they come to your website.

Add and Edit Text

Wix Elements are any editable items on the page. To edit an existing Text Element, double-click on the text box around it. A cursor will appear, just like in a word processing document. A single click will open up a menu of text options for the text box. Once you begin editing text, a bar of style options will appear. When it comes to changing the font of your text, you have two options: you can change each block of text or string of words individually, or, ideally, set different styles for headers, body text, and other types of text. The former option will come in handy if you need to emphasize a single word to indicate that it is a link or italicize the name of a book. The latter will, just like in a Microsoft Word document, update *all* instances of that type of text. For instance, if you want all the body text on your website to be Helvetica 12 pt. black and all your paragraph headings to be Helvetica 16 pt. blue, you can use the information later in this session to change them all in one fell swoop.

Highlight the text you want to edit (changes will *not* be applied to the whole text box, only to highlighted text). From this editing bar, you can change the text style, typeface, size, color, kerning, indentation, justification, alignment, and link properties, as well as adjust line spacing and add bullets or numbered lists. If you are unsure what any of the editing bar items are, hover over them for a second and a description will appear (and if the bar gets

ix Tip #1: Wix provides a ruler and gridlines to demarcate where the header, footer, and body of the website are. Be careful not to build outside the central gridlines, as these areas may not appear to some visitors with smaller screens. You can also turn on the "snap" feature so that elements you add will snap into alignment with other elements of the page or the overall site. If the snap feature is on, thin purple lines will appear to indicate alignment as you move each element around the page. Turn on and off these features in the toolbar at the top of the editor.

Figure 4.2

ix Tip #2: Wix does not autosave your work. You must click
Save or Publish for your changes to be saved. Save your work,
whether or not it is ready to be published, every 5-10 minutes.
Publish when you are ready to share your site with the public.

Figure 4.3

in the way, drag it to a new position by the stripe of gray dots on the left-hand
side.) To add new text, click on the Add button in the Edit menu and then
select Text. Click on Paragraph Text, and you will see a new text box appear,
complete with placeholder text (you do not have to drag the Element onto the
page; just clicking on it in the menu will make it appear). Any time you add
a new Element in Wix, it is automatically populated with placeholder content, so before publishing, *be sure to double-check your site for sample text
or images that never got edited or deleted in the site-construction process.*
Double-click on the text to begin editing it.

Delete or Move Elements

To delete an Element, simply single-click on the element and press delete on
your keyboard. If you are already editing inside an Element, click outside it
and then single-click on the Element. You can also single-click on an Element
and select the trash can icon that appears in the menu of options. If you accidentally delete an object, you can reclaim it using the undo button.

To resize an Element, you have two options. Much like a text box in a
Word document, you can adjust the height and width of your Wix text box
by dragging one of the dots on the edge of the box. Alternatively, you can
drag down the small white box at the bottom of the box. This adjusts the size
of your Element *while maintaining the current page layout,* which is useful

ix Tip #3: The Undo/Redo changes buttons will allow you to
reverse over twenty of your last changes, but do not depend
on it too much. Save frequently and use your site history (found
under Site Shortcuts through your account home page) to revert to
earlier versions of your website.

Figure 4.4

W ix Tip #4: Elements you add to the page will not automatically shift away from other elements already on the page. This means that objects can overlap, fall off the page, and be off-center. As you review your site, make sure you do not have accidental overlaps or other formatting issues caused by odd Element placement. You can always change the dimensions and move the Element if needed.

Figure 4.5

if you have content currently below the element that needs to *stay* below the Element (as opposed to having the Element overlap that content). When adjusting using this method, be aware that content must be completely below the Element to begin with in order to be pushed downward when you adjust the size. In either method, if your text does not take up the entirety of the new dimensions, visitors will see extra space at the bottom or side of your text box.

Similar to the box adjustment button, the white box at the top of the Element box allows you to *move* an Element vertically on the page while maintaining the layout. Using this method, content that is entirely below the Element will move up and down with the element. Content that is above it will remain in its place, and the Element can only move as far upward as the next Element.

You can also freely move an Element horizontally and vertically by clicking outside it to exit the editing functions, then dragging the Element to its new location. As you move Elements, you may see magenta lines appear. These help you line up your Element with elements around it or center an element on the page. When adding or moving Elements, remember to keep them within the gridlines to ensure that they appear to your visitor. Some Elements, such as image Elements, can be rotated by clicking on them once and dragging the circular arrow in the upper-right-hand corner in the direction you want to rotate the object. To return the Element to its original orientation, hover over the same arrow and click the small red X that appears atop it.

Set Default Fonts and Colors

Changing fonts for individual Text Elements should be done while editing the text, as seen above. Changing default fonts for different text styles is best done when you already have some content on your site (whether real or placeholder content) but are not all the way finished. Sometimes fonts look really nice in the sample and are then almost unreadable in a block of text, so waiting until you have substantial blocks of text to test a font out on your site will help you avoid formatting issues later on. To change the default font for headings, body paragraphs, menus, and other styles, click on the Design button in the Edit Menu. From there, click on the Fonts tab. You can choose from preset font schemes or customize your own font scheme. If doing the latter, roll over the font style to see examples of that font highlighted on the current page of your website (if there is any text in that style). At any point, you can return to the default fonts by clicking on Discard Changes at the bottom of the editing menu. If you have already adjusted fonts using the text-editing toolbar, these fonts will *not* revert back to the default—you will either need to change their style in the text editing toolbar or create a new Text Element that automatically incorporates the font styles you just selected.

Under the design tab in the Edit Menu, you can also find preset color palettes for your site. If you click on these palettes, you can see how the new settings will change your site, though you can customize the palette's colors and the way these changes take effect. For example, if you like the Corporate Blues color palette but do not like the new blue of the background, you can click Customize Palette to use suggested colors that match the tone of the rest of the theme or select entirely different colors. If you have specific colors in mind, check out the color history section in Chapter 7 beginning on page 180. You may like the general color scheme, but not the way individual Elements are given colors (e.g., you like the olive green in the color scheme, but it is only assigned to the background, and you would rather have your site title in olive green). If this is the case, you can edit the specific colors of your menus, background, text, and buttons within each Element's editing options as you build your site.

To change the background of your site to a new color or texture, click on the Background button in the Design tab. There are a number of prebuilt background patterns and textures to choose from, and you can also add your own color or image by clicking Customize Background. *If you upload your own image for the background, make sure it is of high resolution, especially if your image is full screen rather than tiled.* Generally, you want your background image to scroll with the site so that visitors scrolling down particularly long pages do not lose the image and end up with white space where you do not intend there to be any. If you upload your own image or select a new background color, changes will only be made to the page your editor is currently on unless you select Apply to Other Pages.

Add Page(s)

Once you feel comfortable with your website theme and colors, you can build it one page at a time or create all your pages and go back and fill them in afterward. The latter allows you to get to know the flow of your site and link between pages right away, filling in images and text after the structure of your site is in place. To add a new page, click on the Pages tab in the Edit menu. Here, you will see a list of pages currently on the site. If you chose a template, there will likely be three or four pages already in the list; if you started from scratch, you should only have one. Click on any page to move the editor to that page, or the blue Settings icon to edit the page title, address, style, and other settings or to delete the page altogether. The Add button at the bottom of the pages menu will give you the option of adding a new page, a link (to an outside web page), or a drop-down menu. When you add a new page, you can add a blank page to build the content from scratch but with the template stylizations. Alternatively, you can select one of the prebuilt pages based on their function, choosing from pages for listing products, providing contact information, writing a blog, putting up a "coming soon" notice, and more. Select the type of page you want, name it, and click OK. It will be added to the bottom of the pages list. When you add a link to the menu, you have the option of linking it to an outside web address, a document, an email, or an anchor on another page (e.g., if you want a visitor to move to a lower location on either the current page or another page).

The menu drop-down option differs from traditional subpages because it allows you to have subpages under a menu item that does not have its own page. Using this, visitors will not be able to click on the top-level menu item of the drop-down menu (because there is nowhere for it to go). For example, you might want a Get Involved menu item with pages for Membership, Volunteering, and Employment, but you do not want a landing page on the Get Involved topic. The drop-down menu allows you to create the Get Involved category without having to build and fill a potentially vague-sounding Get Involved landing page. You can add all your pages now if you are so inclined, or wait until you have built up the existing pages more.

To adjust the order of your pages, drag the page "bar" up or down by its handle (the small dots on the left-hand side of the bar). In a horizontal menu (the default orientation in Wix) pages will appear left-to-right in the order they appear in the page list. Moving a page bar underneath and to the right of another page bar will make it a subpage. Moving a page bar to the left again will make it a top-menu item. You can only have two levels of menu (top-menu items and subpages) in Wix. Your site automatically transitions

ix Tip #5: You can navigate through your site's pages by using the page list in the toolbar at the top of the editor.

Figure 4.6

ix Tip #6: Updating the style of any page or element (rather than clicking on Personalize This) will update the style of every element on your site **with that style**. This is useful if you want to change, for example, all the buttons on your site in the same style. If you want a unique button, however, you will need to click Personalize This Button.

Figure 4.7

by cross-fade when a visitor clicks on a new page. To change the way pages transition, select a new page transition at the bottom of the Pages tab and click on a new page in the list to watch how the pages segue.

To adjust the settings of a page, click the settings gear icon to the right of the page name in the pages list. From here, you can change the name and page address (slug), hide the page from the menu (in case it is a third-level page or you do not want the menu overcrowded with every single page), protect the page (restrict the page to site members or add password protection), hide the header and footer, edit the SEO settings (see Session 8), and change the style of the page.

Add a few pages to your site and fill them with real or placeholder content so you can get a feel for whether the layout and design are suitable for your site. You can use faux Latin as a great placeholder for text, as it allows you to see the design with realistic content and will not distract you. For now, visit lipsum.com to generate text to fill up your site.

SESSION 3

Add or Edit Images

To insert a new image, click on the Add tab of the Edit menu. Select Image. From there, you can add an image (with a default frame), an image without a

ix Tip #7: Within your Image Gallery, you can organize your images into folders by page, subject, or another category. You can also pull images from social networking sites using the buttons below "Upload Images" in your Image Gallery. Note that you cannot add TIFFs—only JPEGs, PNGs, and GIFs.

Figure 4.8

frame, or clip art (good for logos with transparent backgrounds). Any of these options opens up an image uploader box from which you can upload your own image to your Image Gallery, choose an image already in your Image Gallery, select a free image from Wix, or purchase an image from Bigstock.[4] If you upload your own image, it will go into the Image Gallery, which means you can easily find it if you need to use it again.

While you cannot edit images from Wix or Bigstock, any images you upload can be modified in the Wix Image Gallery. You can enter the Image Gallery at any time by double-clicking on an existing Image Element or by adding a new Image Element. To crop the image or to adjust the brightness, contrast, saturation, or other settings, click the settings icon on the bottom right of the image within the Image Gallery. The settings menu includes four options:

- Rename (to make images easier to find within the gallery and help boost SEO—see Chapter 2 for a reminder on SEO points)
- Edit Image (to make basic adjustments like cropping and brightness; this saves a *new* version of the image so you have access to both the original and the modified one)
- Download (in case you lost the original file)
- Remove (which will remove the image from your gallery but *not* from wherever it is placed on the site; to use the image again, you will have to reupload it or copy the Image Element)

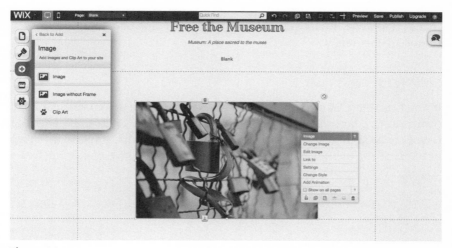

Figure 4.9

Once the image you want to place on the page is selected, click the Add Image button. The image should now appear on the page and you can resize, rotate, or move it. Single-clicking on the Image Element while in the editor will bring up an image menu.

Create Slideshow or Gallery of Images

Adding a slideshow or gallery of images is similar to adding a single image. Under the Add button in the Edit Menu, you will find various arrangements of galleries and slideshows. The image next to each gives you an idea of what the image layout will look like, though there are additional arrangements and settings within each of these. When selecting your gallery or slideshow arrangement, keep in mind that the bigger the image files and the more movement involved in the transition, the longer the loading time may be for visitors with slower browsers or bad internet connections. After adding a Slideshow Element or Gallery Element to the editor, double-click on the Element to bring up the image-organizing menu (which will allow you to replace, rearrange, name, link, and describe each image as necessary). You can draw from your Image Gallery or the Wix or Bigstock image galleries to fill these slideshows and galleries. Add your images and click the Done button. Resize and move your new Slideshow Element or Gallery Element as necessary. Some of these Elements run the full width of the page (e.g., Strip Showcase and Strip Slideshow), so you will only be able to adjust the height. There are two editing areas for slideshows and galleries: the image-organizing menu (accessed by double-clicking on the element) and the element settings menu (which appears when you single-click on the Element). Under the latter, you can change the slideshow or gallery type, change the style, and adjust settings like transition method, timing, and autoplay functionality.

Edit Header and Footer

If you have the gridlines on (the small dotted square in the upper right-hand corner of the editor should be blue) you can quickly see where the header and footer are on your website. Any items placed in the header or footer will have

ix Tip #8: Click Preview in the top toolbar at any point to see exactly how your site functions for your visitors without having to publish it.

Figure 4.10

an orange box, rather than a blue box, when selected. This makes it easier to see what Elements are going to appear in the header or footer on every page. To add Elements to one of these areas, simply add the desired Element to the page and then drag it to the header or footer. Once there, you can edit it as you would any other Element, but be sure to navigate to another page and verify that it appeared. To edit Elements already in the header or footer, simply double-click on them and edit according to the instructions in the sessions mentioned above.

SESSION 4

Add Button

From your editor, click on the Add button in the Edit menu. Select the Buttons & Menus tab, and from there the Button Element. Note that in this menu, you can also add a button made out of an image, a vertical or horizontal button menu, or a PayPal button, all of which may be useful to you as you develop your site further. For now, focus on a plain button, imagining that it will lead visitors from your homepage to the Donate Now page. Double-click the new Button Element on your page to bring up the text, link, and style editor. Rename the button "Donate Now!" Click the link box and then select the Page option. From there, you can select the Donate page. If you like the button style Wix automatically generated, you can move the button to its rightful spot on the page. If you want to edit the button style, click on the blue Change Style option in the Element editor. Remember that *editing the style* (e.g., Default Button or Emphasis Button) rather than *personalizing the button* will change all buttons of that style on your site.

An Image Button Element has no text but rather functions as a clickable image, with the added benefit of rollover and clicked views. That way, visitors are certain that the button links them to new content, and once they have clicked on it, the image changes so they know which links they have visited. In this way, it functions much like hypertext, which changes color after it has been clicked on. If you use an Image Button Element, you will need three different versions of the same image—or three different images—so you can indicate the three stages of the item (unvisited, currently hovering over, and visited). After you are satisfied with the three images, choose your transition, set the link destination, and add your alt text.

Adding a menu, including a button menu, is covered in Session 5, but adding a PayPal button for donations or purchases is a fairly quick process if you already have a PayPal account. If you do not have an account yet, visit paypal.com and set up an account. Make sure you indicate if you have nonprofit status (so you can qualify lower processing fees) and that you select "Option B: Create payment buttons using HTML" when signing up for an account and are asked how you want to use PayPal to accept money. Once you have your PayPal account set up, return to the Wix editor and double-click on the PayPal Button Element. You can then choose one of two PayPal button types: Buy Now or Donation. The Buy Now button requires you to use a set price (e.g., $25) for a single item; it does not function like a shopping cart because it is a one-off purchase of a single service or good. A Donate button, on the other hand, allows visitors to set the amount of their donation.

To set up a new button, select the appropriate button type in the drop-down menu. Enter the email you use for your organization's PayPal account. If you are using a Buy Now button, you will need to enter the item name and the price of the item. If using a Donate button, enter your organization's name along with *either a specific donation amount or a 0 to allow visitors to enter their own donation amount.* When clicked on, the PayPal button you insert here will take visitors to the PayPal transaction site to process their payment. Select whether you want the PayPal processing page to open in a new window or in the same window as your site. You can also elect to use a smaller or visually simplified button (eliminating the credit card logos) by ticking the Use Small Button or Hide Credit Card Logos boxes. Once you are satisfied with your button, click the Update button to make sure your changes are applied.

Add Forum

Website forums can be a great place for community members and museums to engage in discussions about your collections or events. Wix has two third-party forum services available, each of which will suffice for a small, basic forum. You can use either, but for this session, you will be using the Muut Forum. To find it, click on the Wix App Market button in the Edit menu. In the Search Apps bar, type in "forum" and click on the Add to Site button next to Muut Forum. *This will automatically add a new page to your site.* Double-click on the new Muut Forum Element to adjust its settings and look. You will need to create a Muut account before setting up your site's forum. To do so, click on the small Create One link in the top section of the Muut Forum settings box. This will open up a small new window, where you can sign up for an account and begin your forum. Each option that Muut offers you as you create your forum will note if its capabilities are part of a paid plan or the free version. You can use these snazzy paid components for a short time period, but you will have to pay a monthly fee to keep them going—and they are generally unnecessary for a basic forum.

Once you have set up your Muut account, return to the Wix editor and enter the forum name you selected into the Forum Web Address field. Enter into the Prompt New Posts field the text your visitors will see when they want to add a new post. For example, if your forum is gathering responses on an upcoming exhibit about a local community park, you might want to prompt visitors to write a post by asking "What do you like best about going to the park? In which season is the park the most enjoyable?" You can also keep it simple: "Comments? Questions?" Enter your prompt text and then click the small arrow next to Design to see your color and stylization options. The colors and text styles offered should automatically match your Wix site, but you can adjust them as you did colors in Session 2. Changes are reflected in your forum right away, but you should still save your site changes after adding the forum.

Add Poll, Survey, or Form

A number of other Wix apps allow you to pose questions to your visitors, including the Poll app and Form Builder Plus+ app. Though you can use a number of different apps to create questionnaires and polls, these two will be the focus here. The Poll and the Form Builder Plus+ apps both allow multiple questions, which can have answers in the form of text boxes, radio buttons, drop-down menu selections, and more. Both apps are found in the Wix App Market after searching for "poll" or "survey" and *either one can be used to create a single or multipart questionnaire* (they are offered by POWr). Creating a multiquestion form or survey can follow the same process as described below using either the Poll or Form Builder Plus+ apps. Simply add in additional questions or fields to the Element based on what questions you want to ask. For now, click on the Add to Site button next to the Poll app and accept the app onto your site. Double-click on the generic poll question that appears on your site. You will see an app settings menu with tabs for Quick Setup, Content, and Design. The Admin tab is only available with a paid Form app upgrade and the Help tab may answer additional questions you have.

Using the arrows in the Quick Setup tab, select one of the preset poll formats. Use the drop-down menus to select the poll's font and color scheme. Click Apply to confirm any changes you made. Under the Content tab, type in the email address you want the responses to be sent to. You can also see all the responses at once by returning to this menu and clicking View Form Response once visitors have had a chance to respond. Click on the Title and Button title to open up the next fields for editing. Enter in the title, description, and submit button text for your form. Expand the Form Elements field. In the Poll app, the default number of questions is one, but you can add additional form fields (questions) by clicking Add Form

Element. To edit a field, first select the type of response you want. If you are unsure what a format option entails, select it and the poll will reflect the new format. Each format has its own settings, and some come with short explanations of different features. The key setting to look for is the option to make a field required for submission. Most formats have this option. To delete a field you no longer want, click on the X to the right of the format drop-down menu.

The next field for editing is Accept Payments. Here, you can require that visitors submit a payment via PayPal before they can submit the poll or form. This is useful if you plan to accept donations or membership dues (see Session 9 below). As with adding a PayPal button, your form can be used to submit a donation or as a "buy now" transaction. Name your donation association or product and product cost. Make sure that if you need to collect a specific amount, you leave the Allow Buyer to Choose Price box unticked. *Likewise, if you want visitors to be able to select their donation amount, you must check this box, even if you have already selected Donation from the drop-down menu above.* The Quantity Input section is used if you want visitors to be able to add more than one of the item to their purchase. In the next section, add in your submission confirmation text. The last section gives you the option of using captchas to help prevent spam submissions. The Design tab is where you can further adjust the font, colors, and overall style of your poll.

Add Shape or Line

To add a shape or line as a graphic or to help build structure for your site, click on the Add button in the Edit menu. Click on Shapes & Lines and select the Element you want to add. A Strip Element will span the entire width of the page, though you can adjust the color, height, and location of the strip. Similarly, a Full Width Line Element will stretch across the page but can be modified. Adding a Shape Element brings up a menu of shapes and silhouettes, ranging from a simple square or a diamond to lamp posts and laurel leaves. You can browse or use a keyword search to find various shapes. You

ix Tip #9: If you need to add an image with a transparent background, such as a logo, you will need to add a Clip Art Element and then upload the image to the Element. Make sure your image is a PNG or TIFF, the two file types that support transparency.

Figure 4.11

can rotate and resize these shapes and change their colors by clicking on the Shape Element and opening the Settings menu.

SESSION 5

Add Menu

Most templates come with a menu, but occasionally you will want to add an additional menu or one with a different orientation. The easiest method is to let Wix build the menu for you. From your editor, click the Add button in the Edit menu. Click on the Buttons & Menus option and then Menu or Vertical Menu, depending on what layout you want. The new Menu Element will appear on the page, and you can then adjust its size and location. Double-clicking on the menu will bring up your list of pages. Remember that if you do not want a page to appear on the menu, click on the settings gear to the right of the page name and then select the Hide From Menu box. Single-clicking on the new Menu Element and then on Settings brings up the menu settings options. Here, you can change the text and button alignment, as well as the menu style. Note that pages that do not fit in the menu will be grouped under a single label whose default is "More." If you do not want this, you can rename the label, reduce the number of pages present in the menu by hiding them, shorten page names, or adjust the width of each menu item. Click on Change Style to adjust the colors, fonts, spacing, and other aesthetic aspects of the menu.

Preview and Publish Site

Recall that you can click the Preview button at the top of the editor to see your website as visitors will. While clicking Save will keep your progress safe, only clicking Publish will make your site and its updates available to

ix Tip #10: There are two ways to get an Element to appear on all pages of your site. The first is to add it to the header or footer (indicated by an orange, rather than blue, box around the Element when it is clicked on). The second way is to single-click on the Element, then on Settings. Tick the small box next to "Show on all pages" at the bottom of the settings menu that pops up.

Figure 4.12

𝒲 ix Tip #11: If you use the Support Center, be sure you are in the right platform section. Wix originally had both an HTML5 editor and a Flash editor. All new sites are built in the HTML5 editor, but you will often come across what seems to be an answer to your question, only to find out that its solution is for the Flash editor.

Figure 4.13

the public. Once you are ready to share your website, publish it. You will be presented with the option to allow search engines to find it (using your SEO settings) and enable a mobile-optimized view of your site—both of which are highly recommended. Two important things to note: *once your site is published, you cannot unpublish it* (though you can hide pages and hide the site from search engines) and the public will not see any updates you make until you publish your site again (saving it does not update the public view).

SESSION 6

Create Links

Hyperlinks[5] are a convenient way to connect to specific areas of your site or to outside resources. Two of the most common types of links are hypertext— a bit of text that acts as a download button or link—and hyperlinked images, both of which are easily done in Wix. Links can connect to internal pages, external URLs, documents, or email addresses. Wix has preset styles for linked text, generally in the form of underlining, so when you link text, it will stand out a bit from the rest of the text. You can always make the text stand out more using bolded text, colors, or any combination of styles, but you will have to do this to individual links, as Wix does not allow you to edit the over- all default link style. As you create links, remember that your linked items are read by search engines, so choose your links wisely. For example, instead of the sentence "Click here to visit our educational programs page," where the underlined text is the link, use this: "Learn more about our educational programs." Search engines will rate the second sentence higher (more useful).

Both image and text links are created using a simple procedure in Wix. To create an image link, click on the image you want to turn into a link, then click Link To in the small menu that appears. Your link options will then appear. To create a link with text—called hypertext—double click on the Text Element that has the text you want to link. Highlight the word or words that will be linked. In the text editing menu that pops up, click the link icon on the bottom right. Your link options then appear, and you can select:

- Web Address, an outside resource (e.g., Visit the <u>Rocky Mountain Historic Coalition</u> website.)
- Page, an internal page on your website (e.g., If you are interested in booking a field trip, look at our educational programs for <u>middle school students</u>.)
- Email, a new, blank email to a designated person (e.g., Contact our <u>Visitor Services Coordinator</u> for more details.)
- Document, a PDF or other file to download (e.g., Think you're a good fit for us? Fill out our <u>Summer Camp Teacher application</u> today!)
- Page Top, the top of the page (e.g., <u>Return to the top</u> of the page.)
- Page Bottom, the bottom of the page (e.g., <u>Jump to the bottom</u> of the page.)
- Anchor, an specified location elsewhere on the site, generally not at the top of the page (e.g., Learn about our <u>elementary</u>, <u>middle</u>, and <u>high</u> school programs. *[Here, each underlined word links to a different location on the same Education Page.]*)

For Web Address or Email, enter the target URL or email address. For Page, select the page on your site you want to link to. To link to a document, you will need to upload a document to the Document Gallery, then select the document as you would an image from the Image Gallery. Top and bottom links must be added on the page you are currently on.

Slightly more involved is the anchor element. Creating an anchor involves two steps: first, creating an anchor at the location you want your visitor to jump to (called the reference point) and second, creating the anchor around the text that visitors will click on to get there (called the reference). To start, navigate to the location where you want your anchor to lead to—the location of your reference point. Click on the Add button in the Edit menu, then on Buttons & Menus, and finally on Anchor. A thin blue line with a tab and the anchor name will appear, and you can drag the tab up or down to place the anchor exactly as far down on the page as you need it. After double-clicking on the tab and renaming the anchor, return to the page where your reference will be. Highlight the reference text and navigate to the link menu again. Select Anchor, then use the drop-down menus to select the page of the reference point and the name of the anchor.

Add Google Calendar

In order to add a Google Calendar to your website, you will need a Google account. If you already have one, simply make sure you are signed in and navigate to google.com/calendar. If you do not already have an account, sign up for one at accounts.google.com, then visit google.com/calendar. If you have a list of events to add, go ahead and add them to the calendar now, or add a sample event to get started. There are three ways to add an event:

- Click the Create button in the upper left-hand corner and edit the event date, time, and other details from there.
- Navigate to the day and time of the event, click directly on the calendar and drag the box that appears to the correct date and time, then click on the box to edit the details.
- Click anywhere on the calendar itself at any time and adjust the event date, time, and other details from there.

As you add events, you will have the option to create color-coded "sub-calendars." For example, you might have an overall institutional calendar, and within that have subcalendars for Education, Development, and Exhibitions events.

Once you have events on your calendar and are ready to embed it, you will need to make your calendar public so that visitors can see the events. If you have internal events or an internal subcalendar that you do not want shared publicly, you can still add them to the calendar but hide them by editing individual events or deselecting the calendar in the next step. To make a calendar visible, click on the arrow next to its name when you hover over it in the calendar list. Click on Share this Calendar and tick the box next to "Make this calendar public." Do this for each calendar you want to make public. Then, click on the arrow next to "My calendars" and select Settings. Click on the name of one of the calendars you want to share in the list that appears. In the Embed This Calendar section, click on "Customize the color, size, and other options." The main section of the page shows you how the calendar will display. If you are happy with it, copy the HTML code at the top of the page. If you want to include additional calendars or change the look, use the menu of options on the left side of the page to modify your calendar until you are satisfied with it, including adding a Calendar Title. Once you are ready to embed it, click Update HTML at the top of the page and copy the newly generated HTML code.

There are then two ways to add your calendar to Wix. The first is a built-in Google Calendar app, which you can easily add to your site through the App Market. From there, you will need to link your Google Calendar account. Wix will request permission to view and manage your calendars, and you must click Accept to add the calendar. Wix will not change the calendar on your behalf, just use the information you have on your calendar to create a Wix-integrated version of your calendar. Note that if you use this app, you can only display one of your calendars. To include multiple calendars (i.e., sub-calendars), you will need to embed the calendar using the steps mentioned below.

The second method for adding a Google Calendar is to embed the calendar. From your Google Calendar, click on the arrow next to "My calendars" and select Settings. Click on the name of one of the calendars you want to share in the list that appears. Once you are happy with the display, copy the HTML code at the top of the page. Once you are ready to embed it, click Update HTML at the top of the page and copy the newly generated HTML code. Return to Wix. Add an HTML Element to the appropriate location for your calendar. Double-click on it to edit the code and paste in your Google Calendar code. Verify that it displays the way you expect it to, then publish your changes. After adding your calendar to your website, any changes you make on the calendar (e.g., adding, deleting, or editing events) will be automatically reflected in the calendar on your site.

Embed Document

You can add a PDF or other type of document to your website in three different ways. The first is creating a download link to the document using the instructions above. You will need to upload the document to your Document Gallery and then link it to an image or text. The second way to add a document is to add a prebuilt document icon that users click on to download the file. To do this, click on the Add button in the Edit Menu, then click Media and select a Document Element. You will be prompted to select a document in your Document Gallery or add one if the gallery is currently empty. Add a document as you would an image, making sure to give it a clear and identifying title.

The final way to add a document is to embed it on the page so that visitors can view it directly on the site. Generally, you can only use this method to embed PDF documents or images, as word processing documents or spreadsheets require the visitor to have specific plugins that are not commonly installed on browsers. You can convert these other types of documents into PDFs using CutePDF or your word processing application. To embed a document using this third method, you will need to first upload the document to your Wix Document Gallery, then add its location to a bit of HTML code. There are a number of steps involved, but it can all be done within the Wix platform. To start, add a Document Element, as you would using the second method (prebuilt icon) mentioned above. Click on the Preview button at the top of the editor. Right-click on the document icon you just added, and select Copy Link Address (*not* the image URL). This will give you the URL of the actual document as it is hosted on Wix. Return to the Editor. Add an HTML Element by clicking on the Add button in the Edit menu, then on Apps, then the HTML Element. Double-click on the HTML Element. Using the drop-down menu that appears, select HTML code. In the next box, insert the following code exactly as you see it, *replacing the underlined URL with the one you copied*:

   <embed src="http://media.wix.com/ugd/65d_caa18b4.pdf" width="100%" height="100%">

To make sure you have the correct URL, check that your URL ends in .pdf (or whatever file type you intend to embed). Click the Update button. Your document should then appear in the HTML Element, which you can resize to fit your page or the document. Delete the temporary Document Element. Visitors will be able to scroll *within* the HTML Element to see the document even if the document is too wide or long to fit on the page (though you can reduce the document size in the width and height percentages mentioned above).

Embed Video

Wix does not host videos on its platform, so you will need to first find on or upload to YouTube or Vimeo any videos you want to embed. Wix supports both YouTube and Vimeo videos directly, and you can embed videos from another service using an HTML Element. To get started adding a supported video, click on Add in the Edit menu. Then select Media and click on Video. Double-click on the placeholder video to bring up the video settings. Next, visit the published page for the video, and copy the URL. Back in the Wix editor, paste the URL into the video URL field, replacing the placeholder text. You can then use the settings to adjust whether the control bar appears and what its options are. If you want the control bar to be lighter, for example, tick the box next to "Light Control Bar." You can also change the video's visual style by clicking Change Style and then Edit Style or Personalize this Video.

To embed a video hosted elsewhere, you will need to find the embed code. The location of this code depends on the video platform, but it can generally be found under sharing settings. Copy the code and then return to the Wix editor. Click Add, then Apps, then the HTML Element. Double-click on the new HTML Element and use the drop-down menu to select HTML Code. Paste the embed code in the field below and click Update. Your video should then appear in the HTML Element, and you can move and adjust the Element to fit the video.

Embed Map

Wix allows you to quickly embed Google Maps to show your location. To start, click on Add in the Edit Menu. Select Apps, then Google Maps. Double-click on the Google Maps Element that appears. In the first field of the settings menu that opens, type in the address you want the map to pin-point. Retitle the pinpoint in the next field, then select what navigation tools you want visitors to have. At the very least, you should allow visitors to zoom in and out. If you want to construct a map using another service, like Map-Quest, you will need to build it according to that service's instructions. Then, you can copy the embed code and paste it into an HTML Element using the process discussed above in this session.

SESSION 7

Add Blog

Using a blog on your Wix site is an excellent way to keep your website active and engaging. Wix comes with a built-in blog feature, which means you can seamlessly integrate blog entries into your site. You can backdate entries, allow visitor comments and replies, and tag categories, just like in traditional blogs. Blog entries are built on a blog page, so you will first need to add a new page. Click on the Pages button in the Edit Menu and then click Add → Page. Select Blog 1 as your Page Layout and name the blog (of course, the name Blog is perfectly fine). Click OK and look over your new blog page and placeholder content. On the right-hand side, you will see a featured post in the Ticker, as well as your recent posts, an archive of blog entry dates, a list of tag categories, and some social icons for visitors to follow to your Facebook and other social site pages. The Ticker will rotate through your featured posts, and you can adjust its settings by double-clicking on it. Similarly, double-click on the Recent Posts, Archive, and Tag Cloud sections to edit their few settings. Double-click on the placeholder blog entry to bring up your blog settings. The settings in the menu that pops up will apply to all current and future blog entries. Select the layout, padding around the text in a post, spacing between posts, the length of a post's preview text, the date format, image or video size, the "read more" button settings, and the previous and next page button parameters. As you adjust these settings, you can see their changes reflected in the placeholder post.

Once you are ready to add your own posts, scroll back to the top of the settings menu and click on Add & Edit Blog Posts. This opens up your Blog Manager, where you can see a list of your posts (there should be two place-holder posts already there). Unless you plan to put up two posts right away, delete the second post by hovering over it and clicking on the red garbage can. Click on the pencil of the first post to edit it.

Editing your post is relatively straightforward and similar to editing content elsewhere on Wix. Click on any placeholder content to edit it, including

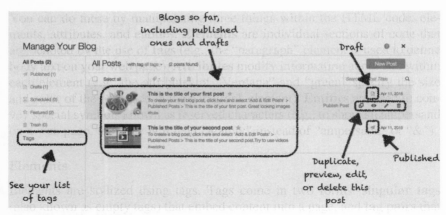

Figure 4.14   The Wix blog manager

the date to select a new posting date. You do not need to add Text Elements in, as the whole editing field accepts text, but to add an image or video, click the appropriate option at the top of the editing window. You can edit or switch out images by clicking on them to reveal alt text, layout, and link options. You can delete unnecessary Elements by clicking on them and then pressing your keyboard's delete key. Any image can be moved or resized by hovering over it and dragging it up or down and dragging the arrow in the bottom right-hand corner.

After you are finished editing your post, you can save it as a draft for future publication, preview what it will look like to visitors, schedule the post for a specific publication date and time (it will self-publish), mark it as a featured post (to appear on your blog main page), and add tag categories. The last is especially helpful for visitors who want to search through your posts by subject.

In your Blog Manager, you can see a list of published, drafted, scheduled, featured, and trashed posts. Once you have a greater number of posts, you can search through them using the search bar in the top right corner. At any time, you can also look at your tag list by clicking on Tags in the left-side menu. You will see a list of tags, as well as what posts they have been assigned to. Tags are important in garnering SEO points, so do not neglect these.

Add or Edit Social Media Buttons

Most Wix templates come with social buttons already in place (e.g., quick links to a Facebook page or Twitter account at the top of the page). If you like the options and placement, all you have to do is link the buttons to your accounts on their respective platforms. Remember that if there is an orange box around the row of buttons, they appear on every page. Locate and double-click on the buttons, generally near the top or bottom of your site in the header or footer.

Once you have the social links menu pulled up, you can change the button style or switch the button out for a different social media site by clicking the Change button over the image in the right side of the panel. This brings up the Social Media Icon Gallery, where you can browse by social media site to see the different styles available. Once you have selected the icon you want, click on Choose Icon. Next, in a separate window or tab, navigate to your social media profile and copy the URL *of your institution's profile* (not the newsfeed or admin URL). Return to the Wix editor and paste the profile URL into the Link To field underneath the appropriate icon. Go through and add any additional social media links by changing existing ones or clicking Add Social Icon. You can delete unnecessary social icons by hovering over them in this menu and clicking on the garbage can. In general, try to pick the same style for all your social media buttons (e.g., if you choose the square, colorful style for Facebook, do not choose the round, all black style for Twitter and the borderless, grayscale style for Flickr).

You may want to add additional social media buttons to specific pages of your site, especially on blog posts. This helps visitors quickly share

Figure 4.15   Social media buttons

interesting content they find on your site. To add, for instance, a quick Facebook Like link to boost your "likes" on Facebook, navigate to your home page (or whichever page you want the button to be on). Click on the Add button in the Edit Menu, then on Social. Click on Facebook Like, and double-click on the new Like button to edit its style. Under the Social Media menu, you can also add the following social media buttons:

- Facebook Like (to like your Facebook page)
- Facebook Page Like (to show a ticker with your Facebook page information, including your recent Facebook posts and the visitor's friends who also like the page)
- Facebook Share (to share your website or a specific page on Facebook)
- Facebook Comments (to show comments about a specific page on your website)
- Twitter Follow (to follow your account on Twitter)
- Twitter Tweet (to share a link to your website on a Twitter feed)
- Google+1 (to share your website with a Google+ circle)
- Social Bar (a grouping of social media icons and links discussed above)
- VK Share (to share a specific page of your website on VK, a Russian social networking site)
- Pinterest Pin Share (to embed a Pin and promote your Pinterest board)
- Pinterest Pin It (to pin one of your images on a Pinterest board)
- Pinterest Follow (to follow your Pinterest account)
- YouTube Subscribe (to subscribe to your YouTube channel)
- Spotify Follow (to follow a specific artist account on the music platform Spotify)

After being added, most of these buttons will then need to be edited and linked to your account for that social media platform.

SESSION 8

Adjust General Settings

Before you post your site for the public, take time to review your general settings. From your editor, click on the Settings button in the Edit menu. The Site Address, Favicon, and Statistics settings are only available if you upgrade, a process discussed more in Session 10. Below, learn how to work around some of this by adding Google Analytics. Additionally, you can edit both the social settings and the SEO settings. The Social Settings tab allows you to upload an image for your website that will appear on a visitor's page when he or she likes or shares your website on Facebook. If you added any Facebook buttons in the previous session, add your Facebook page username (to find this, log into Facebook, click on Profile in the top right corner, then copy the text or ID number in the URL bar that follows "www.facebook.com").

Edit SEO Settings

Review Chapter 2 for SEO best practices before editing your SEO settings. There are two areas where Wix provides easy SEO setting access: general site SEO data and individual page SEO data. The SEO bar in the Settings menu holds the data for your entire website. Make sure that the slider next to "Allow search engines to find my site" is green, otherwise all of your SEO work will be for naught. Insert your site title (limited to 70 characters), site description (160 characters), and keywords (250 characters). Under Advanced SEO Settings, you can insert Meta Tags. Once you have added your SEO content, click Done. To edit individual page SEO data, click on the Pages button in the Edit Menu. Click on the settings gear next to each page in turn and do the following:

1. Click on SEO Page Settings
2. Add the page title (up to 70 characters)
3. Add the page description (up to 160 characters)
4. Add keywords (up to 250 characters)
5. Click Done

Run AddFreeStats

If you do not plan to upgrade your site and get built-in statistics reports, or you want additional visitor tracking information, you can use the free service AddFreeStats.[6] This service traces where your visitors come from, what pages they visit, what their demographics are, and more. To begin, visit addfreestats.com. Follow the site's instructions to set up your account and add your Wix URL. Then, under the Account menu in the upper right-hand corner, click on AFS Code. Copy the code that AddFreeStats generates for you and return to your Wix editor. Click on the Add button in the Edit Menu, then on Apps. Select the HTML Element, and drag it into the header. Reduce the size so it fits comfortably between your header content. Double-click on the HTML Element and switch the mode to HTML code. Paste the AddFreeStats code into the box and click Update. A small AddFreeStats logo will appear in the element. You can resize the HTML Element to hide the logo, but do not forget where you placed the Element in case you need to revisit or delete it later. Once you publish your site and start getting visitors, you can log into your AddFreeStats account and view visitor-tracking data.

SESSION 9

Create Online Store

An online store on your site is a convenient way to give your visitors access to buying memberships, making program reservations, or purchasing products from your gift store. Though an integrated store is only available with a Wix upgrade, you can add PayPal buttons to your site as an alternative. Remember, if you do not already have an account, be sure that you select "Option B: Create payment buttons using HTML" when signing up for an account and are asked how you want to use PayPal to accept money. Use the sections mentioned below as examples to learn how to accept donations and add both individual items (a Buy Now button) and sell multiple items at once (an Add to Cart button). You can then embed the PayPal buttons on your site (discussed below) or add a PayPal button directly from the Buttons & Menus section of the Edit menu.

Accept Donations Online

For those users who have nonprofit status, PayPal offers buttons to collect donations right on your website. *This option is not available for personal or business accounts that do not have their 501(c)(3) status verified, so make sure that you indicate your nonprofit status when you sign up for your account.*[7] To begin, you will need to set up a page to place your donation button(s) on. Navigate to or create the appropriate page, including any text and images you want. Then, click on Add in the Edit menu. Click on Apps, and then the HTML Element.

Next, log into your PayPal account and navigate to the button editing section (Tools → PayPal Buttons). On the right side of the My Saved Buttons home page, click Create New Button. Use the drop-down menu to select Donations. Add the name of your organization, then click the arrow next to Customize Text or Appearance. You can use the default PayPal button or upload your own image, though the second requires that you upload the image elsewhere on the web (on your site, for instance) and copy and paste the image URL into PayPal. If you use the PayPal image, you can change the size of the button and decide whether the accepted credit card logos are displayed. The sample button to the right will reflect the changes you make. Under Contribution Amount, you can allow visitors to select their own donation amount or you can set a fixed donation amount. You may want to look at the settings available in Step 3, namely the option to collect the customer's shipping address and the option to reroute URL after a payment has gone through. The first section determines whether your customer can write you a note (such as whom the donation was made in honor of). The next section allows you to collect your customer's address (in case you need to send them a thank you or other promotional materials). The third section allows you to input a URL to take customers to after they have either canceled a checkout or completed a successful checkout (e.g., a thank you page or a form to fill out in case you need to collect more information).

Once you have these settings adjusted to your satisfaction, click Create Button. On the next page, you will see a field with HTML code. Copy this code and return to your Wix editor. In the HTML Element, change the mode to HTML Code and paste the copied code into the field below. Click Update and make sure your button appeared and looks the way you expect it to. Remember to resize the HTML Element to fit the button. You may want to Preview your site to make sure the button acts correctly.

Sell Memberships Online

PayPal offers good terms for those wishing to sell memberships or other items on their websites. The rate fee for nonprofits is 2.9 percent + $0.30 per transaction. Selling memberships or goods online follows the same process but uses a different button. Navigate to your membership (or other appropriate) page and add in the pertinent information for the item you are selling. There are two main types of buttons you can use for this service (Add to Cart or Buy Now) and you can make a button for each individual item or group similar items together. For example, you might be selling an item with multiple options (e.g., senior membership for $15, individual membership for $20, and family membership for $40) and you expect visitors to be purchasing just one item at a time. To set up a button like this, navigate to the My Saved Buttons home page and click Create New Button. Use the drop-down menu to select Buy Now. Add "Membership" as the item name. *Leave this price field blank* so you can add multiple options and prices in the next area. Under Customize Button, tick the box next to "Add drop-down menu with price/option." In the drop-down menu name field, type "Membership Type" and then add your first three membership types and their prices:

- Senior/Student $15
- Individual $20
- Family $40

Click Add Another Option and add your fourth membership type:

• Corporate $75

Tick the box next to "Add Text Field" and type "Primary Membership Name" in the field. Click Done and then expand the Customize Text or Appearance section. Change the button text to "Pay Now." Expand Step 3 and uncheck the special instructions message option. Verify that your visitor's shipping address will be collected, then tick the box that says "Take customers to this URL when they finish checkout."

Briefly return to your Wix editor and add a new page. Title it Membership Information Form and add a form on the page (see Session 4) that collects new member contact information and any other data you need. Save and publish your site, navigate to the page you just created, and copy the URL. Return to the PayPal window and paste the URL into the field you previously selected. Click Create Button and copy the HTML code you see on the next page. Return to the editor and hide the membership form page from your site menu (see Session 5). Navigate next to the membership purchasing page and add an HTML Element (Add → Apps → HTML) to the page. Double-click on the new Element and change the mode to HTML Code. Paste the copied PayPal code into the field and click Update.

You can follow much the same process for adding items with only one type. To sell a set of ten postcards for $5.00 with $1.50 shipping, add a new page and fill it with an image and description of the item you are selling. Underneath that, add an HTML Element. On the My Saved Button home page in your PayPal account, click Create New Button. Select Shopping Cart from the drop-down menu. Name the item and note the price of $5.00. Expand the Customize Text or Appearance section and tick the box next to "Use Smaller Button." Specify the shipping cost and the tax rate for your area. Expand Step 3 and click the No button next to the special instructions option. Click Create Button, copy the HTML code from the next page, and return to your Wix editor. Double-click on the HTML Element, change the mode to HTML Code, and paste the copied PayPal code into the field. Click Update and verify that your button appeared. Repeat the process for any other items.

Finally, *you will need to set up a View Cart Button*. Return to the same page where you got the HTML code for the button, which you can find again from your My Saved Buttons home page by clicking the Action drop-down menu and selecting View Code. Below the code section, click on the option to create a View Cart button. You can then use your own image or make the PayPal button smaller. Once you are satisfied with the button, click Create Button. Copy the new HTML code on the next page and return to your Wix editor. Add another HTML Element to the page and drag it to the location you want for the checkout button. Double-click on the HTML Element, select HTML Code from the drop-down menu, and paste the new code into the field. Click Update and verify that your new button has appeared.

SESSION 10

Check and Modify Mobile Site

Allowing smartphone-wielding visitors to view the site with a layout specifically made for mobile devices is absolutely necessary. The option to switch back to the full (or desktop) view if desired is important, but Wix unfortunately does not offer this feature. Some visitors will prefer the mobile version of a website because it generally comes with a simplified layout and faster loading times. Others will find that certain Elements do not load correctly in the mobile view and will therefore need to toggle to the full-site version to see desired content. Once you have created your main website, you need to check your mobile version for any formatting gone astray or other issues. If you are worried that your site is unsatisfactory in mobile view, you can disable the mobile view for all users by selecting the Pre-Optimized View (found under the Settings icon → Mobile View).

As you adjust your mobile site, keep in mind that *content changes* will be reflected on both sites, but *rearrangement or resizing* in either site will not affect the other. Be aware that you can only add Elements to your site

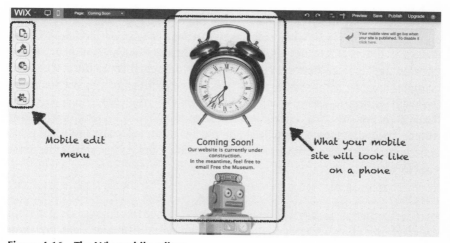

Figure 4.16   The Wix mobile editor

from the *desktop* view. To view the mobile version of your site, click the cell phone icon in the upper left-hand corner of your editor. Your mobile editor will appear (Figure 4.16).

The first step is to go through your site page-by-page and check the layout and look of your content, adjusting and moving Elements as necessary. You can hide any Element from your mobile site (it will not change on your desktop site) by clicking on the Element and then the crossed-out eye in the bottom right corner of the small element window that pops up. Under the Mobile Design button in the Edit Menu, you can change the location of the mobile menu and select a mobile background.

There are two Elements unique to the mobile site. The first is a Mobile Action Bar Element, which gives visitors a quick and easy way to access some of the most commonly sought-after content, such as your phone number, address, and social profile. To add this, click on Add in the Edit Menu, then on Mobile Action Bar. Move the slider at the top to green and tick off the content you want available in the action bar. Select the dark or light color scheme you want, and then click done. The other mobile Element you can add is a Back to Top Button Element. If added, this will appear on every page. This button is a great idea on mobile sites, which tend to be much longer than their desktop counterparts, owing to their narrower screens. Finally, to check whether your pages pass the Google Mobile-Friendly Test, copy each page URL and paste it into the field found at google.com/webmasters/tools/mobile-friendly.

Upgrade Site

You may wish to upgrade your site to take advantage of a number of features unavailable with the free version. You might want to connect a domain, eliminate Wix ads, add more data space to your account, or add features like Google AdSense, an integrated online store, and Google Analytics. If so, click on the Upgrade button in the upper right corner of your editor. This will bring up a list of additional features you can get with each upgrade package. Wix will guide you through the upgrade process. If you want to add your own domain to the site after upgrading, click on the Settings button in the Edit Menu. The site address bar will show you what your current site address is, and you can add your own domain if you purchase the basic Connect Domain upgrade.

∞

As you build your site, feel free to experiment with different Elements. You can save your site over and over again, only publishing for the public after you are satisfied with the changes. Take time to browse through the Apps you can add to your site, especially if you need to add special features like scheduling services or a member login. To view the Wix help pages, visit wix.com/support/html5. Find updated Wix information at freethemuseum.net/wix.

NOTES

1. Note that the option to sign in using Google is using *Google+* (known as "Google Plus"), not a Gmail account. Though your Google+ and Gmail are through the same service and therefore linked, choosing this will create a Google+ profile for you, which you may not want.

2. This can help ensure that no other website will have a site quite like yours, but keep in mind that no two websites will be exactly alike anyway, and your purchase of a template does not forbid other websites from creating a similar look.

3. In Wix, all free packages are assigned a URL based on your account name. This means that every user could have a site named "Test Site" and the URLs would be, for example, http://ransick.wix.com/testsite, http://missoulatapestrymuseum.wix.com/testsite, etc. Keep this URL convention in mind if you choose to use the free package, as it can be cumbersome.

4. Review the image size and copyright info mentioned in Chapter 2.

5. Though there is an occasional and subtle difference between a link and hyperlink (along the lines of "a square is always a rectangle but a rectangle is not always a square") the terms are mostly interchangeable and are used as such in this book.

6. Wix blocks Google Analytics for their subdomains that free account users have.

7. PayPal's terms note that the donation button is strictly "intended for fundraising. If you are not raising money for a cause, please choose another option. Nonprofits must verify their status to withdraw donations they receive. Users that are not verified nonprofits must demonstrate how their donations will be used, once they raise more than $10,000 USD."

Chapter 5

Getting Your Website
Started on WordPress

The first thing to know about WordPress is that there are two forms of WordPress. One is WordPress.com, an online WYSIWYG editor; the other is WordPress, an open-source coding software that users must self-host. This chapter deals with the former, and all references are to the WYSIWYG editor and blogging platform found at wordpress.com. Early on, WordPress was a successful blogging site, and it has since expanded into web publishing for general websites as well. WordPress is a trusted website tool and it steadily adds new features and plugins. Professional designers from around the world write themes for WordPress, and anyone is allowed to use and customize the themes marked as "free" or purchase one of the premium themes. Depending on the theme you choose, widgets (extra tools or content that you can add to your website) allow you to add calendars, images, metadata, upcoming events, and more. Different themes come with different widgets and your options for adding widgets will vary with the amount of sidebar space your theme has. Most themes accommodate popular widgets like images and recent blog posts. The disadvantage to this setup is that you may want to use a widget that is not available in your theme, at which point you have to forego the widget, find a workaround, or change your theme. Overall, WordPress is a good place to start if you like one of the themes and are prepared to use it without too much adaptation and customization. The platform is also ideal for those whose blogs are major components of their website.

This chapter should give you a good push toward setting up a website, but given the variety of themes and their different widgets and capabilities, some of WordPress's features are beyond the scope of this book. By following along in each of the ten sessions, you will soon have a basic grasp of WordPress and its overall capabilities. If you plan to use WordPress as your platform, take a careful look at the themes to make sure that their features and widgets will allow you the flexibility you need for your website. One major bonus of WordPress is that you can easily incorporate HTML into your pages if you feel comfortable with coding—there is convenient toggle between visual and code editing views. WordPress has an extensive help section, but you may quickly come across terms and topics that are quite irrelevant to your site. This is because many of these pages do not specify which form of WordPress they refer to. When looking online for help with WordPress, be wary of the fact that many WordPress help blogs and forums deal with the *downloadable software* rather than the *online platform* covered in this book. For help specifically with the online wordpress.com blogging platform, look first to en.support.wordpress.com.

There are ten website-building sessions in this chapter. Each session goes over different elements of creating a website on WordPress, and you can work through them in sequential order or, once you have the basics set up, jump to relevant topics and skip over irrelevant ones. Some sessions will be quick, taking ten or fifteen minutes. Others may take a few hours, depending on your speed and comfort level with the material. Do not feel rushed to move on to another session if you still want to experiment more with the material in an earlier session. The sessions will cover the following:

- Session 1
  - Create an account
  - Select or create a domain
  - Choose a theme
- Session 2
  - Customize colors, backgrounds, header, footer, and other theme aspects, including linking to social media platforms
  - Add widgets
  - Adjust general settings
- Session 3
  - Add a page
  - Edit or add text
  - Edit or add an image or gallery
  - Delete or move an element
  - Publish your site
- Session 4
  - Add a contact (or other) form
  - Add a poll
  - Add a divider
- Session 5
  - Use HTML to embed a map, video, calendar, document, or download-able file
  - Create links

- Session 6
  - Add a blog
- Session 7
  - Create a menu
  - Edit SEO
- Session 8
  - Create an online store
  - Sell memberships and accept donations online
- Session 9
  - Check and adjust your mobile site
- Session 10
  - Check site statistics
  - Add WordAds
  - Upgrade your plan

All sessions except for Session 1 begin on the account home page.

SESSION 1

Create Account, Select or Create Domain

To begin, you will need to log in or sign up for a WordPress account and add a new site. Navigate to wordpress.com (*not* wordpress.org). Click on the Log In button, then on Register. Do not click on the Create Website button just yet, as you will have to do this step twice if you create a site before you have an account. Enter your new account information, including the website URL you want (referred to as the blog address and, if using a free account, set up as a subdomain of WordPress, such as missoulatapestrymuseum.wordpress. com). If you already own a domain that you intend to use, pick a temporary domain to get started (you will be given the opportunity to purchase a new domain later in the site registration process). Otherwise, use a subdomain of WordPress. Once you have entered a domain that is accepted—that is, not reserved or already in use—you will be prompted to verify your email to finalize your account setup.

After logging in, you will see your account home page. For now, the page is mostly blank, but in future, you will see a list of your sites on this page. Click on the Create Site button to get started. You may need to reenter the subdomain you chose when signing up for your account. In the next step, you will be presented with a few dozen free themes to choose from. You can, and likely will, change themes later, but for now, pick one that you find appealing. Last, select the WordPress plan you want to use. You will then be returned to your account home page. Click on Customize Your Site to get started. This opens up your Customizer, which you will use for future sessions. For now, return to your account home page by clicking the X in the upper left-hand corner.

Choose Theme

After you have set up your account and created your subdomain, you may want to revisit the theme of your site. You can browse through the available themes and pick one that fits your organization, is flexible enough for your needs, and is within your price range—and never fear, there are dozens of free templates on WordPress. From your account home page (which is now your site home page; look at the address bar that now reads https://wordpress.com/posts/yourdomain.wordpress.com), click on Themes under the Look and Feel section on the left. This opens up the full WordPress theme gallery. As you browse, you can click "Demo" below each theme to see how the theme will display in your browser. You can also click on the picture of a theme to see a list of its features, like flexible headers and custom backgrounds, colors, menus, and fonts. Clicking "More" in the browse menu brings up search options so you can search by layout, features, colors, theme name, and price. Some of the most flexible free themes include Typo, Penscratch, Twenty Fourteen, and Writr.[1] *One important feature to look for in your chosen theme is responsiveness*, meaning that it has a preset method for transitioning your site between desktop and mobile versions. If you choose a responsive theme, this can save you a lot of time later as you review your mobile site in Session 9. Refer to the section on layout and design in Chapter 2 as you browse through the themes. Once you have found a theme you like, click Activate, then Customize Your Site.

SESSION 2

When you log into your WordPress account, you will be taken first to your Reader feed, where any blogs you follow will appear. For this and the remainder of the sessions in this chapter, start from your account home page, which can be accessed from this screen by clicking on My Site in the upper left corner.

Customize Theme

Including Header, Footer, and Widgets

To customize the colors, header, and other aesthetic aspects of your theme, you will need to return to the Customizer. From your account home page, click on Customize in the left-hand menu under Look and Feel.

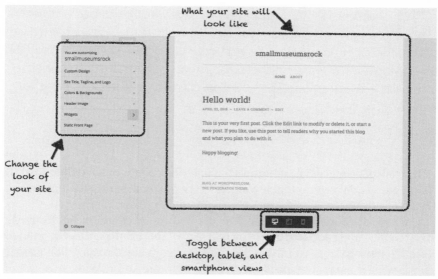

Figure 5.1   The WordPress Customizer

The Custom Design section, which allows you to change the fonts, apply a custom color scheme, and edit the CSS, is only available with a paid upgrade. The Site Title & Tagline are where your website name and institutional motto or tagline go, and they will appear in the header (or other theme-determined location) on every page of your site. Colors & Backgrounds play a major part in the customization of your site. For the background, you can upload an image, choose a preset color, or pick your own color. The first color swatch (possibly white) in this section is the background. Hover over it and click on Change. To upload your own background image,[2] click on Select Image and upload your image. Note that JPEGs, PNGs, and GIFs are the only image-file types accepted. When you upload an image, you can edit its title, caption, alt text, and description (all of which are important for SEO, as discussed in Chapter 2). Once you have edited this information, click Select. When you return to the Customizer, click on Options underneath the background image you just uploaded. From here, you can change the alignment, repetition, position, and underlying color of the image. When you are finished, click Done. To choose a color palette, click on one of the Featured Palettes your theme offers. The header can be adjusted in two ways: by changing the site title and tagline, as above, or by uploading a header image, such as a photograph, logo, or text saved as an image. In the Header Image section, your theme will tell you what the optimal header image size is (e.g., 1260 × 240 pixels) though you can always crop the image after uploading it.

ordPress Tip #1: Some themes have default sidebar widgets. If you add new widgets, the default widgets may disappear, so be prepared to either accept and edit only the default widgets or add all the widgets you want before editing them. There are a few themes that allow deactivation of the sidebar, eliminating this issue, along with any sidebar widgets.

Figure 5.2

Instead of using drag-and-drop elements like many other online WYSI-WYG editors, WordPress uses widgets in its sidebars and footer areas. Each theme has different widgets and different widget areas.

Click on the Widgets section to see your widget area options. For example, your theme might have options for widgets in the Primary Sidebar (on the left), Content Sidebar (on the right), and Footer Widget Area. Click on one of the widget areas to expand its options, then on Add a Widget. A list of available widgets will appear, and you can search by name or browse through them by scrolling. Each widget gives a short description of its function. Click on any widget to add it. The widget's options will appear, and you can adjust each widget and its visibility in that section. The visibility uses an "if → then" formula to determine whether the widget will show up on a given page (e.g., If the page is the front page, then show the widget; if the page is the posts page, then hide the widget). You can generally add multiple widgets in a section and then rearrange them by dragging their bars up and down the list. To move a widget from one sidebar location to another, drag the widget to the new section. If you are interested in adding social media buttons to your site, this is where you will do it. Most WordPress sites have widgets available for Twitter and Facebook likes and pages. Once you are finished adding widgets (you can always come back later to add and adjust more), click Save & Publish.

The Static Front Page section is where to choose what your home page looks like. If you are building a traditional website, make sure that the "A static page" option is selected. You will then have to choose which page is your home page and which one is your posts page (your blog). You may need to revisit this setting after you have added more pages in Session 3. If you choose to keep the home page as your latest posts, the Featured Content section will help you adjust the display of your blog content.

Adjust General Settings

Back in the account home page, click on Settings under the Configuration section. This brings up your general settings, where you can adjust a number of website components. This section of settings is the "fast lane" group— where you can quickly change some of the most important settings. If you need to adjust more detailed areas, there is a second set of settings discussed below. In this current section, you will again see the site title and tagline. The site visibility determines how your site interacts with search engines, and in general, you want your site to be as easy to find as possible. If you have social media presence, such as a Facebook page, also click on Sharing in the Configuration section. By connecting your organization's social media accounts to your WordPress site, your account will automatically publish your new posts to these sites to help alert your followers to your new content.

The second set of website settings to check are found in your site dashboard, which can be found by clicking on WP Admin in the left-hand menu of your account home page. Your site dashboard is only visible to you as the admin, and it is where you will control and edit all your site-specific information, rather than account information that can affect multiple sites under the same account. Before delving into the rest of the site dashboard, scroll down to the Settings section of the editing panel. Start with the general settings, where you will again see your site title and tagline options in addition to date and time formats, calendar settings, website language settings, and a blog picture that visitors will see if they browse for blogs or websites through WordPress.com rather than navigating directly to a URL.

ordPress Tip #2: Once you have opened a section of the editing panel, all of the categories in that section (which you saw as a submenu when scrolling over the panel) will appear below the section title.

Figure 5.3

The rest of the website settings sections cover the following:

- Writing: The way the text of your blog posts is displayed
- Reading: How many and what kinds of posts your visitors see when arriving at your blog, as well as how comments and "followers" can interact with your blog content
- Discussion: Additional commenting and interaction settings for blog posts; note especially the Akismet antispam strictness setting, which helps prevent spam comments on your website
- Media: Default image dimensions, as well as how images and videos are displayed

- Sharing: Which social media platforms your site is automatically publicized to and what shortcuts visitors can use to share the content they find on your site
- Polls: Linked with a Polldaddy account to control how polls are formatted and reported
- Ratings: If users rate your blog content, you can choose to show the ratings on your site
- AdControl: The option to purchase an ad-free upgrade
- Email Post Changes: To notify admins or other relevant persons when the website is published or changed
- OpenID: A service (only relevant if you have a login on your site) to allow admins and visitors to sign in once and have access to their other accounts that also use OpenID
- Webhooks: Used mostly by advanced developers to establish advanced notification settings when a particular action is carried out on the site (e.g., receive a text message when someone comments on a blog post)

SESSION 3

Add Pages, Text, and Images

To begin, navigate to your site dashboard by clicking on WP Admin in the left-hand menu. Click on Pages in the editing panel. You should currently have one page—the About page. In this menu, you can rearrange your pages, look at visitation and comment statistics, and add or delete pages. To edit, view, or delete any of the pages, hover over the page title in the list and click on the appropriate option. Quick Edit gives you access to the page title, slug (the end portion of the page URL), date, viewing permissions, parent page, page order, template, and publish status. View will show you what the page looks like to the public. To add a new page, click Add New at the top of the page. You will then see the page editor (Figure 5.4).

The title of your page will automatically generate a slug for the page (e.g., if your page is Calendar of Events, the slug will likely be www.missoulatapestrymuseum.wordpress.com/*calendar-of-events*). Before adding all of your page content, take some time to establish the individual page settings. If you want the page to be a subpage, select the appropriate parent from the drop-down menu under Page Attributes. The Writing Helper section allows you to copy an existing page to use as a template or request feedback via an emailed link so that collaborators can review the page before it goes live. The Likes and Shares section dictates whether the page will display the

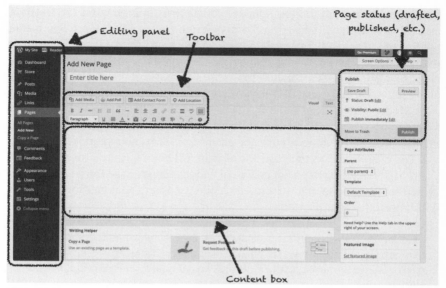

Figure 5.4

ordPress Tip #3: There are distinct zones on your website that you can edit: the header and footer, main content, and sidebars. The layout and format relationships of these zones are determined by your theme, and you cannot change this without paying for an upgrade or using the self-hosted software. The content of your header, footer, and sidebars are managed and edited through the Customizer and Widgets controls. The main content of your pages is edited through the Page section in the website editor panel.

Figure 5.5

number of "likes" your page has gotten and whether visitors will see quick links for sharing your content on Facebook and other social media (as determined in your Sharing Settings in the menu to the left).

You can add all your pages now if you are so inclined, or wait until you have built up the existing pages more. To build the content of your page, return to the content editor below the toolbar. Just like in a word processing document, a cursor will appear in the box and you can delete old text or type new text. The default toolbar options include text formatting and stylization, as well as links, spell-check, and a distraction-free writing mode that clears the rest of the screen's material so you can focus on the text box. The toolbar toggle button has additional text-formatting options, including text paste, clear formatting, indent, undo/redo, and a list of keyboard shortcuts. Just above the toolbar, you will see two tabs, one for Visual Mode and one for Text Mode. Visual mode is the WYSIWYG editing component of WordPress. While in it, content will display in the text box the same way it will appear to visitors. The Text Mode is used for inserting HTML and shortcodes, so you will see everything on the page through its HTML markup. For example, if you add an image to the page in Visual Mode, you will see the image. If you switch to Text Mode, you will see the code used to display the image, which will look something like this:

```
<a href="https://missoulatapestrymuseum.files.wordpress.com/outside-museum.jpg"><img class="alignnone size-medium wp-image-4" src="https://missoulatapestrymuseum.files.wordpress.com/outside-museum.jpg?w=300" alt="outside-museum.jpg" width="300" height="57" /></a>
```

If you feel comfortable editing HTML, this mode makes it easy to embed content and edit text styles just how you want them. For more information on using HTML, see Chapter 7. If you plan to embed videos, maps, or documents, you will use this mode in Session 5. Any changes you make in either mode will be reflected in the other.

To add text in Visual Mode, simply type in the box. Just as you would in word processing software, highlight text and edit its style or impose styles before typing. The Blockquote option will impose a unique style on the selected text, making it stand out from the rest of the page. Adding an image is a little more involved. Before adding the image to the page, your cursor needs to be in the location where you want the image to appear. Though you can delete and re-add an image to change its location, you cannot drag the image to a new position on the page, so placing it correctly from the start is easiest. Once you have your cursor in the desired location, click on the Add Media button above the toolbar. You can select an already uploaded image from the Media Library or upload a new image.[3] To create a gallery of more than one image, select or upload all the images you want to use and click Create a New Gallery. If selected, the Featured Image will appear at the top of the page or post. Once you have inserted the image, you can change its alignment and text wrapping by clicking on the image once. When you do this, you will also see a pencil icon that you can click to edit the image caption, alt text, display settings, and link properties, the last of which is discussed further in Session 5.

ordPress Tip #4: If your page edits are not appearing on your site, make sure you have clicked the Update button on the page or post. Your changes may be saved, but they are not visible until you have published them.

Figure 5.6

Delete or Move Elements

Deleting components on your page is as simple as highlighting or selecting the content and hitting the delete key on your keyboard. If, instead, you want to *move* a page component, you will need to either delete and reinsert or copy and paste the content.

Publish Site

As soon as you create a website in WordPress, the website is viewable by the public. However, you can save individual pages and posts as drafts so that they are not accessible to the public until you choose to publish them. When you are ready, you can change their state to Published. For the current page, if you are not ready to publish it just yet, click Save Draft on the right side of the page. You can always preview the page by clicking View Page or Preview at the top of the page. Once you are happy with a page, click Publish on the page, and it will go live. You can also set the page to publish at a certain date and time using the date-selection tool just above Publish.

SESSION 4

Add Contact Form

Adding a contact form to your site is done in much the same way as adding an image. Your form must be on a specific page and inserted into the content box. To begin, click on WP Admin in the left-hand menu of the account home page. Click on the Pages section and then hover over the page on which you want the contact form to be. Click Edit. To add a contact form, navigate to the location in the page's content box where you want your contact form to appear. Click on Add Contact Form. You can accept the existing fields and click "Add this form to my post" right away, or you can move, edit, or add fields to the form. To delete a field, click the minus sign next to the field.

To move it, hover over the field, then hover over the text that says "move" until you see the dragging cursor appear. Drag the field up or down. To edit the name of the field or to make it required (or not required) for form submission, click on "edit" that appears when you hover over the field. You can rename the field, change the field type (to a checkbox, drop-down menu, radio buttons, and more), and indicate whether the field is required. Click "Save this field" to return to the main form builder. If you need to add more fields, click on the Add a New Field button.

At the top of the form builder, switch to the Email Notifications tab. Enter in the email address you want the form submissions to be sent to and the email subject line you want the submissions to have. When you are finished, save your changes and return to the Form Builder tab. Click on "Add this form to my post" and you will see the shortcode for the form appear in the content box. Though you see the shortcode, your visitors will not. Click on Preview to see how the page and form will appear to visitors. If you need to relocate the contact form, be sure to copy and paste the *entire* shortcode for the contact form, which generally includes a bit of code for each field.

Add Poll

Adding a poll is very similar to adding a contact form. Locate your cursor where you want the form to be, and click on Add Poll. If you already have a Polldaddy account, you can link to it in the Polls Settings menu in the editing panel. If not, get started by clicking Create a Poll Now. You will link it to a new Polldaddy account at the end of this process. Title the new poll and add the number and text of the desired answers. Scroll left and right on the image of the poll in the Poll Style section to select the visual style of your poll. You can also select the width of the poll in this section. Before saving the poll, check the appropriate boxes on the right-hand side to determine answer order, number of answers allowed, how the results are displayed, and whether visitors can vote multiple times and leave comments. Click Save Poll, then click Embed in Post, which appears at the top of the page after you have saved the poll. The shortcode for the poll will appear in the content box, but remember that your visitors will not see the code, just the poll.

Add Divider

If you want to include a thin divider line in one of your content boxes, you will need to use the Text Mode function in your editor. If you feel comfortable looking through the code to find the location for your divider, skip this next step and enter Text Mode now. Should you need help finding this location, do the following: while still in Visual Mode, navigate to the line where you want the divider. In all caps, write, "DIVIDER" and then click on Text Mode. Once in Text Mode, scroll through the code until you see your DIVIDER notation. Highlight the word and delete it, and, leaving the cursor where it lands after the deletion, type *<hr />* as shown here, including the brackets and space between the letters and forward slash. If you return to Visual Mode, you will now see a thin gray line where you placed the code. Unfortunately, you cannot change the color or thickness of the line using this code.[4] However, you can use a different, slightly more complex code to get a line with more flexibility. Use the same method as before to find your place in the code in Text Mode, type the following code instead, exactly as you see here, and replace the underlined portions with components[5] that fit your needs:

<div class="aligncenter" style="width: 225px; height: 3px; background-color: #00007a; font-size: 0;">-</div>

Similarly, for a dashed line, use this code and replace underlined portions with information appropriate for your needs:

<div class="aligncenter" style="width: 225px; height: 0; border-top: 2px dashed #00007A; font-size: 0;">-</div>

If neither of these is producing a line, there are two likely explanations. The first is that the code was mistyped. The second is that the code was typed in a word processing document and then copied and pasted into the WordPress box. The solution to both is to carefully retype the code above exactly as it is directly into the Text Mode box. Then, check that the line appears in Visual Mode. Return to Text Mode to adjust the color, thickness, and other attributes as necessary. This method for inserting code will come in handy again in Session 5. For a list of what other quick codes WordPress permits, visit en.support.wordpress.com/code.

SESSION 5

Embed Map

Embedding items in WordPress involves a process similar to the one already discussed in Session 4 and reviewed again here. WordPress allows for easy embedding of Google Maps. From your account home page, navigate to your site dashboard and from there to the page you want to embed the map on. Identify where you want the map to end up and open up Text Mode. In a separate window or tab, open up Google Maps. Type in the address you want to pin, hit Enter, and wait for the page to load. Once loaded, click on the gear icon in the bottom right corner of the screen. Click on Share and Embed Map. Under the Embed tab, copy the embedding code. Return to the WordPress window and paste the code into the Text Mode box in the appropriate place. Reenter Visual Mode and verify that the map displays correctly. If you see a gray box for the map but no map details, try looking at the page in Preview.

Embed Video

Embedding a video is easily done, especially if the video is from Vimeo or YouTube. To embed the former, navigate to the Vimeo video. Simply copy the URL and return to WordPress, pasting the URL into the correct location in Text Mode. WordPress will read the Vimeo URL and display the video with no further coding. The Visual Mode will not show the video just yet—to verify that it has embedded, you will need to preview the page. If you want to specify a height and width for the video, you will need to use a shortcode to embed the video. Again, copy the video's URL. Paste it into Text Mode in the desired location using the code below and replacing the underlined parts with the URL and the appropriate dimensions:

[vimeo http://vimeo.com/44633289 w=500&h=280]

To insert a YouTube video, copy the video's URL. Then, direct your cursor to the desired location on your site. Paste the URL onto the page in Visual Mode, then preview the page to make sure the video appears where you intend it to.

Add Google Calendar

In order to add a Google Calendar to your website, you will need a Google account. If you already have one, simply make sure you are signed in and navigate to google.com/calendar. If you do not already have an account, sign up for one at accounts.google.com, then visit google.com/calendar. If you have a list of events to add, go ahead and add them to the calendar now, or add a sample event to get started. There are three ways to add an event:

- Click the Create button in the upper left-hand corner and edit the event date, time, and other details from there.
- Navigate to the day and time of the event, click directly on the calendar and drag the box that appears to the correct date and time, then click on the box to edit the details.
- Click anywhere on the calendar itself at any time and adjust the event date, time, and other details from there.

As you add events, you will have the option to create color-coded "sub-calendars." For example, you might have an overall institutional calendar, and within that have subcalendars for Education, Development, and Exhibitions events.

Once you have events on your calendar and are ready to embed it, you will need to make your calendar public so that visitors can see the events. If you have internal events or an internal subcalendar that you do not want shared publicly, you can still add them to the calendar but hide them by editing individual events or deselecting the calendar in the next step. To make a calendar visible, click on the arrow next to its name when you hover over it in the calendar list. Click on Share this Calendar and tick the box next to "Make this calendar public." Do this for each calendar you want to make public. Then, click on the arrow next to "My calendars" and select Settings. Click on the name of one of the calendars you want to share in the list that appears. In the Embed This Calendar section, click on "Customize the color, size, and other options." The main section of the page shows you how the calendar will display. If you are happy with it, copy the HTML code at the top of the page. If you want to include additional calendars or change the look, use the menu of options on the left side of the page to modify your calendar until you are satisfied with it, including adding a Calendar Title. Once you are ready to embed it, click Update HTML at the top of the page and copy the newly generated HTML code.

Return to WordPress. Navigate to the appropriate page and enter Text Mode. Paste in your Google Calendar code and verify that it displays the way you expect it to. Publish your changes. After adding your calendar to your website, any changes you make on the calendar (e.g., adding, deleting, or editing events) will be automatically reflected in the calendar on your site.

Embed Document

There are two ways to insert a document in WordPress. WordPress works well with both Google Docs and Scribd to embed documents for display directly on the page. To use Google Docs, upload your document to your Drive. Make sure that the privacy on the document is set to Public, otherwise visitors will only see a note that they do not have permission to view the document. To do this, click the Share link at the top of the screen while in your Google Document. Click Advanced, then click "Change . . ." next to the access that says, "Private." Select the first option, "On—Public on the web" and then the save button. Return to the document and under File → Publish to the Web click on the Embed tab. Copy the code and return to WordPress. Under Text Mode on the page you want to embed the document, paste the embed code in the desired location. Enter Visual Mode again and check for a

$\mathcal{CC}$ ordPress Tip #5: At any time, you can look at and edit your images, documents, and other media in your Media Gallery by clicking on the Media section of the editing panel.

Figure 5.7

gray box indicating the location of the document. To verify that the document is embedded correctly, enter Preview.

To use Scribd for embedding a document, create a Scribd account at scribd. com first. After doing so, upload the document to Scribd using the upload button in your navigation. Add and edit your document settings in Scribd, then click Save & Continue in the bottom right-hand corner. Do not copy the embed code just yet—click "You're done. View document on Scribd." In the upper right-hand corner, click on the social network sharing icon and then on Embed. Adjust the settings however you want the document to display. Then, under the Format section, select WordPress. Copy the shortcode that appears and paste that code into WordPress' Text Mode in the desired location on the page.[6]

Insert Downloadable File

If you do not want to embed a document, but rather, make it available for downloading, you will need to upload the file to your Media Library. To do this, move your cursor to the desired location in the content box. Click on Add Media. Switch to the Upload Files tab and upload your document. Edit the document title, caption, and description as necessary, then click Insert Into Page. The title of the document will appear as a hyperlink. You may wish to add a small icon or note that indicates the text is a download link.[7]

Create Links

Both text and images can serve as hyperlinks[8] to internal content or external resources. Text that is linked is called hypertext. Hyperlinked images and hypertext can lead visitors to internal pages, external URLs, documents, or email addresses. Your WordPress theme will have a preset style for linked text, generally colored or underlined so that it stands out from other text on the page. You can also manually stylize links after you have created them. Remember as you create links that search engines read your links during their assessment of your site. As such, your hypertext needs to be chosen wisely. For instance, instead of reading "Click here to visit our educational programs page," with the underlined portion serving as the hypertext, a well-linked sentence would read: "Learn more about our <u>educational programs</u>." Any search engines indexing your site will likely rate the second sentence as more useful.

With that in mind, navigate to a page on which you want to create a link. First, create the hypertext. Highlight the word(s) you want to link and click on the link icon in the toolbar. If linking to an external site, insert the URL in the appropriate field. Make sure to include a title and indicate whether you want the link to open in the same or a different window. If you are linking to internal content, click on "Or link to existing content." From here, you can click on the appropriate page. The URL and Title fields will fill in. Once selected, click Update. Your selected text should now be hypertext—possibly indicated by underlining or a different color.

To link an image, insert or navigate to the image in the content editor. Click on the image, then on the pencil icon to open up the image-editing options. Under Display Settings, change the Link To drop-down menu to the appropriate option—most likely Media File (for downloading the file) or Custom URL (for visiting external websites). Below that, paste the appropriate URL. Before clicking Update, expand the advanced options and insert an Image Title Attribute. This is important in helping boost your SEO. If you have created the link successfully, your image will not look any different, but in Preview or after being published, it will take visitors to the linked content when clicked on.

SESSION 6

Add Blog

WordPress.com was originally a blogging platform, so the site's blogging components are among the best in the industry. Posts are built very similarly to pages, but with a few differences in display and formatting. To get started on your blog from your account home page, click on WP Admin. When you create a site, WordPress automatically generates a sample first post called "Hello world!" As with pages, if you hover over the blog post in the list, you will see options for editing, deleting, and viewing the post. Click Edit and look over the blog editor. The blog editor is quite similar to the page editor, though you might notice that the lower right-hand side has a Format section. If your theme allows for post formats, this is where you can select a slightly different layout for your posts so that the blog's display changes based on the content. Though not all themes have post formats, those that do include preset layouts and stylizations for different posts. Background colors, layouts, and even fonts might change. If, in experimenting with post formats, you discover that you like a post format but do not want to use it for the post's intended content (e.g., you like the blue background color of the Video format, but you want to do a post focused on an image gallery), know that the formats are just suggested layouts. You can still put whatever components you want into the post.

Another way the page and post editors differ is that the latter has Categories and Tags sections. Both categories and tags are used to group your posts with like material, but categories are broader. For instance, in a post on a picture of Molly Brown during the time she lived in Leadville, Colorado, your categories might include cabinet card, mining, Colorado, and nineteenth century. Your tags might be Molly Brown, J. J. Brown, Leadville, silver crash, and soup kitchen. Though tags and categories are very similar, traditional bloggers search them differently.[9] For your purposes, you need to assign each post to *at least one category* and just assign tags you find relevant. There is no official list of categories or tags, but you can see a list of the most commonly used tags and you should be *consistent with your naming structure*, much like with your website style guide (e.g., always use MoMA and do not switch between MoMA and MOMA). As you add posts to your blog, you can review the tags and categories you have created by clicking on Categories or Tags in the Posts section of the editing panel.

Edit your first blog post and build your blog up with a few additional posts. You can preview your changes before you post by clicking Preview Changes. If you want to set your posts to publish at a specific date and time, use the calendar in the Publish section on the right-hand side of the page to pick first the date, then the time. Before moving on, take time to review your Discussion settings (in the editing panel), especially the comment and email notification settings, as these will affect how visitors can interact with your blog and also trigger communication with your designated email address when comments are posted.

SESSION 7

Create Menu

As you add pages to your site, WordPress may not automatically create a menu for you. This is to allow you the chance to decide which pages go in your menu, in which order they appear, and in which menus they appear should you have multiple menus. The default menu location varies by theme, but it is generally at the top of the page or in the left sidebar. Note that you cannot add a page to a menu until it has been both created and *published*. If you do not have any published pages yet, you will need to publish them before constructing your menu. To create a menu, enter your site dashboard by clicking on WP Admin in your account home page. From there, click on Menus (under the Appearance section). Enter a menu name and click Create Menu (or edit an existing one if applicable). In your menu editor, you will see a list of pages you can add to the menu. To add a page, check the box next to the page title. You can add multiple pages at once. You can also add links directly to the menu (e.g., a link to the local historical coalition website) if you know visitors will be regularly looking for a resource, especially an outside one. Once you have your page(s) selected, click Add to Menu. Your pages, each with its own bar, will then appear in the Menu Structure section.

Click on a page bar to expand it, and from there, you can rename the menu item or delete it. To move a page up or down (or left or right) in the menu, drag the bar up or down so the pages are in the order you want them. If you have a horizontal menu, your pages will appear here in a top-down order but the final display for your visitors will be left-to-right. Just below, under Menu Settings, you can tick "Automatically add new top-level pages to this menu" so that all new pages are automatically added to your menu when they are published. You may also be able to choose where the menu is located (e.g., your theme may have options for "top primary menu" and also "secondary menu in left sidebar") by ticking boxes next to the locations described in this box. Once you have arranged the menu to your liking, click Save Menu. If your theme does offer multiple menu locations, you will see a Manage Locations tab at the top of the page. If you click on the tab, you will see a list of menus you have added and you can change where each menu appears. As you add items to the menu, be sure to indicate each page's Title Attributes, which give readers—especially visually impaired readers using web readers—more information about the page. For example, on your Calendar of Events menu item, the title attribute might be: "See what events are coming up."

All subpages are indicated by a short indentation of the page bar. You can create a subpage by dragging the page bar underneath its parent and then to the right.

ordPress Tip #6: According to WordPress, "Pages are similar to Posts in that they have a title, body text, and associated metadata, but they are different in that they are not part of the chronological blog stream, kind of like permanent posts. Pages are not categorized or tagged, but can have a hierarchy. You can nest Pages under other Pages by making one the "Parent" of the other, creating a group of Pages."

Figure 5.8

If you want to create a menu item that is an "unclickable" parent (does not have its own page), add a Link menu item and leave the URL field blank. Then, create that item's subpages by dragging the page bars under the item you just created and then to the right.

Edit SEO

Before delving too deep into your SEO settings, review the discussion of SEO in Chapter 2. WordPress.com does not give its users direct access to meta-data, so it is especially important that you title your pages, images, videos, links, and other content appropriately and with an eye to how search engines will read them. Blog categories and tags are especially useful in this sense, as they act almost as key words (as long as you also use the words in your corresponding blog post). WordPress does a good job of making such data easily indexed by search engines. Remember also to submit your site to different search engines for indexing, as covered in Chapter 2. *WordPress sites are open to search engines by default, but just to make sure your settings were not accidentally changed, navigate to Settings → Reading and look under Site Visibility.*

SESSION 8

Create Online Store

An online store on your site is a convenient way to give your visitors access to buying memberships, making program reservations, or purchasing products from your gift store. Though WordPress does not directly support a shopping cart or eCommerce system, there is a way around this by adding PayPal buttons to your site. If you do not already have an account, make sure you indicate if you have nonprofit status (so you can qualify for lower processing fees) and that you select "Option B: Create payment buttons using HTML" when signing up for an account and asked how you want to use PayPal to accept money. Use the sections below as examples to learn how to accept donations and add both individual items (a Buy Now button) and sell multiple items at once (an Add to Cart button).

Accept Donations Online

For those users who have nonprofit status, PayPal offers buttons to collect donations right on your website. *This option is not available for personal or business accounts that do not have their 501(c)(3) status verified, so make sure that you indicate your nonprofit status when you sign up for your account.*[10] To begin, you will need to set up a page to place your donation button(s) on. Navigate to or create the appropriate page on your WordPress site, including any text and images you want. Then, open up Text Mode in the editor.

Next, log into your PayPal account and navigate to the button editing section (Tools → PayPal Buttons). On the right side of the My Saved Buttons home page, click Create New Button. Use the drop-down menu to select Donations. Add the name of your organization, then click the arrow next to Customize Text or Appearance. You can use the default PayPal button or upload your own image, though the second requires that you upload the image elsewhere on the web (on your site, for instance) and copy and paste the image URL into PayPal. If you use the PayPal image, you can change the size of the button and decide whether the accepted credit card logos are displayed. The sample button to the right will reflect the changes you make. Under Contribution Amount, you can allow visitors to select their own donation amount or you can set a fixed donation amount. You may want to look at the settings available in Step 3, namely the option to collect the customer's shipping address and the option to reroute to a URL after a payment has gone through. The first section determines whether your customer can write you a note (such as whom the donation was made in honor of). The next section allows you to collect your customer's address (in case you need to send them a thank you or other promotional materials). The third section allows you to input a URL to take customers to after they have either canceled a checkout or completed a successful checkout (e.g., a thank you page or a form to fill out in case you need to collect more information).

Once you have these settings adjusted to your satisfaction, click Create Button. On the next page, you will see a field with HTML code. Copy this code and return to your WordPress editor. Paste the copied code in the desired location in the content box. Return to Visual Mode and verify that your button appears the way you expect it to. You may want to Preview your site to make sure the button acts correctly as well.

Sell Memberships Online

PayPal offers good terms for those wishing to sell memberships or other items on their websites. The rate fee for nonprofits is 2.9 percent + $0.30 per transaction. Selling memberships or goods online follows the same process but uses a different button. Navigate to your membership (or other appropriate) page and add in the pertinent information for the item you are selling. There are two main types of buttons you can use for this service (Add to Cart or Buy Now) and you can make a button for each individual item or group similar items together. For example, you might be selling an item with multiple options (e.g., Senior Membership for $15, Individual Membership for $20, and Family Membership for $40) and you expect visitors to be purchasing just one type of that item at a time. To set up a button like this, navigate to the My Saved Buttons home page and click Create New Button. Use the drop-down menu to select Buy Now. Add "Membership" as the item name. *Leave this price field blank* so you can add multiple options and prices in the next area. Under Customize Button, tick the box next to "Add drop-down menu with price/option." In the drop-down menu name field, type "Membership Type" and then add your first three membership types and their prices:

• Senior/Student $15
• Individual $20
• Family $40

Click Add Another Option and add your fourth membership type:

• Corporate $75

Tick the box next to "Add Text Field" and type "Primary Membership Name" in the field. Click Done and then expand the Customize Text or Appearance section. Change the button text to "Pay Now." Expand Step 3 and uncheck the special instructions message option. Verify that your visitor's shipping address will be collected, then tick the box that says "Take customers to this URL when they finish checkout."

Briefly return to your WordPress editor and add a new page. Title it Membership Information Form and add a form on the page (see Session 4) that collects new member contact information and any other data you need. Save and publish your site, navigate to the page you just created, and copy the URL. Make sure to remove this page from the menu so that visitors cannot navigate to it without completing the PayPal purchase. Return to the PayPal window and paste the URL into the field you previously selected. Click Create Button and copy the HTML code you see on the next page. Navigate next to your membership purchasing page and switch to Text Mode. Paste the copied PayPal code into the field and save your work.

You can follow much the same process for adding items with only one type. To sell a set of ten postcards for $5.00 with $1.50 shipping, add a new page and fill it with an image and description of the item you are selling. You will insert the PayPal button underneath that image. On the My Saved Button home page in your PayPal account, click Create New Button. Select Shopping Cart from the drop-down menu. Name the item and note the price of $5.00. Expand the Customize Text or Appearance section and tick the box next to "Use Smaller Button." Specify the shipping cost and the tax rate for your area. Expand Step 3 and click the No button next to the special instructions option. Click Create Button, copy the HTML code from the next page, and return to your WordPress editor. Paste the copied PayPal code into the selected location in the content editor (making sure you are in Text Mode). Return to Visual Mode and verify that your button appeared. Repeat the process for any other items.

Finally, *you will need to set up a View Cart button.* Return to the same page where you got the HTML code for the button, which you can find again from your My Saved Buttons home page by clicking the Action drop-down menu and selecting View Code. Below the code section, click on the option to create a View Cart button. You can then use your own image or make the PayPal button smaller. Once you are satisfied with the button, click Create Button. Copy the new HTML code on the next page and return to your Word-Press editor in Text Mode. Paste the new code into the field and switch back to Visual Mode to verify that your new button has appeared.

SESSION 9

Adjust Mobile Site

Allowing smartphone-wielding visitors to view the site with a layout specifically made for mobile devices is absolutely necessary. Equally necessary is the option to switch back to the full (or desktop) view if desired. Some visitors will prefer the mobile version of a website because it generally comes with a simplified layout and faster loading times. Others will find that certain elements do not load correctly in the mobile view and will therefore need to toggle to the full-site version to see desired content. If you selected a mobile-ready theme, WordPress will do most of the work in getting your site ready for mobile viewing. You may still need to make a few adjustments. If your selected theme is not mobile-ready, the standard WordPress mobile theme will be displayed to mobile visitors. Either way, WordPress will provide options for viewers to toggle between the desktop and mobile versions. If you want to disable mobile themes altogether, you can change this setting under the Mobile menu in your site dashboard (found from your account home page by clicking WP Admin → Appearance → Mobile). Make sure you click Update after you change this setting. Visitors will then see only your full website, though this is not recommended, as this may slow down the load time on mobile devices and prevent users with older mobile devices from seeing your content. Should you choose to keep your mobile site option available, make sure you visit each page in your site using a mobile device—or

multiple mobile devices. Check for oddly displayed content (though Word-
Press *should* easily manage this transition) and any content that does not
make sense in the mobile view. To check whether your pages pass the Google
Mobile-Friendly Test, copy each page URL and paste it into the field found
at google.com/webmasters/tools/mobile-friendly.

SESSION 10

Check Site Statistics

When you log into your account, you will see WordPress's built-in statistics
data on your My Site page. The information WordPress gathers includes the
number of visitors and views to your site, the number of likes and comments
on your site, where visitors are coming from, and what pages and posts are
visited most often, among other stats. Other stat programs, including Google
Analytics, are permitted only with a paid upgrade on WordPress.

Add WordAds

WordAds is a product that WordPress uses in cooperation with other businesses so that websites can generate income by showing ads to viewers.
Essentially, what this means for your site is that you can permit WordAds on
your website. Viewers will see targeted advertisements, and you will be paid
a certain amount of money for each view or click the ads receive. You will
not be able to control what ads your visitors see, but you do have a say in the
location of the ads. Again, ads are generally selected based on visitors' cookies and browsing history, so you cannot directly control what is advertised
on your site. If you feel up for having advertising on your site, then this is an
easy and clean way to do it. WordAds does not divulge the number, but there
is a minimum traffic requirement for running ads, so less well-visited sites
that do not meet the requirement may not be approved. To apply for approval,
visit wordads.co and click Apply to get started. If your site is approved, you
will have the option to place ads in one or two locations. WordAds will guide
you through the process of optimizing these advertisements.

Upgrade Plan

Certain features of WordPress are only available with a paid upgrade. Two
of the most common reasons for upgrading are to connect a domain and to
add more data space to your website. If you are interested in upgrading your

site, click on Upgrades in the lower right-hand corner of your account home page. This will show you a list of available upgrade plans and what comes with each upgrade.

∽

As you build your site, feel free to experiment with different elements. You can save your site over and over again, exploring different features and how they manifest on your site. Take time to browse through the widgets you can add to your site. To view the WordPress.com help pages, visit en.support. wordpress.com. Find updated WordPress information at freethemuseum.net/ wordpress.

NOTES

1. "Awesome (and Free) Theme Options You Might Not Know About," accessed April 22, 2015, https://en.blog.wordpress.com/2013/12/04/awesome-theme-options.

2. Review the information on creating graphics in Chapters 2 and 8 for guidelines on making your image large and clear enough for use as a background image.

3. Review the image size and copyright info mentioned in Chapter 2.

4. WordPress Tips, "Divider Lines," accessed April 25, 2015, https://wpbtips. wordpress.com/2010/10/04/divider-lines.

5. For more information on adapting HTML for your needs, see Chapter 7.

6. Note that Scribd accepts the following document types: doc, docx, ppt, pttx, pps, xls, xlsx, pdf, ps, odt, odp, sxw, sxi, txt, and rtf.

7. Note that WordPress accepts the following file types: jpg, jpeg, png, gif, pdf, doc, docx, ppt, pptx, pps, ppsx, odt, xls, xlsx, mp3, m4a, ogg, wav, mp4, m4v, mov, wmv, avi, mpg, ogv, 3gp, and 3g2.

8. Though there is an occasional and subtle difference between a link and hyperlink (along the lines of a square is always a rectangle but a rectangle is not always a square) the terms are mostly interchangeable and are used as such in this book.

9. For more information on the difference, see https://en.support.wordpress.com/ posts/categories-vs-tags.

10. PayPal's terms note that the donation button is strictly "intended for fundraising. If you are not raising money for a cause, please choose another option. Nonprofits must verify their status to withdraw donations they receive. Users that are not verified nonprofits must demonstrate how their donations will be used, once they raise more than $10,000 USD."

Chapter 6

Getting Your Website Started on Google Sites

One of the advantages to using Google Sites is that Google offers an extensive portfolio of services, and almost all of them are easily integrated into their WYSIWYG platform. With a single Google Account, you get access to email, website, calendar, maps, and YouTube. If you choose to use Google Sites for your website, you should also get your single-stream email through Gmail. Google Sites offers good standard templates and lots of tie-in services that allow you to quickly include a Google Calendar, embed YouTube videos, and run Google Analytics on your site. Google Sites is structured in a way that is easy to use for those familiar with word processing programs. Editing text and adding images, for example, is very similar in both Google Sites and Microsoft Word. Google Sites integrates well with other Google products, but it does have some limitations in terms of extra features. For instance, there is no built-in image gallery option, a fairly standard feature on other WYSIWYG platforms.

In the guide here, you will find nine website-building sessions. Each session goes over different elements of creating a website on Google Sites, and you can work through them in sequential order or, once you have the basics set up, jump to relevant topics and skip over irrelevant ones. Some sessions will be quick, taking ten or fifteen minutes. Others may take a few hours, depending on your speed and comfort level with the material. Do not feel rushed to move onto another session if you still want to experiment more with the material in an earlier session. The material covered in each session is as follows:

- Session 1
  - Create an account
  - Choose a theme
  - Select or create a domain

- Session 2
  - Add a page
  - Add or edit text
  - Change fonts
  - Change the page layout
- Session 3
  - Add or edit an image
  - Create a slideshow or gallery
  - Change themes or theme colors and general settings
  - Publish your site (make it visible to others on the web)
- Session 4
  - Edit header and footer
  - Add a divider or spacer
  - Add a Google Calendar
- Session 5
  - Use HTML to embed maps, videos, documents, or files
  - Create links
  - Add social media buttons
- Session 6
  - Add a blog
  - Add a contact form or other survey
- Session 7
  - Hide page(s) from menu
  - Add an online store
  - Accept donations or sell memberships online
- Session 8
  - Check and modify mobile site
- Session 9
  - Edit SEO
  - Run Google Analytics

With the exception of Session 1, all sessions start from the site home page, found by clicking on the name of your site on your account home page. In this context, the site home page does not refer to the landing page on your site, but rather to the admin view of your site.

SESSION 1

Create Account

If you already have a Google account, sign into it. If not, visit gmail.com to sign up for one. Once you are signed into your account, navigate to sites.

google.com. When you signed up for your Gmail account, you were automatically given access to Google Sites, but you will not have any sites started yet. Click on Create in the upper left-hand corner of your Google Sites account home page. You can then select a template, name your site, select your site domain (a subdomain of Google Sites), and add a site description. Google Sites offers the option for either a template or a theme for your site. The former is a newer option and is more robust, allowing you to create custom page layouts and embed gadgets. The latter takes specific colors and images and imposes them on the default Google Sites layout. In general, using a template, even the blank one, is the better choice for your site, as it will allow you to create a distinctive look and feel for your site. Refer to the section on layout and design in Chapter 2 as you browse through the themes. Be sure to add your site description to help boost your SEO (see Chapter 2). Once finished, click Create Site at the top of the page.

Select or Create Domain

If you already own a domain or want to purchase a Google domain for your website, click on the gear icon in the upper right-hand corner of your editor to access the Settings menu. Click on Manage Site. From the menu on the left side, select Web Address. If you own a domain, add it in the field and follow Google's instructions. To purchase a Google domain, visit domains.google. com. If you do not connect your own domain, your website will be a subdomain of Google Sites, and your home page URL will follow this formula: https://sites.google.com/site/yoursitename.

SESSION 2

Add Page(s)

Once at your site home page, you will see your site the way visitors see it, with the exception of the top editing bar.

You should have two default pages on your site, Home and Sitemap. To add a page to your site, click on the Create Page icon in the upper right-hand corner of the screen. Name your page, select a template, and indicate where the page should be placed in the menu (i.e., as a top-level page or as a subpage under an existing page). There are four different page templates you can choose from:

- Web Page (acts as a basic page where you can write content, embed gadgets, and attach documents; it provides standard formatting controls for your text)

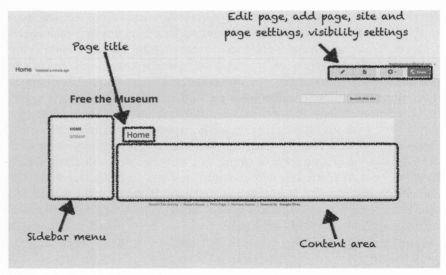

Figure 6.1   Your site home page

- Announcements (displays posts in chronological order, like a blog)
- File Cabinet (hosts files from your computer, allowing you to organize them in different ways so that visitors can easily access your chosen documents; visitors who are subscribed to the page are notified of changes)
- List Page (allows you to make lists of information, organize the lists, and sort information by columns, much like a spreadsheet; visitors who are subscribed to the page are notified of changes)

Most of your website pages will likely be the first (web pages), though you may want to use Announcements pages for a blog, a File Cabinet page for your collections documents so researchers can access your collection, or a List Page so that visitors can find information on affiliated museums in your area. Once you have configured your page, click on Create at the top of the screen. You can edit the page now, or click Save and continue adding the rest of the pages on your site.

As you add pages to your site, if you are using the sidebar menu, these pages should be automatically added to the menu. If using a horizontal menu, you may need to configure the navigation to include these pages. To do this, click on the gear icon at the top of one of your pages, then on "Edit site layout." Make sure that horizontal navigation is enabled, and then single-click on the menu to open up the Configure Navigation box. Add and arrange your pages, using the arrows on the right to move items up and down (left to right oogle Sites Tip #1: There are distinct zones on your website that you can edit, including the header, footer, and main content. The layout and format relationships of these zones are determined by your theme. The content of you header, footer, and main content are managed and edited through the site layout controls. The main content of your pages is edited by clicking the pencil icon at the top of the page. Outside of colors and general settings, pages must be edited one-at-a-time.

Figure 6.2

in the final menu) or over (to make them subpages). Choose the style for your navigation links, and click OK. Remember to add future pages in this way every time you add a new page to your site that you want included in the horizontal menu.

Add or Edit Text and Change Fonts

To edit the text of a page, click on the pencil icon at the top of the page you want to edit. You can navigate between pages by clicking on their title in the site menu of your site home page. Once you have opened the editing options, you can change the title of your page or add content to the main portion of your site. Just like in a word processing document, a cursor will appear and you can delete old text or type new text. Simply click in the field you want to edit and begin typing. The formatting bar at the top of the page allows you to impose styles on your text, including changing the typeface and size and making text italicized, bolded, colored, etc. When it comes to changing the font of your text, you have two options: you can change each block of text or string of words individually, or, ideally, set different styles for headers, body text, and other types of text. The former option will come in handy if you need to emphasize a single word to indicate that it is a link or italicize the name of a book. The latter will, just like in a Microsoft Word document, update *all* instances of that type of text. For instance, if you want all the body text on your website to be Helvetica 12 pt. black and all your paragraph headings to be Helvetica 16 pt. blue, you can use the information in Session 3 to change them all in one fell swoop. From the formatting bar, you can also add tables and bulleted or numbered lists from the formatting menu as well, much like in a word processing document. Remember to save your changes.

Change Page Layout

Google Sites has nine built-in page layouts to choose from. Under the Layout tab in the editing menu, you can add columns to your page and include side-bars. Click on one of the layout options to see what it will look like on your site. If you select a new layout, additional fields will appear in your editor. You can then click on those fields to add content. Choose the layout you want and add your content, making sure to save your changes.

SESSION 3

Add or Edit Images

The process for adding images to your website is very similar to the process for adding them to a word processing document. First, review the image size and copyright info mentioned in Chapter 2. From your site home page, navigate to the page to which you want to add the image. Click the pencil icon at the top of the page. Put the cursor in the field you want to edit, then, under the Insert menu at the top of the page, click Image.

You have two options for adding images: uploading an image from your computer or linking to an image already on the web. Be cautious with the

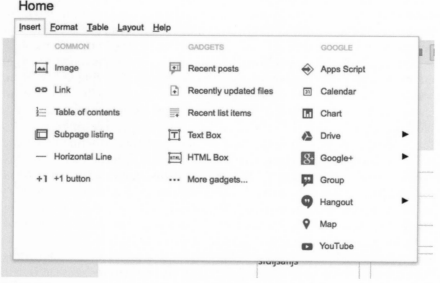

Figure 6.3

℘ oogle Sites Tip #2: Google Sites offers two different menu locations: one horizontal and at the top of the page and one vertical and in the left sidebar. The former presents menu subpages as animated menu items (they appear when the visitor hovers over the top-level page). The latter presents subpages as indented menu items. In the sidebar menu, the top-level page item can be expanded and contracted to show the different subpages underneath it. These two menus do not have to match.

Figure 6.4

second option in terms of both copyright issues and permanence (e.g., should the image be removed from wherever it is hosted, it will disappear from your site as well). To upload an image, click on Upload Images and select the image from your computer. You can only upload JPG, JPEG, GIF, or PNG images files to your site.

To add an outside image using its URL, copy the URL of the image and paste it into the Image URL field after you have selected "Web address (URL)." Whichever method you use, be sure to include alt text (so that your SEO does not suffer and so that visitors using web readers can always understand what the image is). Click OK, and verify that your image is now displaying in the site content editor. You can click on the image once to bring up the image options, which allow you to change the image alignment, size, and text wrapping. If you want the image to act as a link, you can click Change and insert a new URL, a process described in Session 5.

Create Slideshow or Gallery

Your Google account comes with a Google Drive/Docs account, both of which can be used in tandem with your website. Google Drive allows you to host images and other content, and Google Docs is an online document-editing program you can use to create presentations, used here to create an image slideshow for your site. To access Google Docs, navigate to docs. google.com. Click on the Menu button in the upper left-hand corner, and select Slides. You will need to create a new presentation by uploading your images and arranging them, much as you would do if using Microsoft PowerPoint. Once you have created your Google Docs Presentation, open up the File menu and select "Publish to the web." Change the auto-advance and oogle Sites Tip #3: Google Sites uses Gadgets, applications that you can embed into your site. These include PayPal storefronts, slideshows, Google Drive documents, Google Calendar, and more.

Figure 6.5

other setting options, and click Publish. Copy the link that pops up and return to your Google Sites editor.

In the editor on the page on which you want your presentation to appear, click Insert. Select "More gadgets" under the Gadgets column. Search for Slideshow Maker and click on it. Click Select and paste the copied URL for your Google Docs presentation into the URL field. Adjust the other settings as necessary and then click OK. Your slideshow may not appear in full form after this, but once you save your changes and are not in the editing mode, your images should appear. You can edit this gadget at any time from within the editor by clicking on the gadget once and then selecting the gear icon, which brings up the Properties menu.

The simplest way to create a gallery in Google Sites is to change the appropriate page's layout to a two- or three-column one. Then, add your images into each of the columns, entering a hard return or two after each image to add space before inserting the next image. Note, however, that your images will bleed over the columns unless they are shrunken down to fit. The columns just offer a way to add content across the page, rather than to constrain content. If you want the images to be expandable, you will need to add them to your Google+ account (included in your Google account). You can then insert them as a Photo Album from the Google section of the Insert menu.

oogle Sites Tip #4: In looking for help with Google Sites online, you may come across help pages that look relevant but are in fact for Google Business Sitebuilder. This service is not available to everyone, and is being phased out and replaced by Google My Business. If the help page you visit mentions features you cannot find, you may be looking at a Google Business Sitebuilder forum instead.

Figure 6.6

Change Theme, Colors, General Settings

If you want to change the theme, colors, or other overall features of your site, click on the gear image at the top of the page on your site home page. Click Manage Site. The first page is your general site settings. The most important settings are as follows:

- Site Name (the name of your site and where it appears)
- Site Notice (a message that appears to visitors the first time they visit; often seen as a warning about tracking information like cookies)
- Site Description (a brief description of your website; used for SEO reasons)
- Landing Page (designating which page is the home page for your site)
- Site Storage (how much data your site is currently using)
- Statistics (used with Google Analytics, discussed in Session 9)
- Mobile (to easily transform your site to be more mobile friendly when viewed on smartphones and other mobile devices)
- Access Settings (to change who can see your site; useful if your site is still in development; *set on public by default*)

The top portion of the left-hand menu of your Manage Site page allows you to see your site revision history, as well as your sitemap and what images and documents have been uploaded to your site. The lower portion is where you will see your other settings. The General tab repeats many of the settings found on the landing page of your Manage Site settings. The Sharing and Permissions section is another way to modify who can see your site; use this section if you want to send your site to specific viewers or collaborators. The

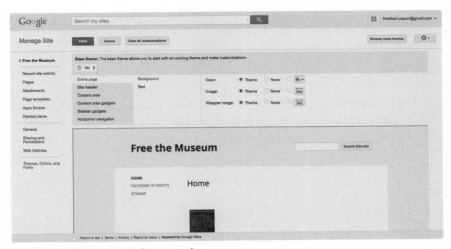

Figure 6.7 Your current theme settings

Web Address section can be used to change your domain. The final section is used to edit the look of your site.

When you click on "Themes, Colors, and Fonts," you will see your overall look settings, which include your current template or theme settings. There are three columns. The first two represent different levels of settings. The first is the *area* you are editing (e.g., entire page or site header). The second is the Background or other specific *types of content* you can edit (e.g., the overall text or a line divider). The third column is where the actual settings are located. By default, all of your settings should be on the Theme setting, rather than on customized settings. As far as areas of your site are concerned, there are six different ones that you can edit. The first is the entire page, where you can change the background to a specific color or image. You can also change the overall fonts on your site, including the fonts for body text and links. Changing the style of different types of text is best done when you have a fair amount of text (whether real content or placeholder text) on the site but are not all the way finished. Sometimes fonts look really nice in the sample and are then almost unreadable in a block of text, so waiting until you have substantial blocks of text to test a font out on your site will help you avoid formatting issues later on. You can also change the background and fonts of your site header, content areas, and gadgets. In both of the gadget areas, you can add a line divider to separate the gadget from the rest of your content. You will need to enable horizontal navigation before any horizontal navigation settings can take effect. To enable horizontal navigation, return to your site home page and click the gear icon at the top of the page. Click "Edit site layout" and click on Horizontal Navigation to enable or disable it accordingly. If you choose to use a horizontal menu, you should disable the sidebar menu so that there are not two competing (though identical) menus on your site.

Publish Site

Once you start editing and saving your site, your changes are automatically saved and shared within your sharing settings. For instance, if you have your site set to private, your site will be published, but no one but you (and your collaborators) can see it. To make your site visible to the public, change your access settings as discussed above.

SESSION 4

Edit Header and Footer

Customized headers and footers are an easy way to include relevant information about your institution on every page. Many museums choose to include their open hours and contact information in the footer, for example. That way, visitors can quickly glean information on visiting your museum no matter what page they are on. To customize your header or footer, click on the gear icon at the top of the page in your site home page. Click "Edit site layout." Here, you have the option to enable or disable the header, horizontal navigation, sidebar (side menu), and footer. You can also adjust your site width (though the theme default is usually the best choice, as the site template is built around that specified width).

To edit the header, click the Header button at the top of the page to make sure it is enabled (you will see a slightly shaded box around each one of these elements that is enabled). Then, single click on the current header in the content area. The header configuration options will pop up, and you can change the height and alignment of the header or add a logo by uploading a file from your computer. Click "Okay" to implement the changes you make. Similarly, to edit the footer, click the Footer button at the top of the page, then on the current footer in the content area. The box that appears is akin to those found in other text-editing areas of your site. You can add images and text and then stylize that content using the formatting menu. Though the actual content you add will display the way you see it in this menu, the footer itself will likely be wider and the line breaks may not fall in the same place.

Add Divider or Spacer

You can quickly add vertical lines to your site to divide gadgets from the rest of your content under the Themes, Colors, and Fonts settings discussed in the previous session. To delineate sections of your page using a horizontal line, click "Horizontal line" in the Insert menu of your editing page. The line will run the width of the content area of your page (not through sidebars or side menus). You cannot edit this line, but it acts as a good rule like those used in newspaper layouts.

Add Google Calendar

Adding a Google Calendar to your site is quick and easy, especially if you already have a Google Calendar set up with events. If you already have one, skip the next few steps about setting up a calendar. If you do not already have a calendar set up, google.com/calendar. If you have a list of events to add, go ahead and add them to the calendar now, or add a sample event to get started. There are three ways to add an event:

- Click the Create button in the upper left-hand corner and edit the event date, time, and other details from there.
- Navigate to the day and time of the event, click directly on the calendar and drag the box that appears to the correct date and time, then click on the box to edit the details.

- Click anywhere on the calendar itself at any time and adjust the event date, time, and other details from there.

As you add events, you will have the option to create color-coded "subcalendars." For example, you might have an overall institutional calendar, and within that have subcalendars for Education, Development, and Exhibitions events.

Once you have events on your calendar and are ready to embed it, you will need to make your calendar public so that visitors can see the events. If you have internal events or an internal subcalendar that you do not want shared publicly, you can still add them to the calendar but hide them by editing individual events or deselecting the calendar in the next step. To make a calendar visible, click on the arrow next to its name when you hover over it in the calendar list. Click on Share this Calendar and tick the box next to "Make this calendar public." Do this for each calendar you want to make public. Then, click on the arrow next to "My calendars" and select Settings. Click on the name of one of the calendars you want to share in the list that appears. In the Embed This Calendar section, click on "Customize the color, size, and other options." The main section of the page shows you how the calendar will display. If you want to include additional calendars or change the look, use the menu of options on the left side of the page to modify your calendar until you are satisfied with it, including adding a Calendar Title.

Return to Google Sites. Navigate to the appropriate page and click on Calendar under the Google section of the Insert menu. Select which calendar or subcalendars you want to use, and click Select. You can then alter your calendar display settings and click Save. Though your calendar will not be visible while you are editing, a placeholder box for it will appear. After adding your calendar to your website, any changes you make on the calendar (e.g., adding, deleting, or editing events) will be automatically reflected in the calendar on your site.

SESSION 5

Use HTML

Whether or not you intend to write HTML code, the HTML element can be very useful for a Google Sites webmaster. You might use it to insert SEO code or you might just want to use Yahoo Maps on your site instead of Google Maps. Whatever the reason, you can quickly insert HTML into

Google Sites by clicking on the pencil icon on the correct page in your site home page. Place your cursor in the field in which you want your HTML content to appear. In the formatting menu, click <HTML>. You will then see the HTML editor, containing the HTML of your current page. You can use this editor to embed maps, videos, and other content, though quicker methods for inserting Google-sponsored services like Google Calendar and YouTube are discussed elsewhere.

Insert Google Maps

To add a Google Map with your institution's location to your page, click on Insert. From there, click on Map in the Google column. In the top field, enter in your organization's title or address (or the address of whatever location you want to pin). Once you are sure that the pin has been dropped in the correct location, click Select and adjust the border, title, and size settings that appear. Click Save and look on your page for a gray box representing your Google Map. Once you have saved the page, the map will appear.

Insert Video

Embedding a YouTube video is very similar process. Navigate to the selected video and copy its URL from the address bar. Return to your Google Sites page and click on YouTube in the Google section of the Insert menu. Paste the URL of the video into the top field and select your display settings. A gray box for your video will appear while you are still editing, but the video will appear after you save the page.

To embed a video from a different service, such as Vimeo, you will need to find the embedding code. The location of this code depends on the video platform, but it can generally be found under sharing settings. On Vimeo, this is the paper airplane graphic on the upper right of the video. If you want to adjust the video size, control options, or adjust other settings for the video before you embed it, click the More or Show Options buttons. Though under the extra options you may be able to remove the volume and other controls, most visitors will want to have the option to adjust volume and video size. Including these controls is a good idea. Navigate to the Vimeo video, copy the embed code, and return to Google Sites. Open up the HTML editor (described above) and paste the embed code into the correct location within the editor. If you need help finding the correct location within the current code, close out of the HTML editor and place your cursor in the desired video location in the content area. In all caps, write "VIDEO" and then click on <HTML> again. Look through the code until you find your VIDEO note.

Delete the VIDEO text and replace it with the embed code you copied. Click Update and look for the gray box of your newly inserted HTML content.

Insert Document

You can insert a Google Doc by navigating to the Drive menu under Google in the Insert menu. Select the type of document you want to insert, and select the document from the list of your Google Docs available. Make sure that the visibility on the document is set to Public if you want visitors to be able to see the document.

Insert Downloadable File

If you do not want to embed a document but rather make it available for downloading, you will need to enable Attachments on the page and upload the file to your Attachments. To do this, navigate to the desired page and click on the settings gear icon at the top of the page. Click Page Settings and tick the box next to "Allow attachments." After the page reloads, scroll to the bottom and click on the "Add Files" option. Browse your computer for the file and upload it. The file will then appear in a list at the bottom of the page. You can click and drag the file name into the body of your content area and then edit the text to make the file integrated as clickable text (e.g., "Download a copy of our Collections Policy to find out more," where the underlined portion acts as a link). You can add a file to the main content area of the page multiple times.

Create Links

Both text and images can serve as hyperlinks[1] to internal content or external resources. Text that is linked is called hypertext. Hyperlinked images and hypertext can lead visitors to internal pages, external URLs, documents, or email addresses. Your Google Sites theme will have a preset style for linked text, generally colored or underlined so that it stands out from other text on the page. You can also manually stylize links after you have created them. Remember as you create links that search engines read your links during their assessment of your site. As such, your hypertext needs to be chosen wisely. For instance, instead of reading "Click here to visit our educational programs page," with the underlined portion serving as the hypertext, a well-linked sentence would read: "Learn more about our educational programs." Any search engines indexing your site will likely rate the second sentence as more useful.

With that in mind, navigate to a page on which you want to create a link. First, create the hypertext. Highlight the word or words you want to link. Click on the link icon in the formatting toolbar. If you are linking to internal content, select the site page on the Sites Page tab. If linking to an external site, insert the URL in the field on the Web Address tab. Either way, make sure to include a title and indicate whether you want the link to open in the same or a different window. Click OK to add the link. Your selected text should now be hypertext—possibly indicated by underlining or a different color.

To link an image, insert or navigate to the image in the content editor. Click on the image, then on "Change" next to the URL that appears in the image settings bar. As with text, select the Google Sites page or insert the URL for the external content. Indicate whether the link should open in the same or a different window and then click OK. Your image will now act as a link when clicked on.

Add or Edit Social Buttons

Adding links to your organization's social media pages may require a few workarounds, but it is possible. Twitter and Google+ are easily added, but some competitor websites, like Facebook, require more steps to integrate. Gadgets for adding a Google+ button, a Twitter follow button, a Twitter widget, and a Tweet button are found under Insert → More Gadgets → Search Gadgets. Navigate to the area on your page where you want the button to be, then open up the Search Gadgets window. Search for the button you want using the name of the social media platform. Click on the gadget you want to use and then on Select. In the next screen, you will configure your button, generally by linking it to your Google+ or Twitter username and adjusting the display parameters.

Adding a link to your Facebook page is slightly more involved. You will need to create a hyperlinked image that users can click on to go to your institution's Facebook profile. Therefore, you will need an image to click on and the URL of your organization's Facebook page. The best image to use is the Facebook logo, or the simplified social media button version. The Facebook social media logo can be found at freethemuseum.net/sample-content. Right-click on the image and save it to your desktop. Navigate to the location in the Google Sites editor where you want the Facebook button to appear and insert the Facebook social media logo as an image. Next, copy the URL of the Facebook page you are linking to. Return to Google Sites and click on the image to change it to a hyperlink (refer to Session 5). Having the link open in a new window or tab is recommended.

SESSION 6

Add Blog

Adding a blog to your website is a great way to keep your online web presence active. To start a blog, click on the Create Page button at the top of your site home page. Name the page, and then select Announcements from the drop-down menu. Click Create at the top of the page. This will bring you to your blog/announcements home page. Click on the pencil icon to edit it. Edit the page content the same way you edit basic web page content, typing in text and adding images from the Insert menu. Once you are happy with your blog home page, click New Post to add your first blog post. For future posts, click New Post on your blog home page. Again, add content using the formatting menu and typing in the content fields. You can save your post as a draft if you are not ready to make it public just yet, or you can click Save to share the post. If you save posts as drafts, you can edit them later by clicking on their titles listed on the blog home page. If you do not want visitors to be able to comment on the page, you will need to adjust your page settings for each post. To do this, click on the gear icon at the top of the page and then on "Page settings." Adjust these settings accordingly and click Save.

Add Form or Survey

Google has a form builder that integrates well with Google Sites. To find it, visit drive.google.com and click New on the left side of the page. Under More, select Google Forms. Title your form and select a theme, if desired. Next, edit the sample question by changing the field title, help text (an explanation of the field that disappears when visitors start typing in it), question type, and options. Indicate whether the question is required for form submission. Click Done when the question is built. If you want to add more questions, click Add Item and edit it accordingly. Once your form is built, adjust the confirmation page settings, including the receipt text (the confirmation text that appears when a visitor has successfully submitted their response). Click Send Form, then Embed. Adjust the size as necessary and copy the embed code that appears. Return to Google Sites and paste the embed code in the HTML editor on the desired page, as described in Session 5. Responses to your form will be sent to your Google Account email.

SESSION 7

Hide Page(s) From Menu

The way to exclude a page from the menu is rather roundabout, but it can be done. Essentially, when you add the page, you will need to make it a subpage of another page. After that, navigate to the parent page. Under Page Settings (found by clicking on the gear icon at the top of the page), you can uncheck the box next to "Show links to sub-pages." Click Save, and the page will no longer be in the menu; visitors will only be able to find the page through the direct URL.

Add Online Store

An online store on your site is a convenient way to give your visitors access to buying memberships, making program reservations, or purchasing products from your gift store. To get started, create or navigate to a store page. You can then use the Simple Storefront gadget found under More Gadgets in the Insert menu. Alternatively, you can embed individual PayPal buttons to your site. Use the sections below as examples to learn how to accept donations and add both individual items (a Buy Now button) and sell multiple items at once (an Add to Cart button). To continue with the Simple Storefront gadget, click on the gadget name and then Select. From there, select the type of button(s) you want to use: Buy Now (for visitors to purchase a single item immediately, such as a membership) or Add Now + View Cart (for visitors to add multiple items to their cart before checking out). Fill in the item details and display settings, then OK to add the storefront to the page.

Accept Donations Online

For those users who have nonprofit status, PayPal offers buttons to collect donations right on your website. *This option is not available for personal or business accounts that do not have their 501(c)(3) status verified, so make sure that you indicate your nonprofit status when you sign up for your account.*[2] To begin, you will need to set up a page to place your donation button(s) on. Navigate to or create the appropriate page, including any text and images you want. Then add an HTML box to the page.

Next, log into your PayPal account and navigate to the button editing section (Tools → PayPal Buttons). On the right side of the My Saved Buttons home page, click Create New Button. Use the drop-down menu to select Donations. Add the name of your organization, then click the arrow next to Customize Text or Appearance. You can use the default PayPal button or upload your own image, though the second requires that you upload the image elsewhere on the web (on your site, for instance) and copy and paste the image URL into PayPal. If you use the PayPal image, you can change the size of the button and decide whether the accepted credit card logos are displayed. The sample button to the right will reflect the changes you make. Under Contribution Amount, you can allow visitors to select their own donation amount or you can set a fixed donation amount. You may want to look at the settings available in Step 3, namely the option to collect the customer's shipping address and the option to reroute to a URL after a payment has gone through. The first section determines whether your customer can write you a note (such as whom the donation was made in honor of). The next section allows you to collect your customer's address (in case you need to send them a thank you or other promotional materials). The third section allows you to input a URL to take customers to after they have either canceled a checkout or completed a successful checkout (e.g., a thank you page or a form to fill out in case you need to collect more information).

Once you have these settings adjusted to your satisfaction, click Create Button. On the next page, you will see a field with HTML code. Copy this code and return to your Google Sites editor. Open the HTML editor and paste the copied code into the field below. Click Update and make sure your button appeared and looks the way you expect it to.

Sell Memberships Online

PayPal offers good terms for those wishing to sell memberships or other items on their websites. The rate fee for nonprofits is 2.9 percent + $0.30 per transaction. Selling memberships or goods online follows the same process but uses a different button. Navigate to your membership (or other appropriate) page and add in the pertinent information for the item you are selling. There are two main types of buttons you can use for this service (Add to Cart or Buy Now) and you can make a button for each individual item or group similar items together. For example, you might be selling an item with multiple options (e.g., Senior Membership for $15, Individual Membership for $20, and Family Membership for $40) and you expect visitors to be purchasing just one type of that item at a time. To set up a button like this, navigate to the My Saved Buttons home page and click Create New Button. Use the drop-down menu to select Buy Now. Add "Membership" as the item name. *Leave this price field blank* so you can add multiple options and prices in the next area. Under Customize Button, tick the box next to "Add drop-down menu with price/option." In the drop-down menu name field, type "Membership Type" and then add your first three membership types and their prices:

- Senior/Student $15
- Individual $20
- Family $40

Click Add Another Option and add your fourth membership type:

- Corporate $75

Tick the box next to "Add Text Field" and type "Primary Membership Name" in the field. Click Done and then expand the Customize Text or Appearance section. Change the button text to "Pay Now." Expand Step 3 and uncheck the special instructions message option. Verify that your visitor's shipping address will be collected, then tick the box that says "Take customers to this URL when they finish checkout."

Briefly return to your Google Sites editor and add a new page. Title it Membership Information Form and add a form on the page (see Session 6) that collects new member contact information and any other data you need. Save your site, navigate to the page you just created, and copy the URL. Return to the PayPal window and paste the URL into the field you previously selected. Click Create Button and copy the HTML code you see on the next page. Return to the editor and hide the membership form page from your site menu (see Session 5). Navigate next to the membership purchasing page and enter the HTML editor. Paste the copied PayPal code into the field and click Update.

You can follow much the same process for adding items with only one type. To sell a set of ten postcards for $5.00 with $1.50 shipping, add a new page and fill it with an image and description of the item you are selling. On the My Saved Button home page in your PayPal account, click Create New Button. Select Shopping Cart from the drop-down menu. Name the item and note the price of $5.00. Expand the Customize Text or Appearance section and tick the box next to "Use Smaller Button." Specify the shipping cost and the tax rate for your area. Expand Step 3 and click the No button next to the special instructions option. Click Create Button, copy the HTML code from the next page, and return to your Google Sites editor. Enter the HTML editor and paste the copied PayPal code into the field underneath the appropriate image. Click Update and verify that your button appeared. Repeat the process for any other items.

Finally, *you will need to set up a View Cart Button*. Return to the same page where you got the HTML code for the button, which you can find again from your My Saved Buttons home page by clicking the Action drop-down menu and selecting View Code. Below the code section, click on the option to create a View Cart button. You can then use your own image or make the PayPal button smaller. Once you are satisfied with the button, click Create Button. Copy the new HTML code on the next page and return to your Google Sites editor. Enter the HTML editor and paste the new code into the field. Click Update and verify that your new button has appeared.

SESSION 8

Modify Mobile Site

Allowing smartphone-wielding visitors to view the site with a layout specifically made for mobile devices is absolutely necessary. Equally necessary is the option to switch back to the full (or desktop) view if desired. Some visitors will prefer the mobile version of a website because it generally comes with a simplified layout and faster loading times. Others will find that certain elements do not load correctly in the mobile view and will therefore need to toggle to the full-site version to see desired content. Google Sites offers the option to quickly optimize your site for mobile viewing. You may still need to make some adjustments after initializing this function, but most of the work will be done. To begin, click on the gear image at the top of your site home page. Click Manage Site and scroll to the Mobile section. Tick the box and click Save at the top of the page. To check how the site adapts for mobile viewing, you will need to use a smartphone, tablet, or other mobile device to visit your site. Look at each page for out-of-place elements or awkward formatting issues that may have arisen. To check whether your pages pass the Google Mobile-Friendly Test, copy the page URL and paste it into the field found at google.com/webmasters/tools/mobile-friendly.

SESSION 9

Edit SEO

Before delving too deep into your SEO settings, review the discussion of SEO in Chapter 2. Google Sites does not give its users direct access to metadata, so it is especially important that you title content appropriately, with an eye to how search engines will read it. The five best things you can do to naturally boost your SEO are:

- Create descriptive, unique, and accurate page titles (e.g., no "Page 1")
- Use description tags for pages (found under Page Settings)
- Do not hide the sitemap
- Provide descriptive alt text for images
- Choose your hypertext wisely

Remember to submit your site to different search engines for indexing, as covered in Chapter 2. Also check your Access Settings (via the Share button in the upper right-hand corner of your editor) to make sure that your site is noted as "Public on the web" so that search engines can find and access your site.

Run Google Analytics

Another option for getting more detailed site stats is to use Google Analytics, another free service from Google. Google Analytics are used to see where your visitors come from, what pages they visit, and what their demographics are. To get started, visit google.com/analytics. Once you have your Tracking ID, return to Google Sites and click on the gear icon at the top of the page. Click on "Manage site" and scroll down to the Statistics section. Select "Use Google Analytics" from the drop-down menu, and paste your Tracking ID into the field below. Click Save at the top of the page. After a few days, your stats should start collecting. Log into your Google Analytics account to view the detailed site stats Google tracks.

∞

As you build your site, feel free to experiment with different elements. You can save your site over and over again, exploring different features and how they manifest on your site. Take time to browse through the widgets you can add to your site. To view the Google Sites help pages, visit support.google. com/sites. Find updated Google Sites information at freethemuseum.net/ google-sites.

NOTES

1. Though there is an occasional and subtle difference between a link and hyper-link (along the lines of a square is always a rectangle but a rectangle is not always a square) the terms are mostly interchangeable and are used as such in this book.

2. PayPal's terms note that the donation button is strictly "intended for fundraising. If you are not raising money for a cause, please choose another option. Nonprofits must verify their status to withdraw donations they receive. Users that are not verified nonprofits must demonstrate how their donations will be used, once they raise more than $10,000 USD."

Part III

EXPAND YOUR WEBSITE

❧

After you have built your website, you may find that you want expanded customizability or features. These can come in the form of writing bits of HTML code or using third-party services like Omeka. You can implement these as you build your site or add them on later as you become more comfortable with your site and its capabilities. Either way, wait to move on to this section until you have developed and at least started designing your site on one of the WYSIWYG editors.

Chapter 7

Basic HTML

If you've ever watched *The Sound of Music* and sung along to "Do Re Mi," you know that the best place to start is, of course, at the beginning. When you code, you begin with **HTML**. If you are reading this section, you may have decided you want to tweak your website a bit using code. Coding a full website requires hours of practice and work, but luckily, you are building your basics with a WYSIWYG editor and using code to specify something like a color or text size that you cannot achieve within your chosen editor. Customized HTML is an option in many WYSIWYG editors, and this chapter focuses on how you can use it to make small adjustments to your site. A few notes about the content in this chapter: First, you may find it helpful to pull up an HTML "testing page" while you read through the chapter and practice. The one found at freethemuseum.net/html-tester[1] is very useful, as it is simple and gives you starting code to work from that reflects your modifications as you go. Secondly, as you work through the chapter, feel free to use either the example content provided or substitute your own content if you feel comfortable doing so. Thirdly, most bolded terms can be found in the glossary, but some are addressed in the appendix.

THE BASICS

Browsing the internet is a lot more work for your computer than you might suspect. When you navigate to a website URL, your computer (henceforth called the receiving computer) sends a request for information to the website's server computer (called the **server**). After the server receives the request, it sends back information to the receiving computer in the form of HTML, **XML**, or a mix of both. These are two common "languages" that computers use to talk to each other over the internet.

HTML stands for Hyper Text Markup Language. It consists of what are called markup tags, each of which defines an element (such as an image or header text) of the web page content conveyed from computer to computer. What is most pertinent to your purpose is that this language defines both *what* is displayed on a web page and also *how* it is displayed. For instance, when you access the web page for kelseyransick.weebly.com, your computer receives data in HTML format that tells it to display the words "Kelsey JS Ransick" in the upper left-hand corner. Below that, it instructs your computer to display a black and white image. Further down is a menu in a blue, sans-serif font. All of this information is sent from the Weebly server computer to yours via HTML.

XML, which stands for eXtensible Markup Language, is related to HTML, but its purpose differs in a significant way. Like HTML, XML is used to send data—to send information on *what* is being displayed. However, it does *not* send information about *how* it is to be displayed. This is useful for a number of reasons. It allows the receiving computer to obtain the data efficiently and display that data according to a separate set of instructions (which may come from the receiving computer, the user's browser, another part of the website, or somewhere else entirely). Because of this, it is hardware- and software-independent, meaning that users with all different devices and software can consistently use it to communicate. Most internet users have used XML, even if they are not aware of it. For instance, if you use Facebook, log in and navigate to your newsfeed, you will see that your computer receives the data content from your friends' posts from the Facebook server. The home page you are looking at has a separate code known as **CSS** (discussed below) with instructions for how to display that content in your newsfeed so all the posts are in the same format. The Facebook server has sent a stream of information on what to display and the page has preset rules for how to display it. The server is using two sets of data—one to note the content of each post and one to direct how it is displayed. This makes the process more efficient because it eliminates the need to send display data (HTML) with every single post. Alternatively, if you have ever subscribed to an **RSS** feed to pull together news stories from various channels, you have been using XML to receive data from the different news sites. Your RSS reader pops that data into a consistent format for you to browse.

To illustrate the difference, imagine that you are creating your annual fundraising gala invites, but you missed the committee meeting. After the meeting, you get an email from your coworker that fills you in on what was discussed about the invites. If your coworker (representing the server) sends you (the receiving computer) a memo about the text the committee wants on the invite, she is sending you the "XML" of the invite—she is sending you the data that you will type on the invite, but you can design the invite however you want. If, however, she sends you the text and specifies that the invite should have red and black graphics on white paper with centered text in Zapfino and Arial fonts, she is sending you the "HTML" of the invite because it includes both content and display information.

So how does the receiving computer know how to interpret the XML or other content data it receives? That is where CSS, or Cascading Style Sheets, comes in. As the name suggests, CSS is essentially a style guide for a given page or website.[2] It is most commonly used by those coding a website from scratch,[3] as it allows a designer to create a single style for the website and then apply it to each page after that, eclipsing the need to redo formatting and styling for every page. CSS also interprets the data sent from the server in XML and HTML and directs your computer on how to display that data by defining fonts, colors, layouts, and more. CSS takes the data you receive and plugs it into that predefined style, much like a mail merge lays out a single document and then plugs recipient information into the appropriate slots. CSS is not used by every website and cannot be altered by viewers; it is more of a development tool than anything else. Because you are using a WYSIWYG editor, you will not have to use CSS to adjust your website, but it is helpful to have an idea of what CSS does should you come across it in your work as webmaster.

HTML, XML, and CSS are all powerful tools with a lot more capabilities than those mentioned here. However, the information most relevant to your endeavor is that:

• HTML sends data about *what* will be displayed and *how* it will be displayed.
• XML sends the data to be displayed but leaves the stylization of that data up to another set of instructions, such as the style sheet.
• CSS is a style guide that unifies the display of data on a website.

HTML FUNDAMENTALS

Now that you know (or have refreshed your memory about) what these languages are, turn an eye to the specifics on what you can do with HTML within your WYSIWYG editor. The most common things you will want to use HTML to do are to:

• Stylize different kinds of text, much like styles in a Microsoft Word document do (e.g., Title, Header, Body, and Footnote styles).
• Produce an effect, such as displaying all text in Helvetica.
• Provide links to outside content.
• Embed content on your page.

You can do these by manipulating three things within the HTML code: elements, attributes, and entities. **Elements** are individual sections of code that are denoted by the use of **tags** (e.g., the "paragraph" element is used to define body text on your web page). **Attributes** modify information about and within each element (e.g., the attributes of "Verdana" and "green" specify the size and color of the font used in the paragraph element). **Entities** are used to convey special symbols known as reserved characters (e.g., to show an ampersand on a web page, the code will read "&" instead of "ampersand" or "&").

Elements

Elements are stylized using tags. Tags come in two forms: **singular tags** (also known as empty tags) that embed content into a page, and **tag pairs** that enclose text or other content within them and impose their defined modifications on only that content. Tag pairs have both an opening and a closing tag, the latter of which is always accompanied by a backslash.

As with any language, there is a predefined set of elements that you can use. You cannot create your own elements, as other computers will not know how to read the code (imagine trying to write a French course book with Egyptian hieroglyphs). Look in Appendix E or visit w3schools.com/tags to see a list of tags you can use in your code. All content—including individual paragraphs, headings, images, and tables—requires some sort of tag designation so that the receiving computer knows what portion of the page it is displaying and therefore how to match it with the correct attributes. For example, below is a short section of code defining a page with one paragraph of text:

```
<body>

<p>

Welcome to the Missoula Tapestry Museum. Have a look around and make sure to visit our new blog page, where we will post updates on what we're doing at the museum, announce upcoming exhibitions, and much more. Please feel free to contact us at tapestrymuseum@gmail.com. Thanks for visiting!

</p>

</body>
```

Table 7.1

	Single Tag	*Tag Pair*
Form	<single />	<pair> Content </pair>
Use	Used to insert or embed content	Used to describe content contained within the tag pair
Examples	Images, line breaks, Google Calendar	Paragraphs, headings, tables

The first thing you see is the **opening tag** of the section of the page called the **body element**. Next, you see the opening tag of a single paragraph (the paragraph tag). There is then the text of the paragraph, followed by the **closing tag** of the paragraph and the closing tag of the body.

It is important that you always close out a tag pair. If you do not, attributes assigned to the content in the tag will run into the next set of content or not display properly, which can cause a lot of confusion. Further into the HTML process, you will likely come across **nested tag** pairs. Nested tag pairs occur when you have multiple levels of tag applicability. When this happens, the tags must close in the same order they were opened. This is discussed more in the attributes section below.

Attributes

Attributes are, as the name implies, visual or other specific styles that you can impose on your content. Whereas the heading is the element, the size 24 and italicization of the text are the attributes. Each element has specific attributes you can use with it, but you cannot pair every attribute with every element—after all, asking an image to display in size 24 Times New Roman would not achieve much. For example, your web page may have two paragraphs of body text, and you want a line in the second paragraph to be bolded. Your code, which has nested tags and a bold attribute, would look like this:

```
<body>

<p>

Welcome to the Missoula Tapestry Museum. Have a look around and make sure
to visit our new blog page, where we will post updates on what we're doing at
the museum, announce upcoming exhibitions, and much more. Please feel free
to contact us at tapestrymuseum@gmail.com. Thanks for visiting!

</p>

<p>

We are open Wednesday through Saturday from 12–5 p.m. <b>Parking is free
but limited,</b> so arrive early to ensure a spot. Visit our directions page to get
detailed directions to our museum.

</p>

</body>
```

This code may look strange, but it can be read with a little practice. The code illustrates nested tags—each paragraph tag nested within the overall **body tag** (the body element). The code breaks down into the following actions:

1. Open the body tag, which begins the body element.
   <body>
2. Open the first paragraph tag.
   <p>
3. Include the first paragraph.
   Welcome to the Missoula Tapestry Museum. Have a look around and make sure to visit our new blog page, where we will post updates on what we're doing at the museum, announce upcoming exhibitions, and much more. Please feel free to contact us at tapestrymuseum@gmail. com. Thanks for visiting!
4. Close the first paragraph tag.
   </p>
5. Open the second paragraph tag.
   <p>
6. Include the second paragraph.
   We are open Wednesday through Saturday from 12 p.m. to 5 p.m. Parking is free but limited, so arrive early to ensure a spot. Visit our directions page to get detailed directions to our museum.
7. Within the second paragraph, open a bold tag around the text, "Parking is free but limited,"
   **
8. Still within the second paragraph, close the bold tag around the text.
   **
9. Close the second paragraph tag.
   </p>
10. Close the body tag.

Notice that the nested tags close in the same order they are opened. The body tag encompasses the entire code: the bolded tag pair is within the paragraph tag pair, which is within the body tag pair, and all of this makes up the body element.[4] It is important to include the closing tag at the end of every paragraph because it tells the receiving computer to insert a space after the text.

Entities

What do £, ¿, €, ©, and → all have in common? They are all special characters that you cannot find on your regular computer keyboard. In HTML, they are known as entities, which require specific strings of text that the computer translates into the **reserved characters** you see. For instance, the British Pound (£) is displayed when the code includes the entity "£".

As with tags and attributes, there are preset entities, each with its own name and number. One of the most commonly used entities is the **nonbreaking space**, represented by the " " entity. The nonbreaking space allows you to insert multiple spaces into your text. If you use two spaces after a period, many HTML readers will remove the extra space.[5] If you type five spaces, it will remove four of them. Should you really want that extra space for formatting reasons, you can insert a nonbreaking space entity into the HTML.

Common Tags and Attributes

Two of the tags you are most likely to use are the link and image tags. You will use these tags if you want to create a link or insert an image into a page but do not or cannot use your WYSIWYG editor's built-in link capabilities or image **W-element**.[6] The link tag allows you to turn specific text or images into a **hyperlink**—a pathway to another resource that is either somewhere else on your site or on an entirely external site. The tag is written thusly:

<a href ="www.linkedpage.com">Text that your visitors will see.</a>

In this case, the opening tag includes the "href" attribute, which directs the receiving computer toward the destination, www.linkedpage.com. The text that follows is the text that will be visible to your readers and will generally say something to the effect of "Click here to visit our <u>new blog</u>," where the underlined text is the link. The closing tag completes the set. In general, you will want the text your visitors need to click on to be bolded or colored or otherwise distinctive from the text around it. Bolding or coloring the **hypertext** clues your visitor in to the fact that the text is clickable. The text your visitors see can say anything and does not have to be text at all; sometimes the link is an image, such as a logo in the upper right-hand corner that always leads visitors back to the home page.

On that note, it is important to understand the **image tag** and its use on your site. The image tag allows you to insert your own image or an image from elsewhere on the web.[7] For your endeavors, the only boon to using an image tag with a WYSIWYG editor is that if you have limited space for your website, you can reuse the same image on multiple pages but only store one data file for it. For example, Wix limits free plan users 500 MB of storage—about enough for 500 images—but perhaps you plan to use a lot of high-quality images or the same image many times. Using the image tag can help you maximize your storage space. You can either link to the high-resolution image on an external image-hosting site or upload the photo to your own site once and link internally to it wherever else it is needed, thus saving your data space.

The fundamental thing to know about image tags is that they do not actually insert an image onto your page; rather, they "call" for an image that is stored elsewhere and then display it in a specific spot on your page. Because you are using a WYSIWYG editor, you will either upload the image to your editor's image gallery or to an image-hosting site like Flickr or Photobucket. When you do this, your image is given its own unique location on the internet (its own URL) that is then referenced in the image tag. The image tag essentially acts as a link to that image, but instead of taking your visitor to a different page, it calls the image to the current page, where it is then displayed. The image tag, which always has both an image **source attribute** and an **alternative text attribute**, is as follows:

```
<img src="http://i.imgur.com/hNMYwY6.jpg" alt="View of museum from Millers Road" />
```

The source attribute directs the receiving computer to the specific image URL. The alt text attribute displays information about the image, which is important for three reasons: first, it appears while the page is loading (even if momentarily) so that visitors can tell what the image will be; second, it is used by screen readers to make the website accessible to the visually impaired; and third, it can be seen when a visitor hovers over the image with his mouse. Information on using the image tag follows in the sections mentioned below.

Another common tag is the line break tag: <br>. The tag inserts a space and, because HTML does not recognize hard returns, the tag is useful for adding a line break between list items, for example. Though the visual result is similar to that of the closing paragraph tag, do not use the <br> tag to separate paragraphs, as this clogs up your code and fails to close out any text attributes that you might apply to that paragraph of text.

PUTTING IT ALL TOGETHER

If you plan to tweak the HTML of your website within the WYSIWYG editor, you will most likely be adding simple elements and attributes to existing content. Each editor has different locations and levels of access to these codes. Once you are inside and ready to edit the code, you will want to "read" the web page to identify the three sections of code—and thereby locate the code that you want to edit. There are four basic HTML elements that every web page should have: the document type (an HTML tag to indicate to the receiving computer that the page is an HTML document), **header** (where information about the page and how to display its content is included), **title** (the title of the page, which usually appears at the top of the tab or URL box, not as part of the page's content), and body (within which are paragraphs, tables, lists, images, and other main content of your page). For example, here is a very basic web page:

```
<!DOCTYPE html>
<html>
<head>
<title>Why Museums?</title>
</head>
<body>
Museums are a great place to go to learn more about the world around you.
</body>
</html>
```

Notice that the tags are nested (opened and closed in the same order). Any computer receiving this information will know to interpret the data that follows as HTML. The receiving browser places "Why Museums?" at the top of the browser (wherever the individual browser usually displays the title). The only thing that the user sees is the sentence "Museums are a great place to go to learn about the world around you." If you have an HTML tester, such as the one found at freethemuseum.net/html-tester, type the code above directly into the tester, then click "See Result." You will see only the sentence, but the rest of the code is still included and read by the computer. These four elements always go in this same order, though their contents will certainly vary and even occasionally be empty.

Next—and before inserting it into an HTML tester—try reading this code that has a more substantial body element.

```
<!DOCTYPE html>
<html>
<head>
<title>Why Museums?</title>
</head>
<body>
<h1>What Museums Can Do For You</h1>
<p>Museums are a great place to go to learn more about the world around
```
you. Whether they deal with science, technology, history, art, or something

else entirely, they care for and interpret valuable evidence from the past and present, and even explore where we're going in the future.</p>
<img src="museumfrommillers.jpg" alt="View of museum from Millers Road" />
</body>
</html>

Can you identify the four basic elements? What else is new? What element is that new content placed in?

To see how this code actually works, open up an HTML tester and type the code above directly into the tester, substituting the URL of an actual image for museumfrommillers.jpg.[8] Going through the elements in order, you can see in the code that the document is an HTML document. The title does not appear anywhere you can see it in the tester, but if it were an active web page, the title would be at the top of the address bar, depending on the browser you use. You can also see that two new HTML elements have been added: a heading and an image. The heading, denoted by <h1> and </h1>, is likely a different size than the rest of the text. It is Heading Style 1, which the tester has conveniently provided attributes for so you can see the difference between the heading and the paragraph below (the text included between <p> and </p>). If the image you use is not stored on your computer, as in this example, the tester must have the direct URL for the image or it will be unable to call for it and display it. If the URL is incorrect, you will see a small blue and green icon of a piece of paper with a white stripe across it. The icon indicates that your image element *code* is correct but the *URL* may be incorrect.

Occasionally, you may want to include information in your HTML code that visitors cannot see but that future webmasters can. These can take the form of HTML comments—areas that are denoted by <!-- and --> whose text does not appear on the actual web page. These are just for passing information to a human reading the code and do not contain data of any value for a computer reading the HTML (which is useful if you are putting in a note about who last updated the page or warnings about difficult areas of the code). For example, type this code directly into your HTML tester and look at the difference between what you see in the code and what you would see as a visitor to the web page it describes.

<!DOCTYPE html>
<html>
<head>
<title>Why Museums?</title>

```
<!-- This page contains an image hosted on another site. If the URL becomes
invalid, the image will need to be replaced. -->
</head>
<body>
<h1>What Museums Can Do For You</h1>
<p>Museums are a great place to go to learn more about the world around
you. Whether they deal with science, technology, history, art, or something
else entirely, they hold and interpret valuable evidence about the past, the
present, and even where we're going in the future.</p>
<img src="http://i.imgur.com/hNMYwY6.jpg" alt="View of museum from
Millers Road" />
</body>
</html>
```

This brings us to two very important things to keep an eye on when you are working with code, especially when inserting images: spaces and quotation marks in your code. Spacing in HTML coding is fairly specific. For example, see the two comment codes below. Type both bits of code into your HTML tester exactly as you see them, noting the extra space before the exclamation mark in the second comment tag.

<!-- This page contains an image hosted on another site. -->
< !-- This comment is for demonstrative purposes only. -->

When the result "appears," you should not see anything displayed for the first comment tag. However, if you added in the space as it appears in the second code between the < and ! in the opening tag, the computer will not recognize it as an opening comment tag. Instead, it will read it as regular text, and your entire comment will appear to anybody visiting your site.

Similarly, as you type in code, *it is very important* that you pay attention to the quotation marks. For quotation marks used in the *code* (not in body text that your visitors will see), you must *always* use straight double quotes. The subtle difference between " and " makes all the difference in how a computer interprets your code, as the straight double quotes are a standard HTML coding character and the curly double quotes are not. For now, if you are typing directly into the HTML tester, you need not be concerned with this, as the tester automatically assumes you mean to use straight double quotes. However, if you are editing HTML, you should *never edit the code in a Word document*, as Word will automatically convert your quotation marks to curly double quotes. Instead, use a simple text editor like Text Edit (on Macs) or Notepad (on Windows) or, better yet, edit the code right in the

WYSIWYG editor in your browser. To illustrate what can change with the wrong quotation marks, type the following code directly into the HTML tester using the straight double quotes:

```
<img src="http://i.imgur.com/hNMYwY6.jpg" alt="View of museum from Millers Road" />
```

The image should appear with no problem. Next, type the following code into a word processor like Microsoft Word:

```
<img src="http://i.imgur.com/hNMYwY6.jpg" alt="View of museum from Millers Road" />
```

Copy and paste the code into the tester. The image will either not display at all, or you will see the blue and green "Cannot load image" icon. What a difference!

HTML TWEAKING

Though it is unlikely you will be working with an entire HTML document through your WYSIWYG editor, it is important to know the basic sections of such a document so that you can locate the elements or attributes you are looking for. Odds are, if you are editing HTML through your WYSIWYG editor, you will be editing an HTML gadget or W-element with the intent of inserting a Google Calendar, image, link, or something similar. This means that you will drag and drop the HTML element box onto the page, copy and paste the code into the box, and adjust it from there. The following section includes instructions on how to:

- Create a hyperlink in your text.
- Turn an email address into a hyperlink so visitors can click on the address and email the address directly.
- Insert an image.
- Insert an image that also functions as a link.
- Embed documents, forms, and other media.
- Change the color, size, and typeface of your text.

Hyperlinks

One of the most useful and quick-to-implement HTML tweaks is the hyperlink—a quick link to external content (either another URL, an email address, or a document). Hyperlinks are easy to spot in PDF documents, as you see text that is underlined and blue. If you click on this hypertext, it takes you to a specific website or opens an email program to send an email. The procedure works the same way with links online, though these links can be denoted by a variety of font styles. Most WYSIWYG editors give you the option of creating hyperlinks easily in the text as part of your basic site-building, and they also typically include the ability to set a style for links, whether bolded or colored. If you have already read the beginning chapters of this book, you will know that whatever denotation you decide on for your links, it should be *consistent* within each type of link (e.g., emails are underlined, URLs are bolded, etc.)

When you insert tags into your text, it is important to keep track of your spaces and punctuation. If you include a space *before* the opening **anchor tag** and another space *after* the opening tag, the final text may display with *two* spaces between the words. Similarly, if you do not want a comma, period, or other punctuation mark to be included in what the visitor sees as a link, you want to make sure that the punctuation comes *after* the closing anchor tag but before the closing paragraph tag (nor do you want to include a space *after* the closing anchor tag in this case). *Remember that, if done correctly, your HTML tags will not appear at all in the text your visitor sees, so when you are coding, keep an eye out for any additional spaces or punctuation.*

External Links

If you are looking to create a link through text or an image and you cannot do it within the regular WYSIWYG editor, you will need to do a bit of coding. To create a link to an outside resource, be it a web page, document, or something else, you will need the URL, the text or an image that you want to act as the link, and an anchor element. Where you can access the HTML will vary with each WYSIWYG editor, but once you have navigated to this area[9] or added your HTML element, you can create a hyperlink by completing these steps:

1. Choose which text you want your visitors to click on to access the linked material. For instance, you want "Missoula Tapestry Museum" to act as the hyperlink.
2. Insert or locate the text *in* the HTML code or element.

   <p>

   We are closely associated with a number of museums in the area. Visit the website for our sister museum, the Missoula Tapestry Museum.

   </p>

3. Insert the opening and closing tags for the anchor/hypertext element
(which is <a>) and a **href attribute** (which is href="www.url.com") on
either side of the exact text you want to make into the link, using the destination URL.

<p>

We are closely associated with a number of museums in the area. Visit the
website for our sister museum, the <a href="www.missoulatapestrymu-
seum.weebly.com">Missoula Tapestry Museum.</a>

</p>

4. Make the hypertext bold using the bold attribute.

<p>

We are closely associated with a number of museums in the area. Visit the
website for our sister museum, <a href="http://www.missoulatapestrymu-
seum.weebly.com"><b>the Missoula Tapestry Museum.</b></a>

</p>

As it is, your link will open in the same window as your website, meaning
that your visitor will automatically be navigated away from your website. If,
instead, you want your website to remain open and for the link to appear in
a new window or tab, you can add a target attribute to the anchor element.
Instead of the opening tag just reading:

<a href="http://www.missoulatapestrymuseum.weebly.com">

you will add in a **blank target attribute** so that it reads:

<a href="http://www.missoulatapestrymuseum.weebly.com" target="_blank">

Everything else about the tag will remain the same, including the straight
double quotes and the closing tag. Lastly, you will want to save your work
and check that the link works by returning to your website as a visitor (not
through the admin portal) and clicking on the link.

Email Hyperlinks

Creating an email hyperlink is very similar. You will choose the text you
want the visitor to click on and use an anchor tag with an href attribute; the
only difference is that you will preface the attribute with "mailto:" and the
email address you are directing them to:

<a href="mailto:tapestrymuseum@gmail.com">

This short bit of text directs the computer to open up a new email using the address provided. Your final HTML text will therefore read:

<p>If you have any comments or questions, please feel free to send us an <a href="mailto:tapestrymuseum@gmail.com">email</a>.</p>

Note that the anchor element is only around the word "email" and does not include the period that follows.

Hyperlinks on the Same Page

One of the handiest HTML tweaks you can implement is the ability to quickly jump around on a single page, especially if the page has a lot of content or is otherwise very long. For example, you may have a page that includes your by-laws and therefore includes a table of contents. You want users to be able to click down to the relevant section and then back up to the top when they are finished. For this, you can use **intradocument hyperlinks**, which, as the name suggests, link to content in the same HTML document (on the same page). They almost act like footnotes or endnotes—there is a specific symbol or character that indicates related content is available further down the document, and the computer will use that information to jump down and find said content. To do this, you will insert two types of anchor elements:

1. An anchor element in the location you want your user to jump to (sometimes called the reference point)
2. An anchor element with an href attribute around the text that users will click on to get there (sometimes called the reference)

Remember that you can include "regular" text of any length in the body of an HTML document; you must do this to incorporate intradocument hyperlinks by placing both your page text and hyperlinks inside a single HTML W-element. The entire regular text in the HTML document that comes between anchor elements must be complete with line breaks in the appropriate locations.[10] Moreover, if you want this regular text to match the rest of the text style on your website, remember to include instructions for its display in the form of text attributes (e.g., font, color, and size) in the HTML element. See Appendix E for a list of text attributes you can choose from and the section below about font attributes to learn how to implement them. For now, focus on defining your anchor elements.

Supposing that you want to include a "Back to top" hyperlink at the bottom of your page, you would place the following anchor code at the top of the body element:

```
<a name="top"></a>
```

This opens and closes the first part of an intradocument hyperlink—the **reference point**. Even if there is no visitor-visible content in the tag, the computer will know to jump to the right place. Next, navigate to the location you want to include the "Back to top" text. It should still be inside the body element. Insert the code below, making sure that the name of the reference point (in this example it is "top") is the *exact same text* as it is in the first anchor element:

```
<a href="#top">Back to top</a>
```

The reference is preceded by a pound sign, which indicates to the computer that the reference point is on the same page, rather than on an external page or site. When creating these intradocument hyperlinks, you can name the reference point anything you want (top, section 1, paragraph 4, etc.) but keeping it simple and obvious is best.

The method for creating any intradocument hyperlink is the same, regardless of where your reference points and references are. You need to place a specific, named reference point using an anchor tag first, then place the hyperlink anywhere on the page to reference that anchor, making sure to use the *exact name* for the reference point in a hyperlink attribute. You can have multiple hyperlinks to the same anchor point, so having a "Back to top" link at the end of every section is easily done by inserting a reference anchor element wherever you want the hyperlinks to be. This can also be done using images as your hyperlink.

Using Images

Inserting images into your site using HTML is useful if you need to be efficient with your storage space. By uploading the image once and then linking to it for any successive uses, you can save significant space, especially if the image is large or has a high resolution. The advantage to storing the image on your site is that the loading speed will not be affected by an outside server, as it would be if you hosted the image on Flickr, for example.

Inserting Images

To insert your image, upload it somewhere on the internet (e.g., to your own site, Flickr, or Photobucket) and capture the URL. It is important to note that the URL for the page the image is on and the URL for the image itself are *not* the same. If you are unsure what the URL is, navigate to the page that the image is hosted on, right click on the image, and select "Copy image URL" or "Open image in new tab," at which point you can look at the address bar for the image URL. It should end in .jpg or another image format. If copied correctly, you should be able to paste the URL into your browser and be taken directly to a page that has nothing but the image on it. Try this out with the URL below:

<img src="http://i.imgur.com/hNMYwY6.jpg" alt="View of museum from Millers Road" />

Here, you can see that the image element does not have a closing tag because it is a single tag, used for inserting content into a page rather than for describing content within a tag pair. The alt text provided is detailed but not overly lengthy.[11] In this circumstance, use the image W-element on your WYSIWYG editing platform or image-hosting site for the first occurrence of the image. For any subsequent occurrences of the image, copy the image's URL (found by visiting the published site and right-clicking on the image) to call for the image using this code.

When you insert an image onto a page using this technique, the image will automatically display in whatever size the file is. If you go one step further and add specific attributes into your image, it will not only keep the display of your image in check, but can also tell a receiving computer with a slow connection how much room to leave on the page for the final image. Often, the automatic size of an image is too large and you will need to downsize the image. There are two cardinal rules for setting size parameters for an image:

1. *Never distort an image.* The ratio of height to width must remain the same; you must never increase or decrease the size of one dimension without increasing or decreasing the size of the other dimension in equal proportion.
2. *Keep images small enough.* This means two things: First, that users do not have to scroll to see all of the images. Second, that the image must not be pixelated. If you try to increase an image's size beyond that which the PPI is intended to display, your image will look fuzzy. This is unattractive and unprofessional—and avoidable.[12]

To adjust the size of an image, you will add two attributes to the image element: height and width. When you add them, keep in mind that the numbers you insert are in *pixels*, not inches. If you are unfamiliar with adjusting images using this unit of measurement, open the image in an image editing or viewing program (most anything will do, as long as you can view data about the image). Navigate to the size section, where you should see the dimensions listed. Alternatively, you can right-click on the image file in your document folder and click on "Get Info" to see the same information. Once you know the pixel dimensions of your image, you can calculate the desired size of your image. If you need to convert pixels to inches or vice versa, try using the tool located at bit.ly/1wvf0CU.[13] Remember to keep the dimensions at the same ratio (e.g., if you reduce the width by 75 percent, you must reduce the height by 75 percent to reduce it proportionately).

After determining the dimensions you need, add in the two attributes to the image tag in this manner:

```
<img src="http://i.imgur.com/hNMYwY6.jpg"alt="View of museum from Millers Road" height="324" width="243" />
```

To see the display difference, enter the following two bits of code into your HTML tester:

```
<img src="http://i.imgur.com/hNMYwY6.jpg" alt="View of museum from Millers Road" height="324" width="243" />

<img src="http://i.imgur.com/hNMYwY6.jpg" alt="View of museum from Millers Road" />
```

The top image is the reduced size of 243 pixels by 324 pixels, and the first is the original image of 500 pixels by 375 pixels. While the *file* size remains the same, the *display* size is greatly reduced and can now fit comfortably in a blog post or on a front page.

Linking Images

Occasionally, you will want to make an image a link to another page, be it on your website or elsewhere. This is especially common for logos on the top or side of a page that link back to your home page. Most visitors expect a quick way to return to the home page of your website, and providing the logo as a link helps prevent them from getting lost while they browse or look for specific information.[14] To do this, you will combine in the code below the two tricks you just learned about hyperlinks and inserting images:

```
<a href="http://www.freethemuseum.net/visit-us"> <img src="http://i.imgur.com/hNMYwY6.jpg" alt="Click to see the Visit Us page" /></a>
```

Notice that this code uses the link tag discussed previously, but instead of having *text* serve as the hyperlink, the *image* serves as the hyperlink. If you type this code into an HTML tester, the image will appear (large, unless you give it size attributes), and you can click on it to be taken to the linked website. Note also that if for some reason your browser cannot display the image, you will still see the alt text, which now reads, "Click to see the Visit Us page." If you wish to add attributes (e.g., size) to an image, these can go in the image tag after the image source attribute.

Linking to and Downloading Files

Using much the same process as linking an image, you can link to downloadable documents. Just as with images, your downloadable PDFs, Word documents, and other files will not actually be placed on a page, but rather called for by a tag. Their tag calls for the link to the content, which is stored elsewhere on the site or online. Almost any file type can be made downloadable (though your visitor may not always have the software to open it), it just requires that you upload the file to a server, be it your site's file gallery, a GoogleDocs account, or another external file hosting site.[15] Once you have the document uploaded to a location of your choosing, you will need to capture the document's URL. Do this by navigating to your editor's file gallery or the direct page of the document.[16] The URL for a page the document or image appears on is *not* the same as the URL for the document or image itself. If you are in the file gallery, there should be an option for copying the URL listed under the document's settings. Alternatively, navigate to the direct page for the image (often right-click → Open Image in New Window) and copy the URL from the address bar. If you are unsure whether the URL you have is correct, check that the URL ends in .pdf or whatever document extension is appropriate. Use the same hyperlink tag and href attribute to insert your document that you would for inserting a link:

<a href="http://i.imgur.com/hNMYwY6.jpg">Click here to download file.</a>

Once the file is clicked on, your visitor's browser will determine whether the file is automatically downloaded or displayed. For example, many browsers, such as Firefox, are automatically set to display PDFs, at which point visitors can choose to download the file to their computers or navigate away. Other browsers, such as Safari, download the document first and then automatically open it in the appropriate software. Still other browsers, like Internet Explorer, ask users if they want to download the file or just save it. You cannot control which of these various actions the browsers will take, but what you can do to help your visitors is to note what the file type is (PDF, .doc, .zip, etc.) on your page so that they know exactly what it is they are downloading. Generally, providing PDFs for non-image files is the best way to go because they are compact and do not allow the user to modify them.[17]

Font Attributes

There are three font attributes you can adjust using HTML: typeface, color, and size. If you are including any of your page text in an HTML element, you will want to specifically define this (most likely to match the rest of the text on the page), otherwise the text will revert to the default text of the visitor's browser and possibly look different than the rest of your text. You can change the style of text in two ways:

1. In-line editing (to alter a word or sentence *within* a paragraph)
2. Text-block editing (to alter an entire block of text made of one or more paragraphs)

This is done by inserting the attribute code in the right spot for each type of edit. In-line editing affects one or more words (by placing the attribute information directly around the words to be affected) and text-block editing affects an entire paragraph (by placing the attributes around the paragraph). For a list of attributes you may want to apply to your text, see Appendix E.

In-line and Text-Block Editing

Using in-line elements, you can change the typeface, color, or size of a single word or short group of words. As you saw at the beginning of the chapter, inserting in-line attributes (such as bold, italic, or hyperlinked text) is a relatively simple matter of placing the desired code around the specific words you want changed. For example, if you want to make one word in a sentence a bolded link, the following code will accomplish it:

```
<p>Check out our <a href="http://www.freethemuseum.net/calendar">
<b>calendar</b></a> to learn more about what upcoming events we have.</p>
```

Note that there are three sets of tags, each opened and closed in nesting order. The first is the opening paragraph tag. Next is the opening link tag, followed immediately (with no spaces) by the bold attribute tag. Immediately after the selected word are the closing bold attribute and link tags. At the end of the paragraph is the closing paragraph tag. If you plug this code into an HTML tester, you will see the sentence in default text with the word "calendar" bolded so that the visitor knows it is a link he can click on.

When you edit the style of a block of text, use the same technique as with in-line editing, but place the attribute code right next to each of the paragraph tags:

<p><i>Check out our <a href="http://www.freethemuseum.net/calendar"> calendar</a> to learn more about what upcoming events we have.</i></p>

If you plan to change the typeface, color, or size of your text, you will need to use the **font tag**. This allows you to define one or more of these attributes for in-line or text-block editing. The code for this is as follows:

<p><font size="3">To learn more about our volunteering here at the museum, send us an email at museumvolunteers@gmail.com.</font></p>

Note that the code above will change the font to size 3, an attribute that will be discussed below.

If you want to change the color or font of the text, use the same formula, including all altered attributes in one tag:

<p><font size="3" color="red" face="Verdana">Check out our <a href="http:// www.freethemuseum.net/calendar">calendar</a> to learn more about what upcoming events we have.</font></p>

After deciding whether you will edit in-line or for a block of text, look at the options you have for altering the text using different typefaces, sizes, and colors.

Typeface

Your WYSIWYG editor will give you a range of typefaces[18] to choose from, but you may find that you want to emphasize certain text or specify the right font for text included in an HTML W-element. If such is the case, you should take time to define the three text attributes for this text to avoid having your visitor's web browser defaulting to an unusual typeface or color. When designating a typeface in this way, stick to what are known as "web-safe fonts." These are typefaces that essentially every computer has—meaning that your intended font will be displayed just as you want. The six most web-safe fonts include Arial, Courier, Courier New, Helvetica, Times, and Times New Roman.[19] The next safest, which both Macintosh and Windows support, are Arial Black, Avant Garde, Bookman, Comic Sans MS, Garamond, Georgia, Impact, Palatino, Trebuchet MS, and Verdana.[20] To define these, include the font element tag and include the name of the typeface (e.g., <font

Check out our calendar of events.

Check out our calendar of events.

Check out our calendar of events.

Check out our calendar of events.

Check out our calendar of events.

Check out our calendar of events.

Check out our calendar of events.

Figure 7.1   Font sizes one through seven

face="Verdana">Your text</font>). If you are not concerned about what specific font the visitor sees but know your page looks best with a serif (or sans-
serif) font, you can also use generic forms of the font typeface attribute to
define the style of the font. Using the same conventions, simply use "serif" or
"sans-serif" as though it were a typeface name (e.g., <font face="serif">Your
text</font>).

Size

There are seven font sizes you can designate using HTML, defined by the
numbers one through seven. The process is straightforward once you understand how the font attribute works. Most browsers default to a font size of
three, so unless you have good reason for using a much larger or smaller
font, keeping close to size three is a good idea. To use this attribute, use the
font element tag and insert the numeral for the size you want (e.g., <font
size="4">Your text</font>).

Color for Fonts and Backgrounds

If you want to define a specific color for your text, you will again use the font
element tag. You have two options for defining a color: using one of about
140 standard color names or using one of sixteen million Hex codes. The first
is simpler because there are significantly fewer options. To use it, just open
the font element tag and type the name of the color you want:

```
<font size="3" color="olivedrab" face="Verdana">Check out our <a
href="http://historicwebsites.weebly.com">calendar</a> to learn more about
what upcoming events we have.</font>
```

For a list of these names, see the Appendix D; for a list with accompanying samples of the color, visit freethemuseum.net/colors.

For the second option, you need some background in color history. When two computers talk to each other via a server, there are two main ways that they can convey information about color: RGB triplets or hexadecimals (often called hex triplets). Though the final display of a given color, whether in RGB or in hex, should be the same, it is worth knowing the difference between the two systems if you plan to pick out specific colors for your website. The RGB color model uses additive light; red, green, and blue light is added together to create all other colors. For each color, a triad of values is displayed (e.g., 0, 0, 102). A value of intensity between 0 and 255 is listed for its red, green, and blue components, and if an RGB color component is given a value of 0, it has no intensity in the resultant color (e.g., if the triad reads R: 0 G: 0 B: 102, the resultant color will be a dark blue with no red or green visible). This model is common in electronic devices like televisions and computers and has long been used in photography, theatre, and other endeavors. However, RGB is not always a reliable color model, as it is device-dependent—different devices display the individual red, green, and blue color values differently.

Hex triplets are ultimately just another way of expressing a color using red, green, and blue values. However, instead of using a single number to represent each red, green, and blue value, the hex system uses a pound sign followed by three couplet values, one for each color component (e.g., the same dark blue mentioned above would be value #000099: red represented by the first 00, green represented by the second 00, and blue represented by the 99). Where RGB color codes can be anywhere from three to nine digits long, hex codes are always seven digits, which makes them a more consistent system.

You may have heard the term web-safe colors in the past when discussing websites and web technology. Even up until five years ago, limited personal computer monitor display capabilities restricted web designers to 216 "web-safe" colors, so named because they would (theoretically) display consistently across all devices. The good news is that this term is no longer a concern for most computer users because most computers have at least a 24-bit display and most mobile devices have at least a 12-bit display—they can interpret and display thousands of color codes. This means that almost any color you pick for your website will display correctly (and consistently) on any device. If you are designing your website using an older computer (think at least six or more years) or know for certain that a large contingent of your viewers will be using such devices, you can consider using some of the calmer web-safe colors available, though keep in mind that they tend to be very bright and harder to incorporate into a modern color scheme.

To incorporate these colors as a font attribute, use the same method as above, but insert the hex code like so:

<font size="3" color="#FF0073" face="Verdana">Check out our calendar to learn more about what upcoming events we have.</font>

You can find an easy color selection tool at w3schools.com/tags/ref_color-picker.asp and a slightly more comprehensive one at paletton.com. By mousing over the color wheels, you can find the color you like, click on a color for its details, and copy the color's hex values. You will also often see suggestions for other colors that go well with the one you select. For a list of other useful color selection tools, see the color resources in Appendix A.

Embedding (Google Calendar, Google Maps, and YouTube)

Many web services, like Google Calendar, Google Maps, and YouTube give you the option of embedding content from their site into your own site. This is very useful if you have content you want available but do not have the capacity to create or host yourself. Each WYSIWYG editor has a different way of handling this embedded content, but most have preset methods for the most common ones.[21] If you need to embed content another way, use the editor's HTML W-element and find the embed code for the content you need. For Google Calendar, navigate to the selected calendar and open up the Calendar Settings menu.

Halfway down on the page is an "Embed This Calendar" option. In a box to the right of this you will see the embed code. Google gives you the option to customize the format and look of your calendar a bit, so take advantage of this to make the calendar suit your needs. Copy and paste this into the HTML W-element, and when you post the changes, you should see the calendar appear. *It is very important that your calendar settings are public if you are sharing the calendar with people outside your organization.* If you keep the calendar restricted to only you (the default), visitors will see an error message when they navigate to your calendar page. To change this setting, select the Share this Calendar menu and tick the box at the top of the page to "Make this calendar public."

To embed a Google Map that has, for instance, your location starred, navigate to maps.google.com. Search for your institution. Once you have found it, click the "Save" star in the upper left-hand corner. Zoom in or out to the desired height on the map. Click on the settings button, and select "Share or embed map."

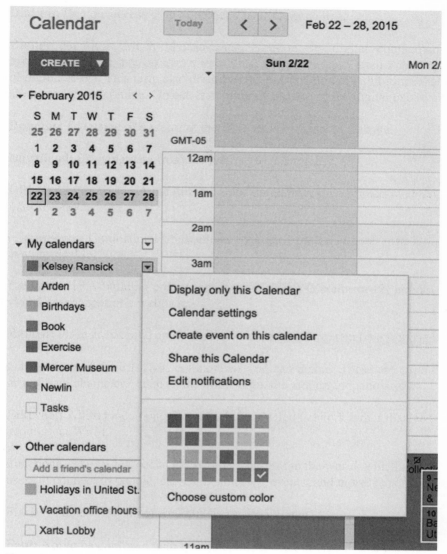

Figure 7.2

Select the size of the box you want your map to display in and then copy and paste the HTML code at the top of the menu into the editor's HTML W-element.

Vimeo and YouTube videos follow a similar process. For YouTube, once you have a video pulled up, click on the Share button just below the video

Figure 7.3   *Source*: Map data ©2015 Google

Figure 7.4

title. There, you will find the option to copy the embedding code, which you can then paste into the editor's HTML W-element. On Vimeo, the share button is a paper airplane icon on the right-hand side of the video.

SEO Header Code

When it comes to drafting your own header code for SEO purposes, keep in mind that most WYSIWYG editors have their own adjustable settings. Using the built-in W-elements for titles is the easiest way to optimize the page for search engines, but sometimes you need a little something more or your editor does not grant you access to the SEO settings you need. If this is the case, insert an HTML W-element on the top of the desired page. Review Chapter 2 to draft your SEO terms, then use an HTML W-element to insert the relevant information:

<head>

<title>Missoula Tapestry Museum - About Us</title>

<meta name="description" content="The Missoula Tapestry Museum explores and celebrates the art and history of tapestry weaving. Our collections include reproductions of the famous Unicorn Tapestries and portions of the Bayeux Tapestry. We feature family-friendly, hands-on education activities like tapestry weaving.">

<meta name="keywords" content="tapestry, Bayeux, Adoration, Magi, Lady, Unicorn, museum, art, history, medieval, education, elementary, programs">

</head>

Note that the keywords are separated by a comma and a space. You can eliminate the space to fit more characters in if needed. Remember that keywords appearing in your SEO data but not also on the page can actually hurt your exposure. Done correctly, this code will not appear to your visitors but will draw search engines to your page in their quest to return relevant search results. The most important pages to do this for are your Home or Visit Us pages, as these are most likely what your visitors are looking for at the beginning, followed by pages for major programs or exhibitions you have. The good news is that even if you do not write SEO code for every page on your website, you can rely on the WYSIWYG-built body of your text to carry a bit of the load. Because <h1> and <h2> tags garner the most attention, search engines should automatically pick up on any title W-elements your page uses.

NOTES

1. You can also use the one found at: http://bit.ly/IT8pAD. Consider bookmarking an HTML tester for easy access.

2. XSLT, or eXtensible Stylesheet Language, is another common way to interpret XML. You will not need to use it if you are creating your website on a WYSIWYG editor, but you can find more information about the language at www.w3schools.com/xsl/.

3. WYSIWYG platforms also use CSS extensively, though not all of them give users the option to edit it.

4. If you ever have trouble tracking down the opening and closing tag order, you can run it through validator.w3.org.

5. Note that if you are just editing text—not HTML—in your WYSIWYG editor, the editor may keep the two spaces. The truncation of extra spaces really only comes into play in HTML or CSS editing areas of the platform.

6. For the duration of this chapter, if the text refers to a *WYSIWYG element* (such as an image element, text element, or HTML element) it will be referred to as a *W-element* (e.g., image W-element, text W-element, or HTML W-element). In contrast, the bits of HTML code that make up the HTML document (header, body, footer) will simply be referred to as elements.

If you have read the beginning chapters of this book, you will already be familiar with the term "element" as a generic term picked by some editors to describe a
WYSIWYG element such as an image, text box, or box containing HTML code. In
the current chapter, this can be confusing, as that type of element is distinct from the
term universally used to describe HTML code that is indicated by tags. The terms are
certainly related—if you could see the full HTML code of your WYSIWYG site, you
would likely see the text box containing your address or the image of your museum
written as an HTML element using tag pairs and single tags. In fact, it is possible that
you will be inserting an HTML element *inside* a W-element; however, the terms are
not used synonymously.

7. As always, be careful when placing outside content on your site. Not only do
you have to check for copyright issues, but the content may also be taken down at any
time, leaving a gaping hole in your own site that you may not immediately notice. It
is always best to use files you actually possess and for which you have permission.

8. You will need to capture the URL of an image first. Search for an image on
google.com, and select an image to use for testing. Right-click on the image and
select "Copy image" or your browser's equivalent. Remember that using an image
that is not your own is generally not recommended because if the image is removed
by its host, *your* image will not display.

9. Session 4 in Weebly, Session 6 in Wix, Session 5 in WordPress, and Session 5
in Google Sites.

10. If you are separating two paragraphs from each other, remember to include
two line breaks (

) in the *code*: one to break the text, and one to insert a line
between paragraphs. It is useful to think of two different kinds of line breaks: coded
line breaks and line breaks created by a hard return. Merely hitting the return key
between the two paragraphs is insufficient because the computer reading the HTML
will not know that the line break is present without the *code* for a line break. It can be
helpful to include the hard returns in your code so that you, as the coder, can visually
keep track of your paragraphs while writing the code, but always double-check that
you have included the *coded* line breaks as well. The same goes for additional spaces
(beyond the first) between words.

11. This will help boost your SEO while also being useful to web readers.

12. To see how an image looks when it offends one of the cardinal rules of
image sizing, enter this code into your HTMl tester: <img src="http://i.imgur.
com/hNMYwY6.jpg" alt="View of museum from Millers Road" height="500"
width="150" />

13. Can also be found at www.unitconversion.org/typography/inchs-to-pixels-y-
conversion.html.

14. With the exception of the linked logo or header, avoid making too many of
your links through images. If the image does not load properly or your visitor is on a
device that cannot read it, your visitor may be unable to navigate to it.

15. Most of these sites, such as filehosting.org, filedropper.com, and tinyupload.
com, will not take your visitor directly to the document, but instead direct them to a
download page where the file can be clicked on. If you are comfortable directing your
visitors to an outside site, these are great ways to share large documents or documents

with a number of people all at once. If you would rather your visitors stay on your site, use Weebly's file W-element, Wix's document gallery, Google Sites' File Cabinet or file attachment, or WordPress' Media Add New screen. All but the first store files on your site for use anywhere on your site. Weebly's is a one-time use element (though you can upload the document multiple times if you need it in more than one place).

16. If your browser automatically downloads the document rather than opening its URL, try navigating to the document in Firefox or Chrome, both of which give you the option of opening documents before downloading them.

17. If the document needs to be editable, be aware that providing a Word document can lead to conversion issues between Macs and **Wintels**.

18. The terms typeface and font are often used interchangeably, but there is a difference. Typeface is the particular design of the type (e.g., Garamond), whereas font is a specific styling of a typeface (e.g., italicized Garamond in size 12).

19. Iggy Ko, "16 Gorgeous Web Safe Fonts To Use With CSS," Web Design Dev, accessed May 1, 2015, http://www.webdesigndev.com/web-development/16-gorgeous-web-safe-fonts-to-use-with-css.

20. Ibid.

21. See the individual WYSIWYG guides for more information.

Chapter 8

Showcasing Your Collection

Having a platform on which to display your institution's collections is one of the most common impetuses for creating a website. Posting images and metadata about your collection on your website offers an excellent way for visitors to engage with your institution. If you have access to a scanner or smartphone and a willingness to spend the time necessary to create quality images of your collections and archives, making your collection accessible on the web is quite feasible. *The first step is to decide how you want to make your collections available.* Think about the display format, level of detail, and number of items you want to include. Similar to the website-development process, identify your goals for online collections access. Do you want to post objects, archival material, or both? Do you plan to include metadata? Will you post your collections as a database or systematically post them as an Object of the Month blog?

The format you choose for your collection influences all steps of the process, so selecting the correct platform for your needs is important. The three formats suggested in this chapter are:

1. A blog
2. A photo-sharing platform, like Flickr or Photobucket
3. Omeka

You can, of course, use more than one platform; each one has its merits. *Blogs* are excellent if you want to feature individual items from your collection over a period of time. You can use categories to tag your featured items. Once you have a number of posts up, visitors can search through your featured pieces by subject, time period, artist, or other tags you set up. Depending on the WYSIWYG editor you select, you may have data limits for your blog or website, so this route is not ideal if you plan to upload lots of high-resolution object images. If you do plan to upload high-resolution images, consider using one of the other two platforms. *Image-hosting sites* are ideal for uploading a large number of high-resolution images and images that you want a large audience to have access to. You can upload images to an image-sharing account, where visitors can search by keyword or browse by user. Many platforms make it easy to upload images as part of the Creative Commons[1] if you have material you want to allow others to download and share (though it is equally easy to mark images as copyrighted). The platform best suited to hosting archival collections is *Omeka.net*,[2] which is a platform built specifically for museums, libraries, and archives to display collections and build digital exhibitions. You can create a database of your collections, including scans, photographs, oral history audio files, and videos. As you can construct "simple pages," institutions occasionally choose to use their Omeka site as their main website. This is not generally recommended if you are using the free package, as you do not have the same flexibility as with online WYSIWYG editors and therefore cannot customize its look and contents much without HTML coding.

Once you know which platform you will be using, you need to gather your materials, including creating quality images and any metadata you wish to use. Depending on your purpose, this may take a significant amount of time. Whereas blogs and image hosting can be edited gradually, as when writing a series of Object of the Month posts, Omeka represents a more substantial time investment to allow for adherence to Dublin Core standards, to adjust the appearance of your Omeka site, and to arrange your items in collections or exhibits. As part of this process, consider purchasing a large external hard drive—at least 1 terabyte if possible—to store all of your new images on.

PREPARING IMAGES

To digitize your object and archival collections, you can photograph or scan them. The three image file details you need to determine are file type, resolution, and dimensions—all of which influence the final file size. The file type (e.g., JPEG, TIFF, or PNG), resolution, and dimensions you need depend on a number of factors, primarily how you plan to store your images. Most basic digital cameras automatically save images as JPEGs and have default resolutions and dimensions that can be adjusted under the camera settings. Once you have the image transferred to your computer, you can adjust the resolution and dimensions downward if necessary. Scanning settings must be inputted before you begin the scan and are based on what you want from your final product. Remember: a flatbed scanner is a must for any fragile archival materials—never run historic paper through a sheet feeder. Most computers and scanners come with built-in software programs for scanning images; check your institution's computer to find the program you need. Though not all scanning software programs have completely customizable options, you should be able to select the three file details mentioned here. *As a rule, initially save both photographed and scanned images as large, detailed JPEGs or TIFFs, knowing that you can resave images later with a lower resolution and smaller dimensions—you cannot go the other direction and make small images larger without sacrificing image quality.*

The information in the following section will help you decide what scanner and save settings to select, based on your answer to two questions:

1. How much data storage space do we have for our online collections? *This limit is set by the account plan of your WYSIWYG editor, image-hosting site, or Omeka.*
2. Do we want visitors to be able to access and save images for their own use? *If your collections policy has a fee schedule that includes reproduction fees, for example, you may want to have informative images online but require researchers to contact and pay you for more detailed study images.*

If you know that the account on your chosen platform has unlimited storage space, the file size of your images is not as important (though keep in mind that larger images may increase page loading time). However, basic plans on WYSIWYG editors, image-hosting sites, and Omeka typically have data limits of 100–500 MB. Wix, for example, allows users 500 MB of storage with the free package, WordPress offers 3 GB, and Google Sites 100 MB. Weebly gives all users unlimited data space. These data limits include all the data on your site, not just images, but pictures and videos can quickly take up much more space than text. Also speak with colleagues, legal counsel, or other people who are knowledgeable about your collections policy to determine how accessible you want your images to be. Before you begin posting, be clear whether the images you are creating will be available for use by visitors or if they will be clearly viewable but with a watermark, low resolution, or other features that would deter visitors from downloading and using the images.[3] If the former, your only image file size restrictions are from your account platform. If the latter, keep images smaller and with lower resolution. Throughout the sections below, keep your target file size and usage in mind.

Selecting the File Type

The three most common image file types used in collections management are JPEGs, TIFFs, and PNGs. Each file format compresses data in a different way, making the final products suited for different purposes.[4] JPEGs typically achieve the smallest file size while preserving image quality, making them good for detailed images that researchers can zoom in on. However, a JPEG may deteriorate over time if you repeatedly edit and save the same image file. This is due to the fact that every time a JPEG is saved, it discards small bits of information in order to meet the compression requirements.[5] In contrast, TIFFs are commonly referred to as "lossless" image files because they are not compressed much, if at all, when saved.[6] This results in rather large image files. PNGs are also predominantly lossless image files, though they do undergo some compression when saved.[7] If you have low data limits, saving images as JPEGs can maintain your image quality while minimizing your data usage.

Selecting Resolution

Recall from Chapter 2 that both DPI and PPI are used to describe image resolution. Because the images you create in this chapter are intended for use on the web, the term PPI is employed, though your camera, scanning program, or image editing software may use either of these designations to describe resolution. Whereas for general website usage, 72 PPI is sufficient, images that are used as part of a collections database may need a higher PPI. If you want visitors to be able to zoom in and see details clearly, a PPI of 300 is adequate. A PPI of 600 is reserved for especially intricate images, as this will make the file size much larger. Alternatively, if you are concerned about copyright of your collections, use 72 PPI. This will still allow visitors to browse your collection, but they will need to contact you if their research requires a more detailed view of your items. They may be able to zoom in a little, but the image will be pixelated if they get too close. PPI alone will not make an image sharp or fuzzy; what determines that is the interaction of PPI to dimensions, given in terms of pixels or inches.

Selecting Dimensions

Images with small dimensions and low resolution will not remain clear when zoomed in on. On the other hand, images with large dimensions may take longer to load for visitors with slow internet connections. To choose the optimal dimensions for your images, consider how closely your visitors will want to zoom in. Recall from Chapter 2 that you want to keep image dimensions small enough that visitors can see the whole image on the screen without scrolling (at least at first). However, many platforms allow for an image to be displayed in a smaller format and then expand after being clicked on.

When photographing an image, your dimensions and resolution are generally preset. When scanning an image, plan for the expanded size and use larger dimensions as necessary. In a WYSIWYG editor, image size can be adjusted within the image element. Omeka, Photobucket, and other image-hosting sites display images in one size while browsing and then expand images after they are clicked on. When you first create your image, start large, *with dimensions at least 100 percent the physical size of the item,* and define your image dimensions in terms of inches. For example, if you are scanning a post card that is 4″ × 5″ your scanned image dimensions should be *at least* 4″ × 5″ with a PPI of 300. Better yet, scan at 200 percent (i.e., 8″ × 10″) with a PPI of 300 to make sure that you can zoom in to see detail.

Adjusting the Image

Once you have a digital version of your image, be it of an object or archival material, you can edit it in an image-editing program like Adobe Photoshop or GIMP.[8] When you make changes to an image, save the new version as a different file. Always keep the original scan or photograph so that if something goes wrong with the adjustment, the quality of the original is not lost. Remember to save your images with clear, descriptive titles. If you wish to change the file type, open the image in an image-editing program and re-save it with the new file type—never change the file type by changing the file name on the desktop. Within the program, you can also adjust brightness and contrast.

Most scanning programs and image-editing programs allow you to edit the image later and define dimensions in terms of pixels or inches, whichever best fits your needs and knowledge. When you adjust the dimensions by changing the pixels, you are adjusting the size of the pixels themselves. For example, if you make the pixels smaller but the PPI remains the same, the dimensions of the image will decrease. When you adjust the dimensions using inches, you are changing the width and height of the overall image but the PPI may remain the same. Within the image resizing menu, you will see the option to "resample" the image. If the resample option is on, the PPI will remain the same. This means that if you decrease the width of an image while the resample option is on, the PPI will remain the same but the total pixels in the image will decrease because you are "deleting" inches from the width and height, and with them, the pixels that they contained. If the resample option is off, the total number of pixels will remain the same but because the dimensions are different, the resolution will change (i.e., decreasing the size of your image and turning off resampling will make the image finer but smaller).

SHOWCASING COLLECTIONS IN BLOGS

Blogs are a simple place to start if you know you want to get parts of your collection online but lack the time or permission to upload large quantities of data and images. All of the WYSIWYG editors included in this book have blog components, as discussed in Chapters 3–6. To adapt these to incorporate collections items, upload and describe items as per the instructions in the previous chapters, then adjust the blog categories to incorporate useful search terms. For example, perhaps you plan to upload a small photograph of Lenore Hall, a famous tapestry weaver in San Francisco in the 1920s. You have already scanned the image at 300 PPI with 200 percent dimensions and saved it as a JPEG in your website folder. Then, you uploaded it into a blog post and wrote a brief story about Hall's life. This is one of five blog posts you have written about tapestry weavers in San Francisco, and you want your visitors to be able to search through the posts to find material relevant to their interests. Therefore, you add the following categories to your blog post on Hall: Lenore Hall, tapestry weavers, San Francisco, twentieth century, women weavers, and photographs. This means that a visitor can enter your blog and click on the category "Lenore Hall" to see a list of blog posts (or items) that are about Hall. A visitor can also click on the category "twentieth century" to see all your posts about objects or people from the twentieth century. Alternatively, a visitor can click on the category "photographs" to see all your posts that are about photographic items. *These categories are not automatically assigned.* Visitors can peruse your posts, but you must sort posts into categories if you want them to be easily searched by subject matter.

SHOWCASING COLLECTIONS ON IMAGE-SHARING SITES

Using image-sharing sites to make your collection available to the public offers a few advantages over the traditional blog post. Because sites like Photobucket[9] and Flickr[10] were originally built as platforms for photographers to share their images, their setup and target audiences are different than those of conventional websites. Two of the most likely concerns for museums and historic sites using these sites are data storage limits and copyright issues. Knowing that most of their users will have substantial amounts of high-quality images (read: large files), these sites often come with lots of data storage space for each account, even at the free level. Photobucket users, for example get up to 10 GB of data storage. As a colorful 300 PPI photo that is scanned at 200 percent (making the dimensions 10″ × 14″) and saved as a JPEG should take up 4–7 MB of space, depending on the color and compression quality. This means that with a free account, you can upload as many as 1,500 large, high-resolution images, if not more. The larger file format TIFF is not accepted by Photobucket. You also have the option to purchase up to 500 GB of data storage. Fickr users get 1 TB of data, even with a free account, which means that the average user will never run out of space on Flickr. Flickr does not accept TIFF either, so any images uploaded with that format will automatically be converted to JPEGs.

Copyright issues are a common concern among users of image-sharing sites, but most concerns can be assuaged by deciding at the beginning how "shareable" you want your collections to be. If you have made your images viewable but small or with low resolution, your images are less likely to be lifted from the site. Feel free to make them large or with a high resolution if you are not concerned about the availability of your images and you want members of the public to be able to share your images. If you have collections that are protected by copyright, most image-sharing sites have settings to allow you to denote copyrighted materials as such, though whether visitors will respect that copyright is largely out of your control. Photobucket notes in its terms of use that members are responsible for their uploaded content. When you post an image to the site, you state that you own the image and have the right to reproduce it (unless it is no longer subject to copyright by anyone). Any images you upload remain your property; Photobucket merely has a license to display the content. Visitors interested in obtaining the images may contact you to ask for permission to reproduce copyrighted material.

Flickr handles copyright similarly, but also has an agreement with Creative Commons, a nonprofit organization that helps individuals and institutions share their materials within an established set of copyright dictates. The Creative Commons website states that

> our free, easy-to-use copyright licenses provide a simple, standardized way to give the public permission to share and use your creative work—on conditions of your choice. CC licenses let you easily change your copyright terms from the default of "all rights reserved" to "some rights reserved." Creative Commons licenses are not an alternative to copyright. They work alongside copyright and enable you to modify your copyright terms to best suit your needs.[11]

If you have materials you want to protect on Flickr, you can use Creative Commons conventions to indicate the level of protection on each image. When you add an image to your Flickr account, you can set the level of copyright. Visitors will see copyright data displayed on the right underneath each image. Visit creativecommons.org and flickr.com/help/guidelines to learn more.

The minor downside to using image-sharing sites is that visitors will need direction to find your collections, most likely in the form of a link on your website. They will be navigated away from your website to one of these platforms, which essentially function as online external hard drives. Image-sharing sites are useful if you plan to host your images online and link to them on your website, but visitors are less likely to stumble across them while browsing the internet. This means that it is unlikely visitors will "discover" your collections merely by browsing Photobucket or Flickr; more commonly, you will need to send them there directly from your website. At the same time, having your collections images publicly displayed on one of these sites makes them available to a broader audience. Flickr users might come across your images in one of their searches, notice that it was posted by a museum, and then search for more information about your institution.

As you upload images to these platforms, you will see fields for describing the image, including tagging map locations and adding keywords or tags. Take advantage of these fields so that browsers and visitors alike can understand more about what they are looking at. Always make it clear what institution the image is associated with and include a link back to your website in the description and account profile. Including a wealth of tags or keywords increases the chance that casually browsing visitors will find their way to your images through related material. Notice also that you can embed your images on other sites and in emails. If you know you have an image with a particularly large file size and you are concerned about it taking up room in your WYSIWYG account, post it to one of these sites and embed or link the image to your website proper using an HTML element. Consider using Google+ or Dropbox for the same purpose, especially if you want to keep the images away from the public eye when they are not on your website.

If you want to host images on these sites and then embed them in your own website, you will need to capture the embed code. On Photobucket, the code is found by clicking on the desired image in admin view and copying the code listed in the HTML box in the right-hand side Share Links menu. Embed codes for Flickr images are found by clicking on the share button (a white arrow in the bottom right corner of the photo) and copying the code provided when Embed is selected.

SHOWCASING COLLECTIONS WITH OMEKA.NET

As an open-source collections-sharing platform designed specifically for museums, libraries, and archives, Omeka stands out as a superior way to upload information about your collection. Omeka hosts images, videos, oral histories, and metadata from cultural institutions across the country. Users can even create online exhibits and organize their items into virtual collections. Omeka describes itself as "fall[ing] at a crossroads of Web Content Management, Collections Management, and Archival Digital Collections System."[12] It combines the web content management style of WordPress and Wix with the collections management capabilities of PastPerfect and Pachyderm and the digital collections systems of CONTENTdm and Fedora. Much like the online WYSIWYG editors discussed in this book, Omeka was created specifically for non-IT specialists with the purpose of "allowing users to focus on content and interpretation rather than programming."[13] Its built-in templates give users the freedom to spend time creating quality content and be secure in the knowledge that such content will be displayed a clean and professional manner. Best of all, Omeka is standards-based, employing Dublin Core and Library of Congress authorities.

On its website, Omeka suggests that museums use its services to launch online exhibits, share collections that are otherwise inaccessible to the larger public, and allow visitors to mark favorite objects and contribute their own stories and content. Libraries might also use Omeka to build online exhibits or publish content that complements online catalogues. Like museums, archives can share their diverse collections, which might include documents, oral histories, photographs, and visitor-generated materials. Omeka is open to all these users, and the ways to use the platform are constantly expanding. The platform also offers "Use Cases" on its website, so you can see examples of other institutions' Omeka sites and walk through the steps of creating a similar site.[14]

There are two versions of Omeka: Omeka.org, a downloadable software program for users with their own servers, and Omeka.net, for an all-online administrative experience. With the former, you can download the open-source software and configure the online database and exhibits as much as you like, though this requires some coding and web development knowledge. Data limits are set only by your own server and FTP client. The latter operations on a freemium principle, and users with very little web development experience can upload content and curate exhibits. This chapter focuses on using Omeka.net, the online system for institutions with no server of their own. It is organized around five key sessions that will guide you through the process of setting up an Omeka.net account and get started posting your content. Except for Session 1, all sessions start from the Account Dashboard.

- Session 1
  - Create an account
  - Choose and set up a theme
  - Install plugins (free extra features)

- Session 2
  - Create a collection
  - Create an item, including adding tags
- Session 3
  - Add a simple page
  - Embed multimedia
- Session 4
  - Add users
  - Adjust search options
  - Add Google Analytics
- Session 5
  - Create an exhibit

SESSION 1

Create an Account

To get started, navigate to the Omeka.net home page and click the Sign Up button. You will immediately be presented with a number of different packages to choose from, with the free Basic plan at the bottom. The free plan offers 500 MB of storage (enough for 125 JPEG images at 300 PPI and 10" x 14"), which is a good starting place if you are not yet sure how many collection items you will be posting. After you fill in your information for whatever plan you choose, you will receive an activation link in your email inbox.[15] Once you activate your account through this link, you will be taken to your Dashboard. From here, you can click on My Account to see your data usage and other account features, or click on Add a Site to get started constructing your online database. When you are ready to add a site, fill in your new site information. The subdomain you choose should bear a clear relation to your institution or, if you are using Omeka for a specific collection within your institution, the collection name (e.g., missoulatapestrymuseum.omeka.net or chriscarlislecollection.omeka.net). Include the site title and a brief description too, as these will count toward your SEO points. After saving, you will be taken back to your Dashboard and your new site will appear.

Click on Manage Site to start building your browsable database. You will now see your Site Dashboard, from where you can add plugins, change the site's appearance, invite collaborators, adjust settings, and manage your collections items. A summary of your items, collections, tags, plugins, and site settings appears in the center (at this stage they should be at 0).

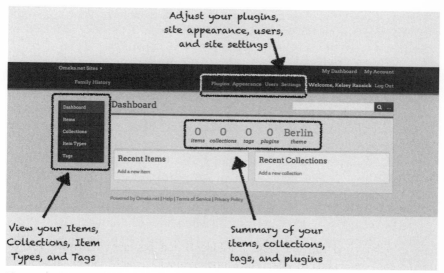

Figure 8.1

Choose and Set Up a Theme

From your Site Dashboard (the page you come to after you click "Manage Site" on the Account Dashboard), click on the default theme name, usually Berlin, Rhythm, Seasons, or Minimalist. The next page is the Appearance Menu. Here, you can see the four (or more) themes available for your account package, alongside a small preview of what they will look like. Generally, you cannot adjust colors or layouts much, as the real focus of these sites is the collections content. By clicking "Configure Theme," you can adjust the home page content, header image, and footer text. If you have an institutional logo, upload it in the Logo File section, keeping in mind that your logo will display at the dimensions listed in the file (e.g., if your logo file has dimensions of 300 pixels by 500 pixels, Omeka will not reduce those dimensions to fit in your site). If your logo is too large, you will need to resave the logo with smaller dimensions by using Photoshop, GIMP, or another image-editing program.

Though you will not need to alter all fields in your Omeka site settings, general information for the rest of the settings in the Themes tab of the Appearance Menu is as follows:

- Footer Text: The footer text will appear on every page of your Omeka site, so this is an ideal location to list your website, address, email, and hours. Do not add your copyright information into this box, as this can be more easily done in the setting just below.

- Display Copyright: This is where you can elect to have your copyright information automatically included in the footer. This will be added in Session 4 when you adjust the account's general settings.
- Use Advanced Site-wide Search: Unless you have a compelling reason not to, allow your visitors to search using Advanced Site-wide search.
- Display Featured Item/Collection/Exhibit: If you want to have a featured item, collection, or exhibit on your site's home page (generally the most recent addition, though you can select a specific item, collection, or exhibit too) check the corresponding boxes.
- Homepage Recent Items: The number you put in here determines how many of your recent item additions are displayed on your home page (up to ninety-nine).
- Homepage Text: This is a great place to mirror your website's About Us page by including your mission statement, a brief institutional history, and a link to your website. To make a word or phrase into a link, highlight the appropriate text and click the link button in the toolbar on the top of the box. A new box will open, and you can paste the URL of your website, and set the link to open in the same window or in a new window.

Save your changes, then click on the Navigation tab in the Appearance Menu.

The Navigation tab comes with two automatic pages in your Omeka site menu (the site that visitors will see): Browse Items and Browse Collections. The menu items appear as tabs near the top of the page, and visitors who click on them can search through your online database by individual items or by collections. In admin view, you can rename menu items, rearrange the order of menu items, and remove or add more menu items. To rename a menu item, click the arrow to the right of the page title (e.g., Browse Items). To rearrange the menu order, drag a menu item up or down in the list, as you do with pages if you use Weebly, Wix, or WordPress. If you want to remove a default page from the menu, simply uncheck the box next to the menu item. To delete menu items you added but no longer want (aside

O meka Tip #1: Audio files uploaded as items in your database will automatically be downloaded when a visitor clicks on the item's Show Page (the page that presents all the metadata for a specific item).

Figure 8.2

from the default menu items) just click the X to the right of the page title. Including external links (e.g., to your website), you can add almost any item or page to your site menu. For example, if you have a collection that is very popular or large, you may want to include a link to it in your menu for easy access. Type the page title in the Label box. In a new window or tab, navigate to your Omeka site (the visitor view) and from there to the specific page you want to include. Copy the portion of the URL that follows your Omeka site home page (e.g., copy "items/show/3" from the URL "http://missoulatapestrymuseum.omeka.net/items/show/3") and return to the window with the Navigation tab open. Paste the URL into the URL box. To add an external link, copy the full URL of the link and paste it into the URL box.

The Settings tab in the Appearance Menu is the place to set image sizes and other display settings for your entire Omeka site. The full size and thumbnail sizes for all your images (except the logo) can be constrained here in terms of pixels. If you need to test how large the limits you set are, input test values and then add a few visual items to your database (see Session 2). Set the maximum sizes, save the changes, and navigate to the items' pages to see how the dimensions appear on your device.[16] If you are unsure what pixels are most appropriate, leave the defaults of 600 px for full-size images, 300 px for thumbnails, and 200 px for square thumbnails. Whatever you choose, these settings will only affect *new* uploads, they will not retroactively resize previously uploaded materials. As such, it is good to pick a standard for these dimensions before you upload a lot of material.

The admin and public Results Per Page settings adjust how many items a viewer can see at a time. The default of ten is by-and-large a good setting because it will not force viewers to click to see every result, nor will it overwhelm them with too much information at once. Similarly, you can check or uncheck the Show Empty Elements box based on whether you want viewers to see all fields describing an item or collection even if the fields are empty. Remember to save your changes.

Install Plugins

Plugins are free extra features you can add to your database. The free Omeka. net comes with thirteen optional plugins, including Coins (to make your metadata readable by Zotero), CSV Import (so you can upload a CSV file of your items instead of entering them individually), Docs Viewer and PDF Embed (which enable you to embed various documents), Exhibit Builder, GoogleAnalytics, and Simple Pages (used to create web pages that act as landing pages, as opposed to item or collections pages). For each plugin, you have the ability to:

- Install (initially activates the plugin)
- Uninstall (deletes the plugin, along with any information associated with that plugin; this may delete data on your site or in your items records that are dependent on the plugin)
- Deactivate (makes the plugin components inaccessible to visitors but retains the data associated with the plugin in case you decide to reactivate it later)
- Activate (reactivates the plugin if you deactivated it earlier)

Take this opportunity to install any plugins you want to use or to see the capabilities of plugins you are interested in. Remember that you can uninstall, deactivate, or activate these plugins later if needed. Some installed plugins, such as Simple Page, create a tab for that plugin that appears in your Database Editing Menu. Others can be edited using the blue Configure button that appears next to the plugin name in the Plugin menu. Using activated plugins is covered in various sessions throughout this chapter, though not all plugins are discussed.[17] You can enable or disable these plugins at any time by clicking on the Plugins option in the Admin Menu.

SESSION 2

Create a Collection

Not all of your database items have to be sorted into a collection. However, if you know you will be adding groups of material that go together thematically or because of who their donor was, consider creating collections, even if they are informal (e.g., Sports Memorabilia Collection or the Jean Ransick Collection). From your Account Dashboard, click on Manage Site to see your Site Dashboard. Click on the Collections bar in the Database Editing Menu and then on Add a Collection. This brings up the Dublin Core metadata page. If you are adding an archival collection, you may already have all this information collected in a finding aid. If you do not have a finding aid for this collection, you should determine the data for these fields (called elements) before making the collection visible to the public. Each element comes with a brief explanation of what its contents should be, but for a more detailed description of what each of these fields should encompass, visit omeka.org/codex/Working_with_Dublin_Core for Omeka-specific advice or dublincore.org/documents/dces for more universal Dublin Core information.

Once you have the information prepared, look over the metadata page. The Add Input button below each element title will add an additional field of that category in case you need more room or have two data sets for a given field. The Use HTML box underneath each field converts the box into an HTML field so you can include links, adjust the text alignment or style (e.g., bold or italic), and add bullet points or numbering. If you do not need to use the HTML option, Omeka will fit your text into an agreeable preset style. Finally, the Public and Featured options will, respectively, make your new collection visible to the public and place your new collection in the Featured Collection section on your site home page. Until you make your collection public, it will only be visible in the admin view. If you plan to have multiple collections that you want to feature, you can switch them in and out by editing them later.

Once you have added pertinent information, click Add Collection to save your work. If you need to edit the collection metadata or settings at any point after this, click on the Collections bar in the Database Editing Menu. You will see a list of your collections, along with a summary of contents. You can click directly on the Edit option underneath a collection, or you can click on the collection name to see its detailed metadata and specific item list and to see options to edit it, delete it, or view its public form. When you choose to edit it, you should see the Dublin Core metadata entry page you used to create it, along with the options to make it public or featured. Remember to save any changes you make.

Create an Item

Whether you add individual items to specific collections in your database or you keep them as standalone pieces, the process for adding items is the same. Before adding items, click on the Item Types bar in your database editing menu. Omeka has sixteen built-in item types, along with a description of what items fall into them. Once you have added items to your database, the far column will tally up how many of each item type your site has. Click on any item type title to see what elements (what metadata fields) of information you can capture for that item. Though the built-in list is fairly comprehensive, if you do not see an item type you plan to use, you can add an item type along with its own description and unique elements.

Once you are ready to add an item, click on the Items bar in the Database Editing Menu. When you click on Add an Item, you will be taken to a Dublin Core metadata screen. As with the collections metadata page, you will see a list of elements and options for entering data using HTML, creating additional fields for a given element, making items public or featured, and sorting the item into a collection. If the item will stand alone, do not select a collection in the collections drop-down menu below the Add Item button. This page is generic for all items, regardless of item type, so the elements listed here are not specific to the item type—those elements will be edited next. Once you

O meka Tip #2: When you are logged into Omeka, your default view is the admin view (you are behind the scenes of your site). If at any point you want to see your Omeka site as visitors will see it, click on the site title found at the top of your Omeka admin window or type in the URL of your Omeka site (e.g. missoulatapestrymuseum.omeka.net).

Figure 8.3

have completed the fields on this page and adjusted the visibility of the item, click on the Item Type Metadata tab near the top of the page.

On the Item Type Metadata page, select the appropriate item type[18] and look for item type-specific elements to appear. Some item types will only have one or two elements specifically for them, while others may have seven or eight. Some do not have any additional elements. Omeka's Dublin Core standards note that for physical objects, "digital representations of, or surrogates for, these objects should use Moving Image, Still Image, Text or one of the other types."[19] Complete these element fields, using omeka. org/codex/Working_with_Dublin_Core if you need more information on an element. After you complete the elements, click on the Files tab near the top of the page. If you have images, audio files, video footage, or other files to upload for this item, add them here. You can add multiple files for each item if necessary. Once you have added all files for the item, move on to adding tags.

Create an Item: Add Tags

Tags are used to make items more easily found when a visitor wants to search your collections by subject, geographical area, or people. These labels function the same way categories do on blogs. They are nonhierarchical terms you apply to your content so that a person searching your database can click on one of the tags and immediately see all items in your database with that same tag. For example, a person browsing your site for information on women's suffrage movements in Colorado might find on your site a letter from the governor of Colorado in the 1920s. He can click on the tag "women's suffrage" next to that item and see your other letter written by a local resident at the time of the suffrage movement, view your interview with the daughter of a famous Colorado suffragette, and look over a series of photographs from voting rallies in Denver. Each item has an unlimited number of tags, so especially long items or those with broad scopes can be tagged with as many applicable subjects as you need.

To add a tag, type the chosen term into the tag field, separating each *term* with a comma. Most tags should be no more than two words long. Keep a running list of your tags handy, as tags only work if they are entered exactly the same way every time (e.g., if you enter the tag "Colorado" once and the term "CO" once, they will not cross-reference). Names should be written "First Last" rather than "Last, First" because the comma will trigger two separate tags. You can always return and add more tags as you add additional related items to your site. Once you are satisfied with your tags, click Add Item.

In admin view, you can look at a list of your tags and edit them by clicking on the Tags bar in the Database Editing Menu. Here, you will see a list of all your tags to date, including a note of how many items are associated with that tag (indicated by the number just to the left of the tag name in the green tag box). If you click on the tag name in the green tag box, you can change the text there, and all items with that tag will be updated to reflect the new name. You can also delete unnecessary tags by clicking the X to the right of the tag name in the green tag box. Once you have a healthy list of tags, you can sort through them by the most- and least-used, see them in alphabetical order, or look at your most recently used tags. *This section is not for adding tags*; tags will only appear in this list if you have already created them by associating them with items in your database.

SESSION 3

Add a Simple Page

The Simple Pages plugin is used to create a web page or pages with content that is not necessarily associated with a specific item or collection. For example, you might want a landing page for your information about your institution. Because an "About Us" page is not an item or collection, you might need the Simple Pages plugin to add a few paragraphs about your museum and staff, along with images of your gallery. Some institutions, especially those that are collaborative between multiple museums or are without a physical site, use the Simple Pages plugin to create enough web pages that they do not need a separate website. However, this does not allow for the flexibility and full capabilities of WYSIWYG editors like Weebly and Wix, so most users will want to use Omeka as a supplement to their full website.

From your Account Dashboard, click on Manage Site. To add a Simple Page to your site, you will need to have the Simple Page plugin installed on your site—a process discussed in Session 1. Once added, click on the Simple Page bar in the Database Editing Menu. When you add the plugin, a single

Simple Page called "About" is automatically added. You can add additional Simple Pages by clicking Add a Page or edit existing pages by clicking Edit below the page title. The title is the name of the page as it will appear at the top of the page and in the tab menu on your Omeka site. The slug is the ending part of the URL for that page (e.g., in the URL "http://missoulatap-estrymuseum.omeka.net/about" the slug is "about" after the backslash). You can create your own slug, which should be related to or the same as the page title, or let Omeka automatically generate one for you (it will be based on the page title).

The HTML editor option will show an editing toolbar you can use to stylize text in a specific way or to write parts of your page using code. For example, you can add bolded text, adjust the alignment of text, create bulleted lists, add images and links, insert lines to break up the page, or embed HTML code. If you do not select the HTML editor option, all your text will appear in a simple stylized format determined by the Omeka theme you selected. For more information on adjusting HTML code for your own purposes, see Chapter 7. To adjust the HTML code of the page, click on the small HTML icon in the editing toolbar. The HTML editor accepts what Omeka calls short-codes. These allow you to quickly add information from your Omeka site, such as a list of your featured items, to your Simple Page. For a complete list of built-in shortcodes available for use, visit omeka.org/codex/Shortcodes. These shortcodes act much like mail merge fields; they are entered on your Simple Page in the exact location you want the information and are automatically filled in on the public view of your site using the appropriate content from your database.

Once you have added content to the fields on your Simple Page, you can adjust the settings on your new page. On the right side of the editing page, you will see the option to make your page public (visible to everyone once you are ready to share it) and a Parent Page drop-down menu. If you only have one Simple Page, its parent is the site's home page. However, if you add additional Simple Pages, these will be added to the list so you can create subpages if needed. Having more than one subpage will require you to apply an order to the pages. For example, if you want a landing page introducing the twentieth-century tapestries in your collection and three subpages discussing the weaving techniques, famous tapestries of that time period, and a list of events at your museum over the next year that explore tapestries in your collection, you will create four Simple Pages. The Weaving Techniques, Famous Tapestries, and Tapestry Events pages will all be designated as subpages of the parent Twentieth-Century Tapestries page. As you add the subpages, add an order number to each of them (1 will be the top subpage, 2 the middle subpage, and 3 the bottom subpage). Visitors will then see the pages appear as a submenu when they roll over the top menu item.

Embed Multimedia

Depending on the media you plan to embed, you may need to install a plugin. For example, the PDF Viewer plugin eliminates the need for visitors to click on download links to view any PDFs you upload to your database as part of an item. The plugin automatically renders the PDF document visible to viewers directly on the page. Once you install the PDF Viewer plugin, you can adjust the height of the PDF viewer (the default of 500 pixels is a good place to start), but you do not have to do anything more for it to run.

To embed audio or video, you will need to generate an embed code and paste it on the page where you want the item to appear. This requires that your embedded content is hosted elsewhere (such as on YouTube or Photobucket) and is therefore useful if you do not want to max out your data limits on Omeka. Capturing an embed code depends on the resource you are embedding. For Google Calendar, Google Maps, and YouTube videos, visit Chapters 3–7. Embedding procedures for images and audio files hosted elsewhere vary with each platform, but the code can generally be found in the Share menu or section of any image-hosting site. For example, to find the embed code for a Google Docs document, open the document up and find the code under File (not the browser File menu, but the Google Docs file menu) → Publish to the web → Embed. Click the Publish button and copy the code that appears.

It is possible to insert embedded content as part of an item by clicking Use HTML underneath an existing element, clicking the HTML icon in that menu, and then pasting the embed code in the editing box. However, your embedded content will generally fit much better on a Simple Page. To add embedded content to a Simple Page, create or navigate to the Simple Page you want to edit through the Simple Page bar in your Database Editing Menu.[20] Check the Use the HTML Editor box above the Text field and then click the HTML icon to bring up the HTML box. Paste the embed code in the appropriate location, using Chapter 7 if you are unfamiliar with basic coding techniques. Click update, and notice that a large yellow box appears in the text field where your code will appear. Save the changes to your page and then visit it from the Public view to make sure that the content embedded correctly.

SESSION 4

Add Users

If you have multiple employees or volunteers who will be adding content to the site, or if you plan to let community members contribute content (as part of a community exhibit, for example), you can add and manage users. Click on Manage Site in your Account Dashboard, then on Users in the Admin

Menu. To invite a new user, type the user's email address into the email field
and select the appropriate Role.

- Super users are:
  - Able to access all pages via the admin view.
  - Allowed to choose and configure themes.
  - Permitted to add and edit users.
  - The only type of user with ability to change site settings.
- Admin users are:
  - Able to access and edit Items, Collections, and Tags.
- Contributor users are:
  - Able to add and edit items, but only those that they have created.
  - Allowed to create exhibits using any item in the archive.
  - Permitted to view public exhibits from the administrative side.
- Researcher users are:
  - Able to see both public and private Items, Collections, and Item Types
    pages.
  - Not allowed to edit any content.

The user type can be changed later by those with Super privileges. Users will
not be added to the list until they accept their invitation via an email sent to
the listed address.

Adjust Search Options

To adjust the search options available to your visitors, click on Settings in
the Admin Menu at the top of your Omeka page. Click on the Search tab and
check the boxes next to each record type you want to be searchable. In general, the more record types that are available to be searched, the easier it
will be for your visitors to find the information they want. Always save your
changes after updating the search settings.

Visitors can then search your collections using one of three methods: keyword, boolean, or exact match. Searching via keyword is similar to using
a search engine like Bing or Google. The visitor types in a word or phrase
related to her research needs and the records the search returns are prioritized
by relevance to the entered keyword. For example, a keyword search for the
phrase "Molly Brown" will first return records that include both words, then
list records that include only "Molly" or only "Brown." A boolean search is
useful for more specific search parameters. For example, a visitor looking for
information on women's suffrage movements across the United States can
use the boolean search for "Englewood-Colorado" to return letter regarding
a suffrage rally in Englewood, New Jersey, but will not list the video footage

of a similar rally in Englewood, Colorado because of the preceding minus sign. The exact match search will return records that match the exact order of the word or phrase as it is typed (ignoring upper- or lowercase). An exact match search for "New Jersey Englewood" would return nothing in the example above, but a search for "Englewood, New Jersey" would return the video. If you anticipate your visitors being unfamiliar with these search techniques, consider alerting them to the search options by including the information found at omeka.org/codex/Managing_Search_Settings_2.0 on one of your Simple Pages.

Add Google Analytics

Using Google Analytics is an excellent and completely free way to track visitor data. To use the service, make sure that the Google Analytics plugin is installed on your site. You will then need to obtain a Tracking ID in a separate window or tab. You may have set up a Google Analytics account when you constructed your WYSIWYG site, and though it is possible to use the same Google Analytics code on two different sites, it may be easier and make more sense to use separate codes for each site. You are allowed multiple Google Analytics codes for each Google account, so this is not an issue. Log into your Google Analytics account (or create one). If you already have one Property (i.e., you already setup Google Analytics on your website) click on the Admin tab. In the second column, labeled Property, click on the drop-down menu and select Create New Property. Using the information for your Omeka.net site, fill out the form and click Get Tracking ID.

Copy the Tracking ID (which should start with "UA-") and return to your Omeka window. Click on the Plugins option in the Admin Menu, then select the Configure button next to the Google Analytics plugin. Simply paste the Tracking ID into the field and click Save Changes. You should then be able to log into your Google Analytics account as review site traffic and visitor data. For more information or support for Google Analytics, visit support.google.com/analytics.

SESSION 5

Create an Exhibit

The ability to create online exhibits is a major draw of the Omeka platform. Your exhibits use customizable layouts to display items from your database alongside narrative text. Often, you will create a landing page to introduce the exhibit and then add additional pages for individual pieces or group items. These pages can be made hierarchical to easily manage layers of information.

Exhibit pages consist of content blocks, available in three different types: file with text, gallery, and text block. To get started, you will need to make sure the Exhibit Builder plugin is installed. Click Manage Site on your Account Dashboard, and then on the Plugin option in the Admin Menu. Install the plugin if necessary, or click Configure next to the already installed plugin. Determine the sorting order for exhibits (Date Added, Alphabetical, or Recent) and save your changes. Then, click on the Exhibits bar in the Database Editing Menu. Click Add an Exhibit.

When you add a new exhibit, you will first be prompted to enter the exhibit's metadata. Enter the title, slug (the ending part of the URL, which should be an abbreviated version of the exhibit title, as discussed above), any applicable credits or other acknowledgments, a description of the exhibit, and relevant tags (which will be searchable by visitors). By default, the theme for your exhibit will match the theme of your Omeka site. Should you want it to be slightly different (e.g., with a different header logo to acknowledge a joint effort between two musuems) or visually distinct, select a new theme from the drop-down menu and click Configure. Once you are satisfied with the initial setup of your exhibit, save your changes and click Add Page to get started compiling your items and other data.

As with the overall exhibit, you will need to add title and slug data for each exhibit page. Then, you can construct the page block-by-block. You can combine one or more of the three block versions in any order, using multiple blocks of each type or only one block on a page. Click on the layout of the first block you want to add and then click Add New Content Block. A bar with the block title will appear, and below that, the block's editing field. In the field, you can enter and configure text (in a Text content block), select one of your database items and provide a caption (for Gallery content blocks), or do both (in a File With Text content block). If you want to include HTML in a Text or File With Text content block, click the HTML icon at the top of the editing field. The Gallery and File With Text content blocks come with multiple layout options. On these blocks, you will notice a bar at the bottom for Layout Options. Click on the small arrow to the right of that text to expand the layout options. For a Gallery block, you can showcase a particular file, adjust the width and alignment of the gallery, change the image cropping, and set the position of captions. In a File With Text block, you can determine the position of the file, set the file size and cropping, and change the position of the caption. You can delete and rearrange content blocks using the bar that holds the block title. To delete blocks that you no longer need, click the X to the right of the block header (e.g., the portion that says Block1 [Block Type]). The small arrow to the right of the block header will expand or collapse a block. To rearrange the blocks (though they will retain their block number from the order they were added), drag the bar with the block title up or down. Make sure to check the Public and Featured boxes on the right side of the page when you are ready to share your exhibit and to save your changes frequently.

Once you have added and filled out multiple pages, you can rearrange their order. Click on the Exhibits bar in the Database Editing Menu, and then Edit below the title of the exhibit you want to edit. As with content blocks, you can rearrange the order by dragging the bar with the page title up or down. Click on a page title to edit content on the page.

∽

Posting parts of your collection online is an excellent way to make your institution visible and accessible to your visitors. Long-distance researchers especially appreciate the ability to use the internet to locate resources and even view details of documents or photos. Just like having a website, making your collections available through your website or another platform can boost your reach. It will not detract from visitor experience but rather serve as a complement to your museum or historic site. Taking the time to prepare your collections for use online is worth the effort. Moreover, it does not have to be done all at once. Pieces can be released one-at-a-time as you process more and more of your collection. Visitors (and board members) will appreciate the opportunity to watch your collection grow.

NOTES

1. Creative Commons (CC) is a nonprofit organization that helps institutions and individuals develop copyright terms with the goal of enabling the sharing and use of creative materials and knowledge. CC can help you modify the terms of your copyright to suit your needs. For more information, visit creativecommons.org.

2. Not to be confused with omeka.org, which requires institutions to have their own server.

3. For more information on this topic, see Marilyn E. Phelan, *Museum Law: A Guide for Officers, Directors, and Counsel*, 4th ed. (Lanham: Rowman & Littlefield, 2014).

4. Look at http://users.wfu.edu/matthews/misc/graphics/formats/formats.html for more information.

5. Sue Chastain, "JPEG Myths and Facts,"accessed March 29, 2015, http://graphicssoft.about.com/od/formatsjpeg/a/jpegmythsfacts.htm.

6. Ibid.

7. Ibid.

8. GIMP is a free image manipulation program, available for both Macs and Wintels.

9. Found at www.photobucket.com.

10. Found at www.flickr.com.

11. About Creative Commons, accessed April 1, 2015, http://creativecommons. org/about.

12. About Omeka, accessed March 30, 2015, http://omeka.org/about/.

13. Ibid.

14. Visit info.omeka.net/omeka-net-help/use-case-museum-professional, info. omeka.net/omeka-net-help/use-case-archivists, info.omeka.net/omeka-net-help/use-case-librarians for more information.

15. Make sure you are using your single, streamlined email account to sign up for Omeka.

16. Because different computers have different pixel sizes, visitors may see these images with slightly larger or smaller dimensions. In general, the size will be similar, if not the same.

17. For information on plugins not discussed here, visit the Help Pages on Omeka at info.omeka.net. Not all plugins listed in the Help Pages are available to free account users.

18. If you do not see the type you need:
   1. Click Add Item.
   2. Return to the Item Type bar.
   3. Add the desired Item Type.
   4. Click on the Items bar in the Database Editing Menu.
   5. Click on Edit below the item you were just editing.
   6. Return to the Item Type Metadata tab and continue following the instructions.

19. DCMI Type Vocabulary, accessed February 15, 2015, http://dublincore.org/ documents/2004/06/14/dcmi-type-vocabulary.

20. You will not see this bar unless you have the Simple Page plugin installed.

Chapter 9

Moving Forward

"Once we accept our limits, we go beyond them."

—*Albert Einstein*

These words ring as true for the small museum worker as they did for the brilliant physicist who penned them. The local historical society cannot host the same large traveling exhibition that the large art museum next door does. The historic house museum that is open Wednesday through Saturday cannot reach all visitors that pass through the town. The living history farm has livestock that sometimes prevent staff from attending faraway conferences. And yet, what limits these institutions also gives them their uniqueness. Such distinctiveness puts them in a position to offer their visitors up-close experiences and personal connections to the stories they tell. No matter how small the staff or budget, each and every one of these institutions has the potential to make a meaningful impact in the preservation of the past and the telling of historical narratives.

Do not squander this potential. Hesitation to adopt new techniques is natural but, when paired with pragmatism, is not necessary. This book aims to help you construct a plan that begins within your limits but helps you stretch them just enough. Staying relevant and connected to a community requires routine examination of your organization's limits and looking for ways to push beyond them when logical. To move forward, a worthy institution cannot be held back by trepidation. Taking the time to evaluate your institution's audience, abilities, and goals is well worth the effort. Like the city itself, Rome's website was not built in a day.

Small museums and historic sites have good material in their historical arsenal. It is the duty of every museum docent, volunteer, intern, and professional to make sure this material is preserved and presented to the public—and that it continues to be accessible. Though the techniques for doing so vary by institution and opportunity, maintaining an active online presence is an achievable step that all institutions can take. Take heart that others have faced the same struggles to adapt to new and ever-changing technology. Creating a website is an important task, not without its difficulties unique to every museum. Perhaps identifying your new audience seems like an intangible task. Maybe finding a computer with fast enough internet is a challenge. Whatever the issue, ask advice from your colleagues and volunteers (whose expertise might surprise you) and make progress whenever possible. Through it all, acknowledge that every step forward is just that—an improvement and a way to keep your organization meaningful and relevant. As Louisa May Alcott once proclaimed, "I am not afraid of storms, for I am learning how to sail my ship."

Appendix A

Additional Resources

Table A1.1   Design

99designs *99designs.com*	If you are looking for a logo, you can submit a description of your institution and what you are looking for to 99designs.com, a contest-driven logo design platform. You choose a payment level and your contest is launched and open to thousands of designers around the world. You select the design you like best and can download it and use it however you like.
DesignCrowd *designcrowd.com*	If you are looking for a logo, you can submit a description of your institution and what you are looking for to designcrowd.com, a contest-driven design platform.
FreeLancer *freelancer.com*	Post a call for logo designs and a price you are willing to pay. You will receive bids for your project. You can compare proposals and prices and select the one you like best.
colorcombos.com *color.hailpixel.com* *color-hex.com* *colorschemedesigner.com* *colourlovers.com/palettes* *paletton.com*	These color design sites provide good examples of color deployment and may inspire your own site. There are also color-selection tools so you can identify the Hex and RGB codes of colors you like.

Table A1.2   Fundraising

AmazonSmile *org.amazon.com*	AmazonSmile is a division of Amazon where customers can shop the same selection of products found on amazon.com, but 0.5% of their eligible purchases will go to charitable organizations. Sign up to be one of these organizations at org.amazon.com.
Google AdSense *google.com/adsense/start*	AdSense is a simple way to earn money through your website or blog by displaying targeted ads next to your online content. Visitors will see ads relevant to their interests, and you can customize the look of the ad display to fit with your site.
Indiegogo *indiegogo.com*	Indiegogo is a great way to raise funds for specific projects. Launch a campaign for free, garner donations, and receive all the pledged money minus a small fee (6.75% for nonprofits).

Table A1.3   Software (Various)

CutePDF *cutepdf.com*	CutePDF helps you quickly convert any printable document into a PDF file.
GIMP *gimp.org*	GIMP is a freely distributed software program that can be used to retouch photos, compose images, and convert image formats.

Table A1.4   Online Content, Website Plugins

Google for Nonprofits *google.com/nonprofits*	Google for Nonprofits offers nonprofits access to institution-specific email, Google Calendar, and other products for free or at highly discounted rates.
Google SEO Guide *http://bit.ly/1icyyHR*	Google shares its tips for SEO best practices.
MailChimp *mailchimp.com*	A mailing list platform for sending emails and other newsletters. Free for institutions with fewer than 2,000 subscribers.
Nabble *nabble.com*	Offers free, embeddable forums, mailing lists, photo galleries, and blogs.
PayPal *paypal.com*	Accept payments and donations online (or in-person with PayPal Here). Lower rates for nonprofits (2.2% + $0.30 per transaction).
SustainingPlaces *sustainingplaces.com*	A collaborative resource project from the Museum Studies Program at the University of Delaware and the Tri-State Coalition of Historic Places. The website collects examples of good ideas and best practices for small historical organizations.

Appendix B

Website Planning Guide

OUR AUDIENCE(S)

Current Audience(s)—Physical Site
Current Audience(s)—Website
Audience(s) to Reach

OUR IDEAL VISITORS

Website Access Routes

Characteristic *Age, access device,* *interests, etc.*	Ideal Visitor #1	Ideal Visitor #2	Ideal Visitor #3

OUR SITE GOALS, PART 1

1. Whom do we want to reach with our site?

2. What are our expectations for the site?

3. What will our audience(s) expect from the site?

4. How will people access our site?

5. How much time can we commit to our site each month? How often will we update it?

6. What are the limitations of our online presence? What does our physical site offer that our website cannot? Vice-versa?

7. What can our site offer visitors who cannot come to our physical location?

8. How can the website engage with or supplement in-person visits?

9. How can we engage new visitors? Maintain current visitors?

10. How will we measure the effectiveness of our site?

OUR SITE GOALS, PART 2

Goal	Timeline	Assessment
Sell $10/month from online gift shop	*Ongoing*	*Visitor Services Coordinator check PayPal account monthly*

OUR SITEMAP

Top-Level Pages

Second-Level Pages

Third-Level Pages

Draw sitemap here

ELEMENT LIST

Page	Images	Documents	Other Multimedia
Calendar of Events	*Slideshow of 2014 Events (15 photos)*	*None*	*Embed Google Calendar*

RESPONSIBILITIES CHECKLIST

Page	Responsibility	Draft Deadline	Submitted to Webmaster
Calendar of Events	*Visitor Services Coordinator*	*June 14*	*June 13*

Appendix B

CONTENT EDITING CHECKLIST

Initial next to each when checked. Consult style guide as necessary.

Page: _____

_____ Grammar	_____ Verb tense	
_____ Punctuation	_____ No run-on sentences	
_____ Times/dates correct	_____ Important info at top	
_____ Spelling	_____ Other:	

Page: _____

_____ Grammar	_____ Verb tense	
_____ Punctuation	_____ No run-on sentences	
_____ Times/dates correct	_____ Important info at top	
_____ Spelling	_____ Other:	

Page: _____

_____ Grammar	_____ Verb tense	
_____ Punctuation	_____ No run-on sentences	
_____ Times/dates correct	_____ Important info at top	
_____ Spelling	_____ Other:	

Page: _____

_____ Grammar	_____ Verb tense	
_____ Punctuation	_____ No run-on sentences	
_____ Times/dates correct	_____ Important info at top	
_____ Spelling	_____ Other:	

SITE EDITING CHECKLIST, STYLE 1

Page: _____ Device and browser: _____

_____ Grammar, Punctuation,   _____ Image captions
Spelling, etc.   (if applicable)
_____ Times/dates correct   _____ High-quality images
_____ Formatting consistent   _____ Paragraph spacing
_____ Links working   _____ Content still up-to-date
_____ Images displaying   _____ Other: Forms

Page: _____ Device and browser: _____

_____ Grammar, Punctuation,   _____ Image captions
Spelling, etc.   (if applicable)
_____ Times/dates correct   _____ High-quality images
_____ Formatting consistent   _____ Paragraph spacing
_____ Links working   _____ Content still up-to-date
_____ Images displaying   _____ Other:

Page: _____ Device and browser: _____

_____ Grammar, Punctuation,   _____ Image captions
Spelling, etc.   (if applicable)
_____ Times/dates correct   _____ High-quality images
_____ Formatting consistent   _____ Paragraph spacing
_____ Links working   _____ Content still up-to-date
_____ Images displaying   _____ Other:

SITE EDITING CHECKLIST, STYLE 2

Example

Name: *Kelsey*
Specifications: *ex. Macbook Air, Chrome*

Page	Spelling & Grammar	Content	Images (pixelated, rotated, cropped)	Embedded Content	Links	Forms	Style	Formatting	Other
Home	✓	✓	x	✓	X	✓	✓	✓	✓
About Us	x	✓	✓	✓	✓	✓	x	✓	✓
Blog	✓	✓	x	✓	✓	✓	✓	✓	✓
Location & Directions	✓	✓	✓	x	✓	✓	✓	✓	✓
Volunteer	✓	✓	✓	✓	✓	x	✓	x	x
Employment	✓	x	✓	✓	✓	✓	✓	✓	✓

Spelling and Grammar Notes
About Us: The second paragraph should read, "We love to hear from our visitors . . ." not "We loves to hear from our visitors."

Content Notes
Employment: The educator position has been filled, so the call for applications should come down.

Image Notes
Home: The image of the waterfall is very pixelated and cropped oddly—use a higher-quality image and perhaps move it to the left.

Blog: The third photo down, of the school visit last month, is very large and takes up the whole page—perhaps make it smaller so it fits within the blog box.

Embedded Content Notes
Location & Directions: The Google Map will not show up in my browser.

Links Notes
Home: The link to the American Association of State and Local History website does not go through—double-check URL.

Forms Notes
Volunteer: I submitted a test "Volunteer with us!" form and did not receive a confirmation email.

Style Consistency Notes
About Us: The font on this page is Times New Roman, but all the other pages have Helvetica.

Formatting Notes
Volunteer: The way the image is placed next to the paragraph causes a strange cutoff in the text—perhaps move the image to the right.

Other Notes
Volunteer: This page is missing your contact information at the bottom of the page.

Appendix C

Webmaster's Keyboard Shortcuts

Command	On Mac	On Windows
Bold	Cmd + B	Ctrl + B
Close Window/Tab	Cmd + W	Ctrl + W
Copy	Cmd + C	Ctrl + C
Cut	Cmd + X	Ctrl + X
Hide Program	Cmd + H	Ctrl + H
Italic	Cmd + I	Ctrl + I
Paste	Cmd + V	Ctrl + V
Print	Cmd + P	Ctrl + P
Redo	Cmd + Y	Ctrl + Y
Right-click/Equivalent	Ctrl + Click	On mouse
Save	Cmd + S	Ctrl + S
Save As . . .	Cmd + Shift + S	Ctrl + Shift + S
Select All	Cmd + A	Ctrl + A
Select Multiple (as of files)	Cmd + Click (on each file)	Ctrl + Click (on each file)
Select Range (as of files)	Shift + Click (on first and last file in list)	Shift + Click (on first and last file in list)
Underlined	Cmd + U	Ctrl + U
Undo	Cmd + Z	Ctrl + Z
Zoom In	Cmd + + (plus sign)	Ctrl + + (plus sign)
Zoom Out	Cmd + − (minus sign)	Ctrl + − (minus sign)

Appendix D

Color Names for HTML

Color Name	Hex (RGB)
Alice Blue	#F0F8FF
Antique White	#FAEBD7
Aqua or Cyan	#00FFFF
Aquamarine	#7FFFD4
Azure	#F0FFFF
Beige	#F5F5DC
Bisque	#FFE4C4
Black	#000000
Blanched Almond	#FFEBCD
Blue	#0000FF
Blue Violet	#8A2BE2
Brown	#A52A2A
Burlywood	#DEB887
Cadet Blue	#5F9EA0
Chartreuse	#7FFF00
Chocolate	#D2691E
Coral	#FF7F50
Cornflower	#6495ED
Cornsilk	#FFF8DC
Crimson	#DC143C
Cyan or Aqua	#00FFFF
Dark Blue	#00008B

Dark Cyan	#008B8B
Dark Goldenrod	#B8860B
Dark Gray	#A9A9A9
Dark Green	#006400
Dark Khaki	#BDB76B
Dark Magenta	#8B008B
Dark Olive Green	#556B2F
Dark Orange	#FF8C00
Dark Orchid	#9932CC
Dark Red	#8B0000
Dark Salmon	#E9967A
Dark Sea Green	#8FBC8F
Dark Slate Blue	#483D8B
Dark Slate Gray	#2F4F4F
Dark Turquoise	#00CED1
Dark Violet	#9400D3
Deep Pink	#FF1493
Deep Sky Blue	#00BFFF
Dim Gray	#696969
Dodger Blue	#1E90FF
Firebrick	#B22222
Floral White	#FFFAF0
Forest Green	#228B22
Fuchsia or Magenta	#FF00FF
Gainsboro	#DCDCDC
Ghost White	#F8F8FF
Gold	#FFD700
Goldenrod	#DAA520
Gray	#BEBEBE
Green or Lime	#808080
Green Yellow	#00FF00
Honeydew	#008000
Hot Pink	#ADFF2F
Indian Red	#F0FFF0
Indigo	#FF69B4
Ivory	#CD5C5C

Khaki	#4B0082
Lavender	#FFFFF0
Lavender Blush	#F0E68C
Lawn Green	#E6E6FA
Lemon Chiffon	#FFF0F5
Light Blue	#7CFC00
Light Coral	#FFFACD
Light Cyan	#ADD8E6
Light Goldenrod	#F08080
Light Gray	#E0FFFF
Light Green	#FAFAD2
Light Pink	#D3D3D3
Light Salmon	#90EE90
Light Sea Green	#FFB6C1
Light Sky Blue	#FFA07A
Light Slate Gray	#20B2AA
Light Steel Blue	#87CEFA
Light Yellow	#778899
Lime	#B0C4DE
Lime Green	#FFFFE0
Linen	#00FF00
Magenta or Fuchsia	#32CD32
Maroon	#FAF0E6
Medium Aquamarine	#FF00FF
Medium Blue	#B03060
Medium Orchid	#7F0000
Medium Purple	#66CDAA
Medium Sea Green	#0000CD
Medium Slate Blue	#BA55D3
Medium Spring Green	#9370DB
Medium Turquoise	#3CB371
Medium Violet Red	#7B68EE
Midnight Blue	#00FA9A
Mint Cream	#48D1CC
Misty Rose	#C71585
Moccasin	#191970

Navajo White	#F5FFFA
Navy Blue or Navy	#FFE4E1
Old Lace	#FFE4B5
Olive	#FFDEAD
Olive Drab	#000080
Orange	#FDF5E6
Orange Red	#808000
Orchid	#6B8E23
Pale Goldenrod	#FFA500
Pale Green	#FF4500
Pale Turquoise	#DA70D6
Pale Violet Red	#EEE8AA
Papaya Whip	#98FB98
Peach Puff	#AFEEEE
Peru	#DB7093
Pink	#FFEFD5
Plum	#FFDAB9
Powder Blue	#CD853F
Purple	#FFC0CB
Rebecca Purple	#DDA0DD
Red	#B0E0E6
Rosy Brown	#A020F0
Royal Blue	#7F007F
Saddle Brown	#663399
Salmon	#FF0000
Sandy Brown	#BC8F8F
Sea Green	#4169E1
Seashell	#8B4513
Sienna	#FA8072
Silver	#F4A460
Sky Blue	#2E8B57
Slate Blue	#FFF5EE
Slate Gray	#A0522D
Snow	#C0C0C0
Spring Green	#87CEEB
Steel Blue	#6A5ACD

Tan	#708090
Teal	#FFFAFA
Thistle	#00FF7F
Tomato	#4682B4
Turquoise	#D2B48C
Violet	#008080
Web Gray	#D8BFD8
Web Green	#FF6347
Web Maroon	#40E0D0
Web Purple	#EE82EE
Wheat	#F5DEB3
White	#FFFFFF
White Smoke	#F5F5F5
Yellow	#FFFF00
Yellow Green	#9ACD32

Appendix E

HTML Tags

GENERAL HTML TAGS[1]

Tag	Purpose
<!--...-->	Defines a comment
<!DOCTYPE>	Defines the document type
<a>	Defines a hyperlink
<b>	Defines bold text
<big>	Defines large text. Not supported in HTML5, so use CSS if possible
<blockquote>	Defines a section that is quoted from another source
<body>	Defines the document's body
 	Defines a single line break
<caption>	Defines a table caption
<center>	Defines centered text. Not supported in HTML5, so use CSS if possible
<div>	Defines a section in a document
<em>	Defines emphasized text (italicized)
<embed>	Defines a container for an external (non-HTML) application
<figcaption>	Defines a caption for a <figure> element
<figure>	Specifies self-contained content
<font>	Defines font, color, and size for text. Not supported in HTML5, so use CSS if possible
<footer>	Defines a footer for a document or section
<h1>, <h2>, <h3>, <h4>, <h5>, and <h6>	Defines six different HTML headings

<head>	Defines information about the document
<header>	Defines a header for a document or section
<html>	Defines the root of an HTML document
<i>	Defines italicized text
<img>	Defines an image
<li>	Defines a list item
<mark>	Defines highlighted text
<meta>	Defines metadata about an HTML document
<object>	Defines an embedded object
<ol>	Defines an ordered list
<p>	Defines a paragraph
<q>	Defines a short quotation
<small>	Defines smaller text
<source>	Defines multiple resources for media elements (e.g., <video> and <audio>)
<strike>	Defines strikethrough text. Not supported in HTML5, so use <del> or <s> instead.
<strong>	Defines important text (bold)
<style>	Defines style information for a document
<sub>	Defines subscripted text
<sup>	Defines superscripted text
<table>	Defines a table
<tbody>	Groups the body content in a table
<td>	Defines a cell in a table
<tfoot>	Groups the footer content in a table
<th>	Defines a header cell in a table
<thead>	Groups the header content in a table
<time>	Defines a date/time
<title>	Defines a title for the document
<tr>	Defines a row in a table
<u>	Defines underlined text

SPECIFIC HTML TAG USES

Three of the most likely types of tags you will be dealing with are for images, text, and links. The most common attributes for these include:

Image Attribute Tags	
Alt text	<img src="url.jpg" alt="Text" width="104" height="142">
Height	<img src="url.jpg" height="142">
Source	<img src="url.jpg">
Width	<img src="url.jpg" width="104">

Link Attribute Tags	
URL (the location of the link)	<a href="http://www.url.com">Link text</a>
Target: open link in new window	<a href="http://www.url.com" target="_blank">Link text</a>
Target: open link in same window	<a href="http://www.url.com" target="_top">Link text</a>

Text Attribute Tags	
Bold	Text
Highlighted	<mark>Text</mark>
Italicized	<i>Text</i>
Font size	<font size="3">Text</font>
Font color	<font color="blue">Text</font>
Font face	<font face="verdana">Text</font>
example	*<font size="3" face="verdana" color="green">Text</font>*

HTML ENTITY TAGS

Result	Description	Entity Name	Entity Number
	Nonbreaking space		
<	Less than	&lt;	&#60;
>	Greater than	&gt;	&#62;
&	Ampersand	&amp;	&#38;
¢	Cent	&cent;	&#162;
£	Pound	&pound;	&#163;
€	Euro	&euro;	&#8364;
®	Registered trademark	&reg;	&#174;
©	Copyright	&copy;	&#169;

Appendix E

NOTE

1. These lists, compiled from w3schools.com, are tailored to match the content discussed in this book. Additional tags, attributes, and entities can be found at www.w3schools.com/tags, www.w3schools.com/html/html_formatting.asp, www.w3schools.com/Html/html_attributes.asp, and http://dev.w3.org/html5/html-author/charref.

Appendix F

Stop Words

a
able
about
above
abroad
according
accordingly
across
actually
ad
after
afterwards
again
against
ago
ahead
all
allow
allows
almost
alone
along
alongside
already
also
although
always

am
amid
amidst
among
amongst
an
and
another
any
anybody
anyhow
anyone
anything
anyway
anyways
anywhere
apart
appear
appreciate
appropriate
are
aren't
around
as
aside
ask
asking

associated
at
available
away
awfully
back
backward(s)
be
became
because
become(s)
becoming
been
before
beforehand
begin
beginning
behind
being
believe
below
beside(s)
best
better
between
beyond
billion

both
brief
but
buy
by
came
can
cannot
cant
can't
caption
cause(s)
certain
certainly
changes
clearly
click
co
com
come(s)
comes
concerning
consequently
consider
considering
contain(s)
containing

239

copy
corresponding
could
couldn't
course
currently
dare
daren't
definitely
described
despite
did
didn't
different
directly
do
does
doesn't
doing
don
done
don't
down
downwards
during
each
edu
eg
eight
eighty
either
else
elsewhere
end
ending
enough
entirely
especially
etc
even
ever
evermore

every
everybody
everyone
everything
everywhere
ex
exactly
example
except
fairly
far
farther
few
fewer
fifth
fifty
find
first
five
followed
following
follows
for
forever
former
formerly
forth
forty
forward
found
four
free
from
further
furthermore
get
gets
getting
given
gives
go
goes

going
gone
got
gotten
greetings
had
hadn't
half
happens
hardly
has
hasn't
have
haven't
having
he
hello
help
hence
her
here
hereafter
hereby
herein
hereupon
here's
hers
herself
he'd
he'll
he's
hi
him
himself
his
hither
home
homepage
hopefully
how
howbeit
however

htm
html
http
hundred
I
ie
if
ignored
immediate
in
inasmuch
inc
indeed
indicate(s)
indicated
information
inner
inside
insofar
instead
into
inward
is
isn't
it(s)
itself
it'd
it'll
it's
I'd
I'll
I'm
I've
join
just
keep(s)
kept
kg
km
know(s)
known
last

lately
later
latter
latterly
least
less
lest
let
let's
like
liked
likely
likewise
little
look(s)
looking
low
lower
made
mainly
make
makes
many
may
maybe
mayn't
me
mean
meantime
meanwhile
merely
mg
Microsoft
might
mightn't
million
mine
minus
miss
more thus
moreover
most

mostly
mr
mrs
ms
mt
much
must tries
mustn't
my
myself
name
namely
near
nearly
necessary
need(s)
needn't
neither
net
Netscape
never
nevertheless
new
next
nine
ninety
no
no-one
nobody
non
none
nonetheless
nor
normally
not
nothing
notwithstanding
novel
now
nowhere
obviously
of

off
often
oh
ok
okay
old
on
once
one(s)
one's
only
onto
opposite
or
org
other(s)
otherwise
ought
oughtn't
our(s)
ourselves
out
outside
over
overall
own
page
particular
particularly
past
per
perhaps
placed
please
plus
pm
possible
presumably
probably
provided
provides
quite

rather
re
really
reasonably
recent
recently
regarding
regardless
regards
relatively
reserved
respectively
right
ring
round
said
same
saw
say(s)
saying
second
secondly
see
seeing
seem(s)
seemed
seeming
seen
self
selves
sensible
sent
serious
seriously
seven
seventy
several
shall
shan't
she
she'd
she'll

she's	the	toward(s)	welcome
should	their	tried	well
shouldn't	theirs	trillion	were
since	them	truly	weren't
site	themselves	try	we'd
six	then	trying	we'll
sixty	thence	TV	we're
so	there	twenty	we've
some	thereafter	twice	what
somebody	thereby	two	whatever
someday	therefore	um	what'll
somehow	therein	under	what's
someone	thereupon	underneath	when
something	there'd	undoing	whence
sometime(s)	there'll	unfortunately	whenever
somewhat	there's	unless	where
somewhere	there've	unlike	whereafter
soon	these	unlikely	whereas
sorry	they	until	whereby
specified	they'd	unto	wherein
specify	they'll	up	whereupon
specifying	they're	upon	wherever
st	they've	upwards	whether
still	thing(s)	us	which
stop	think	use(s)	while
sub	third	used	whither
such	thirty	useful	who
sure	this	using	whoever
take	thorough	usually	whole
taken	thoroughly	value	whom
taking	those	various	whomever
tell	though	versus	whose
ten	thousand	very	who'd
tends	three	via	who'll
test	through	want(s)	who's
text	throughout	was	why
than	thru	wasn't	will
thank(s)	till	way	with
that	to	we	within
that'll	together	web	without
that's	too	webpage	won
that've	took	website	won't

would	yes	yours	you'll
wouldn't	yet	yourself	you're
www	you	yourselves	you've
ye	your	you'd	

Glossary

All definitions are given in terms of their use in this book, and as such, additional uses and details may be omitted or simplified. Unless otherwise noted, they are compiled and adapted from www.w3schools.com, www.techopedia. com, and the Apple Inc. native Dictionary program.

Accessible/accessibility: Allows people with disabilities to perceive, understand, navigate, and interact with online content. Accessibility encompasses all disabilities that affect access to the internet, including visual, auditory, physical, speech, cognitive, and neurological disabilities.[1]

Alt text/Alternative text attribute: Specifies alternative text for any image that cannot be displayed.

Anchor tag: Consisting of a reference point and a reference, anchor tags allow users to jump from one specific location on the page to another (e.g., from the bottom of the page to the top).

Attribute: One of three HTML components you can define, attribute modifies specific characteristics of HTML elements (e.g., size 12 is an attribute of a paragraph element).

Blank target attribute: When linking to an outside resource or page, a blank target attribute will open the page in a new window or tab rather than in the current window or tab.

Blog: Short for weblog. Regularly updated internet content written in an informal or conversational style, typically one run by an individual or small group.

Body tag: This tag defines the main element of an HTML document (a web page).

Browser: A program with a graphical user interface for navigating the internet.

Captcha: A program in the form of an image or audio transcription used to distinguish between human and machine visitors. Used to thwart spam and automated extraction of data from websites.

Closing tag: *See Tag*.

Cloud: When something is stored or run "on the Cloud" its computing takes place on the internet rather than on your computer. Many common services and software, such as Dropbox and Google Drive, run on the Cloud.

Color scheme: An arrangement or combination of colors on your website.

Color chord/color harmony: Two or more colors that work together to produce a pleasing aesthetic effect.

Compatibility mode: A setting in Microsoft Word that enables documents to be opened in earlier versions of Word, as well as on different operating systems.

Cookies: A small bit of data that a website sends and stores in the visitor's web browser for the duration of the visit and for return visits. Cookies help websites present custom pages for return visitors, such as when you log in to an email account once and, when you return later, you have your username already filled in.

Crowdsource: To obtain information by enlisting the help of a large number of people via the internet.

CSS (Cascading Style Sheet): A markup language used in conjunction with a programming language like HTML or XML to describe the look and format of a web page.

Dial-up: Remote access to the internet via a telephone line.

Digital curation: Much like in-house curation, its digital counterpart involves selecting, preserving, maintaining, collecting, and often archiving of digital assets. This term also describes the presentation of exhibitions that are hosted purely online. Omeka is commonly used to create digital exhibits.

Domain: The name of a website; the URL used to access a website.

Download: Copying data from the internet to a computer.

DPI (Dots Per Inch): A measure of color dot density on a printed medium. *Also see PPI.*

eCommerce: Commercial transactions conducted on the internet instead of at a physical location.

Element: (1) A building component in a WYSIWYG editor or (2) an individual component of a webpage.

Embed: Place an external application or other external content on a webpage.

Entity: One of three HTML components you can define. These are special or reserved characters, such as the dollar sign, the ampersand, and arrows.

Ethernet: Allows a computer to connect to a wired network rather than connecting via Wi-Fi.

Facebook: The largest social networking platform in the world, which allows users to connect to people, causes, businesses, events, and more.

Flash: Enables viewing of multimedia on the internet.

Font: Not to be confused with typeface, this is a set of type of one particular face and size.

Font tag: Used to impose specific attributes on a text (e.g., paragraph) HTML element. A font tag can define the color, typeface, and size of a specified text.

Footer: The bottom section of a website, typically containing contact information and commonly used links.

Freemium: A pricing system in which the main or basic product is available for free, but premium versions or upgrades are sold to a smaller part of the user base.[2]

FTP client: A software that transfers files to and from a remote computer using a specific protocol called File Transfer Protocol.

Functionality testing: A process used to ensure that a website displays properly and conforms with access requirements.

Google AdSense: A Google program that allows websites to host targeted third-party advertisements.

Hardware: Machines and other physical components of a computer system.

Header: The top section of a website that is the same across all pages. It typically includes the organization's logo and navigation.

Hexadecimal color: A color in HTML and CSS that is defined using a hex triplet, a six-digit, three-byte number. The three bytes represent the amount of red, green, and blue in the color. *See also RGB.*

Homepage: A website's introductory page.

Host(ing): A company that provides server space for another organization's website data.

Href attribute: Specifies the URL destination for a link.

HTML (Hypertext Markup Language): A standardized system for creating files that result in webpages with specific fonts, colors, graphics, and hyperlinks.

Hyperlink: *See Link/Hyperlink.*

Hypertext: Text that contains a link to other text online. Often used in place of term "HyperMedia," which is a text link to videos, graphics, or sound.

Ideal visitor: The concept of an unnamed visitor with specific attributes (e.g., male, 25, using an iPhone) used to direct the construction of a website or business. The developer takes those specific attributes into account when designing the flow, content, and look of a website.

Image tag: Used to impose specific attributes on an image HTML element. An image tag can define the dimensions of an image.

Intradocument hyperlink: A link that takes the user to another location in the same HTML document (i.e., another location on the same web page). An anchor.

JPEG (Joint Photographic Experts Group): A standard for image files that defines how an image file is compressed. It is a "lossy" file format, so JPEG images may deteriorate over time with excessive editing and re-saving.

Keyword: A particular word or phrase that describes the content of a page or website. It is part of a site's metadata that is used by search engines to match search queries with relevant sites.

Link/Hyperlink: A link from an image or text, activated by clicking, to bring the visitor to new content.

LinkedIn: A social networking platform used for professional purposes to associate with businesses, colleagues, schools, and professional groups.

Linux: An open-source operating system.

iOS: The operating system of Apple's mobile devices.

Menu/submenu: The list of site pages and links one can navigate to. The submenu includes subpages to top-menu items or may be a secondary menu on a discrete set of pages.

Multimedia: Non-text elements on a website, including slideshows, videos, Flash animation, audio, and more. Often involves a level of interactivity.

Nested tags: Several pairs of tags that are closed in the same order they were opened in. Important for restricting attributes to the correct content.

Nonbreaking space: An HTML entity used to create additional space *within* a line of text.

Omeka: An open-source online platform for publishing library, museum, and archival materials, especially in collections and exhibitions.

Online presence: Having a website and/or social networking profile that is regularly updated.

Page title: More than just the name of the page, the page title is a piece of metadata that search engines read to return relevant search results.

PDF (Portable Document Format): A file format that can act as an unalterable image file.

Pinterest: A personalized media platform wherein users curate groups of links and images ("pins") on various subject-based "pinboards."

Pixel/pixelated: One point of illumination on a display screen. A pixelated image is one whose dimensions have been increased without a corresponding increase in the number of pixels, the result of which is that the viewer can see individual pixels and the image looks distorted.

PNG (Portable Network Graphics): A standard for image files that defines how an image file is compressed. PNG is a mostly lossless file form, though there is some compression when saved. This file form maintains transparency.

PPI (Pixels Per Inch): A measure of resolution on a screen. *Also see DPI.*

Primary color: One of the three colors from which all other colors can be created (red, yellow, and blue).

Publish/post: As opposed to just saving, publishing or posting a page or blog article makes it visible to the public.

Reference point: Used in intradocument hyperlinking to indicate where an anchor tag will take the user.

Reserved characters: *See Entity.*

Resolution: The degree of detail visible in an image.

RGB (Red, Green, Blue): A color model that uses additive light to reproduce a variety of colors through electronic media. It is device-dependent, meaning that different devices may reproduce the color values differently. Colors are defined using three numbers, one for each of the color values (e.g., white is 255, 255, 255 or #FFFFFF).

RSS/RSS Feed (Rich Site Summary or Really Simple Syndication): A standardization system used in the distribution of online content, especially from news sites and blogs. A feed is a ticker of such content pulled from other sites or pages.

Safari: Apple's native web browser.

Sans serif (font): A typeface that does not have serifs—slight projections off a stroke of a letter.

Screenshot: An image that captures the display of a computer screen.

Search engine: A program that uses keywords to search for items in a database, especially for finding sites online.

Secondary color: A color resulting from the mixing of two primary colors.

SEO (Search Engine Optimization): The process of improving the ranking of a website on search engine results.

Serif (font): A typeface that has serifs—slight projections off a stroke of a letter.

Server: A computer that manages access to a centralized resource or service in a network.

Singular tag: *See Tag.*

Site description: A description of an entire website. It is a piece of metadata that is used by search engines to match search queries with relevant sites.

Site stats: Data about the number and frequency of visits your website receives. May also include demographic and behavioral data about your site visitors.

Sitemap: A list of a website's pages, typically in hierarchical order, that is accessible to search engine crawlers and sometimes visitors.

Smartphone: A cell-phone that performs like a computer so that users can access the internet and other services available online.

Social icons: Small buttons, usually in the upper right-hand corner or at the bottom of a web page, that link directly to an institution's social media profiles on Facebook, Twitter, and the like.

Source attribute: Used to specify a media resource for media elements (e.g., to direct an image element to the correct image stored elsewhere on the web).

Style (font): An attribute, such as bold, italic, or underlining, applied to text.

Style guide: A set of standards used in the writing of website pages to ensure consistency in voice and grammar across the site.

Tag: singular, pair, opening, closing, nested.

Tag pair: *See Tag.*

Tertiary color: A color made by mixing either a primary and secondary or two secondary colors.

Theme or template: A preset layout and design for a website or webpage. The individual generic components can be changed out for the user's own material.

Thumbnail: A smaller version of an image that usually has a lower resolution so it takes up a minimal amount of storage space.

TIFF (Tagged Image File Format): A standard for image files that defines how an image file is compressed. TIFF is a lossless file form. This file form maintains transparency.

Title: *See Page title.*

Top-level page: A web page that is a top menu item that usually acts as a landing page for a group of related subpages that have more detail.

Twitter: A social networking platform wherein users can send short 140-character messages ("tweets").

Typeface: A particular design of type. Not to be confused with font, which is a specific size and stylization of a given typeface.

Upload: To add a file to another system, especially via the internet.

URL (Uniform Resource Locator): The address of a specific web page.

Vimeo: A video-sharing website on which users can upload, share, and view videos.

Visibility (search engines): A setting in WYSIWYG editors that allows your site to be searchable by search engines, such as Google and Bing. You can submit your site to these search engines to optimize your visibility.

W-Element: *See Element.*

Webmaster: A single person who gathers, edits, and puts a website's content online.

Web reader: Also known as a screen reader, a web reader is important in making the internet accessible to visually impaired persons. The reader conveys website content to the user, often through text-to-speech technology.

Web-safe color: A mostly defunct concept that defines a set of 216 colors that are supposed to be consistently readable by every computer. With higher-bit displays on almost every personal device, web-safe colors are no longer necessary.

Wi-Fi: Allows computers, smartphones and other devices to access the internet wirelessly within a particular range.

Windows: A very common operating system for computers.

Wintel: Personal computers with an Intel processor that runs the Windows operating system.

WYSIWYG (What You See is What You Get) editor/platform: An online website-building program that hosts and builds websites. Allows users to see the content onscreen as it will be displayed to website visitors rather than only showing users the website code.

XML: A computer-to-computer language that defines the content of a web-page but not its display.

YouTube: A video-sharing website on which users can upload, share, and view videos.

NOTES

1. https://www.w3.org/WAI/intro/accessibility.php.
2. www.freemium.org/what-is-freemium-2.

Bibliography

1stwebdesigner.com. "Empathizing Color Psychology in Web Design." Accessed November 10, 2014. http://www.1stwebdesigner.com/design/color-psychology-website-design/.

American Association of Museums – Center for the Future of Museums, Museums & Society 2034: Trends and Potential Futures. Last updated December 2008. http://www.aam-us.org/docs/center-for-the-future-of-museums/museums-society2034.pdf.

Bigman, Alex. "PPI vs. DPI: What's the Difference?" *99 Designs*. Last updated February 13, 2015. http://99designs.com/designer-blog/2013/02/26/ppi-vs-dpi-whats-the-difference/.

Chapman, Cameron. "Color Theory for Designers, Part 1: The Meaning of Color." *Smashing Magazine*. Last updated January 28, 2010. http://www.smashingmagazine.com/2010/01/28/color-theory-for-designers-part-1-the-meaning-of-color.

Charalambous, Alex. "Understanding How Internet Explorer Affects Website Design." Last updated March 18, 2014. http://www.business2community.com/online-marketing/understanding-internet-explorer-affects-website-design-0814809.

Chastain, Sue. "JPEG Myths and Facts." Accessed March 29, 2015, http://graphicssoft.about.com/od/formatsjpeg/a/jpegmythsfacts.htm.

Cousins, Carrie. "Color and Cultural Design Considerations." Last updated June 11, 2012. http://www.webdesignerdepot.com/2012/06/color-and-cultural-design-considerations.

Cousins, Carrie. "DPI vs. Pixels: What Do I Use?" *DesignShack*. Last modified May 21, 2012. http://designshack.net/articles/graphics/dpi-vs-pixels-what-do-i-use.

Cousins, Carrie. "Serif vs. Sans Serif Fonts: Is One Really Better Than the Other?" *Design Shack*. Last updated October 28, 2013. http://designshack.net/articles/typography/serif-vs-sans-serif-fonts-is-one-really-better-than-the-other.

Creative Commons. "About Creative Commons." Accessed April 1, 2015. http://creativecommons.org/about.

Dacey, Andrew. "Image Size Resolution." Accessed February 18, 2015. http://www.andrewdaceyphotography.com/articles/dpi.

de Valk, Joost. "WordPress SEO." Last updated September 8, 2014. https://yoast.com/articles/wordpress-seo.

Design Your Way. "Internet Explorer in a Web Designer's Life—Problems and Solutions." Accessed February 20, 2015. http://www.designyourway.net/blog/resources/internet-explorer-in-a-web-designers-life-problems-and-solutions.

"Digital Image File Types Explained." Accessed March 17, 2015. http://users.wfu.edu/matthews/misc/graphics/formats/formats.html.

Dublin Core Metadata Initiative. "DCMI Type Vocabulary." Accessed February 15, 2015. http://dublincore.org/documents/2004/06/14/dcmi-type-vocabulary.

Dublin Core Metadata Initiative. "Dublin Core Metadata Element Set, Version 1.1." Last updated February 2013. http://dublincore.org/documents/dces.

Farrell, Betty and Maria Medvedeva. "Demographic Transformation and the Future of Museums." American Association of Museums – Center for the Future of Museums. Last updated 2010. http://www.aam-us.org/docs/center-for-the-future-of-museums/demotransaam2010.pdf.

Freemium.org. "What is Freemium." Accessed February, 15, 2015. http://www.freemium.org/what-is-freemium-2.

Friedman, Vitality. "10 Principles of Effective Web Design." Last updated January 31, 2008. http://www.smashingmagazine.com/2008/01/31/10-principles-of-effective-web-design.

Gillikin, Jason. "Importance of Logos in Business." *Small Business Chronicle*. Accessed November 3, 2014. http://smallbusiness.chron.com/importance-logos-business-577.html.

Google AdWords Help. "Using Keyword Planner to get keyword ideas and traffic forecasts." Accessed April 19, 2015. https://support.google.com/adwords/answer/2999770?rd=1.

Google. "Search Engine Optimization Guide." Last updated 2010. http://static.googleusercontent.com/external_content/untrusted_dlcp/www.google.com/en/us/webmasters/docs/search-engine-optimization-starter-guide.pdf.

Griffiths, Jen. "Why I Think Small Museums Should Have a Web Presence." *Historian @ Work* (blog). Last updated November 3, 2010. http://historianatwork.wordpress.com/2010/11/03/why-i-think-small-museums-should-have-a-web-presence.

Haley, Allan. "Serif v. Sans for Text." *Fonts.com*. Accessed November 3, 2014. http://www.fonts.com/content/learning/fontology/level-2/making-type-choices/serif-v-sans-for-text.

Haynes, Judy and Dan Zambonini. "Why Are They Doing That!? How Users Interact With Museum Web Sites." In *Museums and the Web 2007: Proceedings, Toronto: Archives & Museum Informatics*, edited by J. Trant and D. Bearman. Last updated March 1, 2007. http://www.archimuse.com/mw2007/papers/haynes/haynes.html.

Honigman, Brian. "The Psychology of Color in Logo Design." Last updated March 26, 2013. http://www.huffingtonpost.com/brian-honigman/psychology-color-design-infographic_b_2516608.html.

Hot Off the Press. "Awesome (and Free) Theme Options You Might Not Know About." *Wordpress.com* (blog). Accessed April 22, 2015. https://en.blog.wordpress.com/2013/12/04/awesome-theme-options.

Institute for Dynamic Educational Advancement. "Newton and the Color Spectrum." *Color, Vision, & Art.* Accessed February 23, 2015. http://www.webexhibits.org/colorart/bh.html.

Intelligent Editing. "Writing a Style Guide: What You Need to Know." Accessed November 10, 2014. http://www.intelligentediting.com/writingastyleguide.aspx.

Ironspider. "HTML Color Chart / Font Color Codes." Accessed February 22, 2015. http://www.ironspider.ca/format_text/fontcolor.htm.

Karlins, David and Bruce Hopkins. *Adobe Dreamweaver CS3 How-Tos: 150 Essential Techniques.* Berkeley: Adobe Press, 2007.

Ko, Iggy. "16 Gorgeous Web Safe Fonts To Use With CSS." Web Design Dev. Accessed May 1, 2015, http://www.webdesigndev.com/web-development/16-gorgeous-web-safe-fonts-to-use-with-css.

Kole, Stacey. "Serif vs. Sans: The Final Battle." Last updated March 15, 2013. http://www.webdesignerdepot.com/2013/03/serif-vs-sans-the-final-battle.

Kronkosky Charitable Foundation. "Museums Research Brief." Last updated December 2013. http://kronkosky.org/research/Research_Briefs/Museums%20%20December%202013.pdf.

Larson, Julia. "50 Beautiful Color Palettes for Your Next Web Project." Last updated July 9, 2013. http://www.dtelepathy.com/blog/inspiration/beautiful-color-palettes-for-your-next-web-project.

Logo Design Team. "Why You Must Have a Logo." Accessed November 3, 2014. https://www.logodesignteam.com/why-logo-design.html.

McNeil, Patrick. *The Web Designer's Idea Book.* Cincinnati: F&W Publications, Inc., 2007.

Mukhopadhyay, Sounak. "Microsoft To Discontinue Internet Explorer, To Launch New Browser For Windows 10" *International Business Times.* Last updated March 18, 2015. http://www.ibtimes.com.au/microsoft-discontinue-internet-explorer-launch-new-browser-windows-10-1430604.

National Education Foundation. "10 Principles of Basic Web Design." Accessed November 3, 2014. http://www.nea.org/home/10-Principles-of-Basic-Web-Design.html.

Nielsen, Jakob. "How Little Do Users Read?" Nielsen Norman Group. Last updated May 6, 2008. http://www.nngroup.com/articles/how-little-do-users-read.

Omeka.org. "Working with Dublin Core." http://omeka.org/codex/Working_with_Dublin_Core.

Patel, Neil. "How To Write A Meta Description That Gets Click-Throughs." Search Engine Land. Last updated November 26, 2014. http://searchengineland.com/write-meta-description-gets-clickthroughs-207922.

Phelan, Marilyn E. *Museum Law: A Guide for Officers, Directors, and Counsel.* 4th ed. Lanham: Rowman & Littlefield, 2014.

Teague, Jason Cranford. "Choosing the Right Color Value." *Peachpit.com.* Last updated December 14, 2009. http://www.peachpit.com/blogs/blog.aspx?uk=Choosing-the-Right-Color-Value.

Tiger Color. "Color Harmonies." Accessed November 11, 2014. http://www.tiger-color.com/color-lab/color-theory/color-harmonies.htm.

Tittel, Ed and Jeff Noble. *HTML, XHTML, & CSS For Dummies*. 7th ed. Hoboken: Wiley Publishing, Inc., 2011.

W3schools.com. "HTML Element Reference." Accessed December 9, 2014. http://www.w3schools.com/tags.

W3schools.com. "HTML Entities." Accessed December 9, 2014. http://www.w3schools.com/html/html_entities.asp.

Web Science: How the Web is Changing the World. "Homophily in Social Networks." Accessed December 10, 2014. https://www.futurelearn.com/courses/web-science-2014-q3/steps/13421/progress.

WebNots. "Limitations of Free Weebly Forum Site." Last updated July 17, 2014. http://www.webnots.com/limitations-of-free-weebly-forum.

Weebly.com. "The Power of Sites in 2013." Accessed October 20, 2014. http://www.weebly.com/power-of-sites.

WordPress Tips. "Divider Lines." Last updated October 4, 2010. https://wpbtips.wordpress.com/2010/10/04/divider-lines.

Yeung, Ken. "DIY Web builder Weebly launches an Android app, along with a mobile and HTML5 site creator." *The Next Web News*. Last updated May 2, 2013. http://thenextweb.com/insider/2013/05/02/diy-web-builder-weebly-launches-an-android-app-along-with-a-mobile-and-html5-site-creator.

Zakas, Nicholas C. "It's Time to Stop Blaming Internet Explorer." Last updated July 12, 2012. http://www.smashingmagazine.com/2012/07/12/its-time-to-stop-blaming-internet-explorer.

Zambonini, Dan. "The Museum and Gallery Website a Thing of the Past?" Box UK Blog. Last updated March 18, 2009. http://www.boxuk.com/blog/museum-gallery-websites.

Index

icons, 70, 97, 98–99, 100, 124, 252
spacer, 49, 50, 145
statistics, visitor, 71, 72, 101–2, 132,
 154–55, 251
style:
 guide, 10, 12, 126, 161, 224, 252;
 text/font, 21–22, 44–45, 51, 79,
  81–82, 83, *84*, 89, 92, 118, 124,
  139, 144, 148, 161, 168, 171, 173,
  178–82, 203, 252
subdomain. *See* domain

tag, 48, 162–67, 169, 171–80, 185,
 186n5, 189;
 blog, 97–98, 204–5, 235–37, 245,
  246, 247, 249, 250, 251, 252
tax, sales, 65, 66, 67, 104, 131, 153
theme, 23, *34*, 37, 40, 41, 48, 52, 59, 70,
 77–78, 82, 109, 112–14, 124, 125,
 126, 127, 131, 133n1, 137, 143–44,
 145, 148, 199–201, 206, 210, 252
TIFF, 24, *25*, 190–92, 195, 252
Twitter, xi, 13, 19, 27, 48, 55, 61, 98,
 99, 100, 114, 149, 252
typeface, xxi, 21–22, 79, 139, 170, 178,
 179–80, 187n18, 247, 251, 253

unique visitors. *See* statistics, visitor
unpublish your site, 48, 63, 92,
upgrade your plan, xiv, 43, 53, 58, 62,
 63, 65, 66, 67, 72–73, 89, 100,
 101, 102, 106, 113, 116, 132–33

URL, resource (image, document,
 web page), 46, 53, 56, 57,
 59, 68, 69, 73n2, 95, 96,
 102, 103, 104, 122, 125, 129,
 130, 141, 142, 147, 151–52,
 153, 154, 166, 167, 168, 169,
 170–71, 174–75, 177, 186n8,
 187n16

video, add a. *See* embed
Vimeo, 26, 53, 96, 122, 147, 183,
 184, 253
volume controls, 26, 53, 147

webmaster, xiv, 9, 12, 28, 29, 30, 48,
 49, 51, 59, 70, 72, 106, 132, 146,
 154, 161, 168, 223, 227, 253
web reader, 14, 21, 25, 127, 141,
 186, 253
widget, 75, 109, 100, 110, 112–14, 133,
 149, 155
Windows (operating system).
 See Wintel
Wintel, xx, 187n17, 211n8, 253

XML, xx, 56, 160–61, 185n2, 246, 254

Yahoo, 4, 6, 13, 15n10, 27, 30,
 51, 146
YouTube, xiii, 8, 13, 26, 44, 53, 54, 96,
 100, 122, 135, 147–48, 182–84,
 207, 254

About the Author

Kelsey Ransick received her Bachelor's Degree from University of San Francisco and her Master's Degree from University of Delaware, focusing on museum studies and medieval and early modern European history. She has done curatorial and archival work, web design, and sundry other tasks that come up when working at a small museum. Originally from Colorado, she is currently a museum professional in the Philadelphia area. When not writing about websites or women's education in early modern England, she enjoys traveling.